RICK STEIN'S SPAIN

RICK STEIN'S SPAIN

BBC
BOOKS

This book is dedicated to Edward, Jack and Charles and Sarah, Zach and Olivia.

This book is published to accompany the television series entitled *Rick Stein's Spain*,
first broadcast on BBC TWO in 2011.

This series was produced for BBC Television by Denham Productions
Producer and Director: David Pritchard
Assistant Producer: Arezoo Farahzad
Executive Producers for the BBC: Jo Ball and Amina Razaq

10 9 8 7 6 5 4 3 2 1

Published in 2011 by BBC Books, an imprint of Ebury Publishing.
A Random House Group Company

The Random House Group Limited Reg. No. 954009

Addresses for companies within the Random House Group can be found at
www.randomhouse.co.uk

A CIP catalogue record for this book is available from the British Library.

ISBN 978 1 849 90923 5

The Random House Group Limited supports the Forest Stewardship Council® (FSC®), the leading international
forest−certification organisation. Our books carrying the FSC laber are printed on FSC®−certified paper. FSC is
the only forest−certification scheme supported by the leading environmental organisations, including Greenpeace.
Our paper procurement policy can be found at www.randomhouse.co.uk/environment

MIX
Paper from
responsible sources
FSC® C008047

Commissioning editor: Shirley Patton
Project editor: Mari Roberts
Assistant editor: Laura Higginson
Home economist: Debbie Major
Design and art direction: Smith & Gilmour
Photographer: James Murphy
Props stylist: Penny Markham
Map illustration: Debbie Powell
Production: David Brimble

Colour origination by: XY Digital Ltd
Printed and bound in China by C&C Offset Printing Co., Ltd.

To buy books by your favourite authors and register for offers, visit www.randomhouse.co.uk

CONTENTS

If you go to La Coruña, there's a place I think you should visit. It won't fill you with a sense of modern Spain, the country that dazzles the eye with its forests of electricity-generating windmills on the tops of hills, its new motorways with dark blue crash-barriers and dizzying spaghetti intersections with just-completed roads that sometimes seem to be going nowhere. Neither will it give you a shred of information about the new Spanish cooking, with its emulsions of roasted piquillo peppers and foams of langoustines. This place does octopus and, not unnaturally, it's called Mesón do Polpo; it's in the Calle de la Franja, a narrow street packed with little seafood restaurants whose names hardly seem to matter, though if you're doing a bit of a tapas trek, there's another one called Mesón o Galego, which has very wobbly tables and is rated by the locals as the best in Galicia. Do Polpo specializes in *pulpo a la feria*, slices of tender octopus boiled in salted water and served on a pine platter sprinkled with extra virgin olive oil, sea salt and pimentón, the smoky paprika from La Vera in Extremadura, which is the most distinctive flavour of Spanish food. I can't think of any dish in Spain I enjoy more, especially with a glass of albariño wine or, if I'm feeling very local, a white bowl of cloudy Ribeiro.

I might also have mentioned a tapas bar a few streets away called La Traida. It was run by two sisters, Mari Carmen and Sisi, in their seventies. They took over when their father died and ran it for fifty years. I went there last February. Now it's gone. The Galician beer was ice-cold and their tuna empanadas were pretty special, as were the slices of *tetilla* cheese which, when whole, come in the shape of a small breast. As is often the way in such old bars, the floors were uneven flagstones and the walls adorned with pictures of Galician rias, sunken valleys flooded by the sea where a lot of Galician seafood is caught or farmed. There were pictures of King Carlos and Queen Sofia, and lots more of their own, much-loved father. Such places are going fast, replaced by modern bars or clothes shops.

My Spain is fixed in those older places. I first went there in 1955, to Cantabria; the Civil War had finished only sixteen years earlier. Childhood memories are so strong. I remember the poverty, the shock of seeing that the fishermen had no toilets. And the Guardia Civil, the national police, were everywhere in the countryside, standing motionless, watching the roads with their grey uniform and distinctive black two-cornered hats. One of them roughly pushed me back into the crowd at the annual Battle of the Flowers in the fishing port of Laredo where we were staying, and that, and the darkness of Burgos cathedral, seems like yesterday. I can still see the frighteningly lifelike images of Jesus battered on the cross, the galloping statue of El Cid outside with sword outstretched, and his coffin high on the wall inside. On the way back from Burgos to Laredo there were griffon vultures circling high above the mountains. All formed a slightly grim but romantic view of Spain that I can't shake off. It was still a world to which the English author Laurie Lee walked out one midsummer's morning in 1934 and found a poor but beautiful country, 'a landscape pure as the sea, ancient, wind-ravaged and bare', isolated from the rest of Europe by the Pyrenees and a history of ardent Catholicism brought about by a fanatical desire to build a Christian nation after eight hundred years of Moorish rule. This influence of the church, and the riches and produce from the Americas – potatoes, tomatoes, chillies, tobacco – were what made Spain what it was, so well personified in the character of Don Quixote. For although Cervantes wrote the book in the sixteenth century, not much changed until the Civil War. Quixote, the idealist, a man of quality but desperately poor, thinking of food all the time and dreaming of times past when knights performed dazzling acts of chivalry, setting out to put a baffling world to rights – this seems to me to be how Spain was.

Since General Franco died in 1975, Spain has become a completely different country, prosperous, sexy even, and confident. Cities like Barcelona and Valencia are exciting places with entertaining architecture, like the all-glass Gas Natural building by the sea in Barcelona, which has part of its complicated mirror-like elevations built as though it has had a gigantic bite taken out of it by a shark. A marine theme results in the shimmering silver scales of the Guggenheim Museum in Bilbao, too, which has transformed a rather grey northern industrial city in the Basque country into somewhere stylish.

Both buildings engage the viewer and give a sense of optimism and hope for the future. My problem is not that I don't enjoy this new Spain, it's just that I'm still imbued with memories of Spain over my lifetime. As an eight-year-old I had cuttlefish stewed in its own ink with garlic and tomato and I still remember it. Spanish cooking has been for me over the years a memory of simple but completely satisfying flavours. In the north, in what they call Green Spain, I think of the white thickness of a fillet of hake cooked in fragrant albariño wine with peas and asparagus, or the cheerful acidity of Asturian cider, freshly aerated from being poured into a glass from a great height, and served with a tapas of fresh slices of monkfish, deep-fried in egg batter. In the Basque Country, I love the scent of charcoal on the rib of beef chops they grill rare and slice for you. I yearn for the plates of wild mushrooms quickly fried in olive oil then served with an egg yolk to stir in as a sauce in a pintxos bar in San Sebastián. In contrast, in the hot and dry south, there are the reds and yellows of the Spanish flag everywhere: the strong red wine from Rioja, the warm smoky red of pimentón, sweet tomatoes, the deep red of ibérico ham with its melting fat and the flecked lean with its slight grittiness and tartness, the orangey-red of spicy chorizos with yellow chickpeas or butter beans, and the colour of saffron and lemon, golden garlic and eggs. Eggs in tortillas, in soups and scrambled with asparagus, aubergine, tomato and courgette. With the slippery green of peppery olive oil and the scent of orange and orange blossom, you realize that the heart of Spanish food lies in the simplicity of the cooking and their belief in the quality of raw materials. Food for me is a memory of happy times in Spain tied in with thoughts of old musty cathedrals, vast horizons and fishing boats somewhere in the Mediterranean unloading wooden boxes of dark red prawns, a scent of fish scales, black tobacco and diesel in the air.

I was talking to an Italian chef in Sydney last year who suggested that, in the world order of cuisine, Italian food was in the first division, Spanish in the second. I didn't like to ask him where he thought British food was; I was pretty irritated anyway. How typical of an Italian, I thought. They believe they have the best food and cooking but how can you really judge what's best? For the TV series I made to accompany this book, I was filmed cooking fifteen of the recipes I had written up from my observations during the journey through Spain. We were in a rambling villa in the hills behind Málaga, looking out over olive and citrus groves that reached nearly to the top of a series of limestone ridges. None of the Spanish people who watched what I was doing complained that my recipes were wrong, though I was making a lot of it up from what I had seen. They made a few friendly suggestions for improvements, but that was all. The same thing in Italy would have been a scene of much animated chat and gesticulation about how I had got it so wrong. My confidence would have been sapped and the filming would have become a chore. As it was, I became more optimistic, more aware of the subtleties of how things are done and full of respect for the thoughtful hospitality of the Spanish.

I love Italians and their exceptional food, but they do think that no one else can cook it with such passion. I enjoy their enthusiasm but I also like the Spanish understatement, the way they rather roughly drop a plate down in front of you in a tapas bar. They know it's good; they don't need to make a fuss about it. We filmed a chef in La Mancha cooking garlic soup, *sopa de ajo*. The restaurant was just outside Las Pedroñeras, a town known for its purple-skinned garlic and indeed called the garlic capital of Spain. The restaurant was called Los Angeles, so named because the couple who ran it were Angel and Angela; he ran the restaurant and Angela cooked, and angels they were, friendly, bustling and beaming. In La Mancha they grow lots of garlic, lots of olives, lots of red peppers and lots of wheat. That's all there is to the dish, with an egg. It takes about two minutes to make. You heat olive oil in pan, throw in a lot of sliced garlic and hot smoky pimentón. You fry it a little, then pour on stock or water, season, break an egg into it, stir it up a little, then pour it over some grilled crusty bread in a bowl and finish with a lick of good olive oil. It's as good a soup as you're likely to get anywhere. When I got to make the recipe I didn't break the egg up, just lifted it out of the soup and put it on the toasted bread in the bowl then poured the hot garlic and smoky pimentón-flavoured broth over it, because I wanted my guests to break into the egg and have the yellow yolk flow into the soup as they ate. I'm sure Angela would have quietly raised an eyebrow but no more than that. The soup summed up what is best about Spanish cooking: colourful, robustly flavoured and very easy to cook.

I can see a lot of similarity between that and our own cooking in the British Isles. Not in the specific flavouring at all. Spanish food, even in the north, has lots of influences from the hot and dry country to the south. No, it's more in the simplicity of the cooking and the respect for the quality of the raw materials. In Galicia, for example, they wouldn't dream of serving a *necora* (velvet swimming crab) or *centolla* (spider crab) with anything like lemon, hollandaise or mayonnaise, having just boiled them in seawater; they say that something so good needs no embellishment. Again, in Valencia, a true paella is made with rabbit, chicken and snails, beans, shallots, garlic, tomato, saffron, rice, stock and pimentón. All the main ingredients come from the watery deltas around the city. In England, I'm often excited to cook something like cod in parsley sauce, or steak and kidney pudding, or a roast goose with sage stuffing, using the best quality produce and recognizing how first-class ingredients change everything. In Spain, you don't need to encourage people to cook using great local produce. It's what they do anyway. Sometimes when you are sitting in a restaurant in Seville and you've ordered *revueltos* – scrambled eggs with ham and asparagus – and a rather unsightly pile of scrambled egg is put in front of you on a fairly nondescript patterned plate, you can yearn for something with a bit more finesse, but a Spanish-Australian friend of mine, Frank Camorra, summed it up perfectly in just such a place. 'It's down to whether you like your romano pepper skinned hot from the charcoal or prefer to drink it through a straw.' Spain is ruggedly real.

I think that's a big reason why the country's been so popular with tourists for so long. It's easy to be a bit patronizing about the food because, apart from the new gastronomy and some hallowed dishes like paella, the locals have a sort of take-it-or-leave-it attitude to their cuisine. In truth, it's not always good. But good or bad, you feel unintimidated by it, as you are sometimes in countries like France or Italy. The Spanish will be delighted if you share their passion, but they are more reserved than that. That's why I've felt relaxed about calling the book *Rick Stein's Spain*. The recipes are not always completely authentic. They've been slightly altered to reflect my memory of how a particular gazpacho or paella tasted, or equally how something that was overcooked, stale or just badly prepared could have tasted if they'd tried harder. You're getting my Spain, in other words.

Chapter One

GALICIA

Though it was very cold, dark and gloomy at the time, I'm glad I arrived in Galicia in February. You can tell what a place is really like out of season. I drove over the Ría de Ribadeo with my son Jack and Debbie, who helps me with these books, on a blustery, rather melancholic afternoon and found a cheap hotel in the town smelling strongly of tobacco smoke, with a small radiator in the bedroom which heated it not at all. We walked around town in our overcoats. I had been reading a book about the Galician's love of pork by an English writer, John Barlow, who lives in La Coruña. It's called *Everything but the Squeal* and in it he describes the distinctly unenthusiastic welcome you are likely to get in country bars and restaurants, so when we went into a little tapas bar called Casa Villaronta, virtually next door to our hotel, I was expecting just that – and was not disappointed. The bar specializes in *pulpo a la feria*, octopus with paprika and olive oil, and *calamares* (deep-fried squid). It was an indication we were in the real Galicia when the patron behind the bar made it quite clear he was not pleased to see us. It was a pretty scruffy place but packed. I felt we should humour him by leaving but he pointed to a tiny table and we squeezed in. I ordered a jug of white Ribeiro and some china bowls to drink it, and the specials. Both dishes were exquisite, so fresh you could almost smell the sea in them. Then another customer recognized me. Apparently some of my old programmes are shown on a cable TV channel, and soon he had the barman beaming at our presence. John Barlow says the locals are not actually hostile at all, it's rather a sort of constitutional pessimism: 'Galicians enjoy negatives like no one else.' They are quite similar to the Cornish in that respect, and very appropriate too, what with the grey Celtic weather outside. My new fan told us you could buy a cottage overlooking the sea in the town for 25,000 euros. Padstow must have been like that once. I was tempted; the place had a rather spiritual if melancholic atmosphere about it, and an undeniably beautiful view across the wide sunken estuary, the ria. Rias, half-submerged valleys, occur all the way down to the Portuguese border beyond Vigo and are responsible for a lot of the seafood for which Galicia is so famous: crabs, lobsters, mussels, and particularly scallops.

The scallop shell is the symbol marking out all the pilgrim routes that lead across western Europe to the cathedral at Santiago de Compostela. I'm sure that anyone going to Galicia, even in summer, would feel themselves to be in a place inhabited by ghosts and spirits, with a history of hardship and poverty. When we came back filming in May, in the rain, we found an isolated graveyard out on the Costa de la Muerte, the 'coast of death', entirely occupied by the small bodies of teenage cadets from a training ship from Plymouth. One stormy night towards the end of the nineteenth century, all but three drowned when the ship went down on the savage rocks there.

But it's not depressing, just full of atmosphere. The feeling is also in the dark green of the vegetation and the grey of the granite outcrops and the somewhat sepulchral look of the low, stone storage sheds called *hórreos* that you see everywhere, with a cross at one end. They are raised off the ground by granite mushrooms to keep the rats out. If you were looking for a hot holiday you would certainly give Galicia a miss, but if you value a rather haunting spirituality, it is very special. You will eat well, too, on arguably the best seafood in the world, and not only all those lobsters, crabs and scallops but *percebes* too, the weirdly shaped goose-necked barnacle that the locals revere so much, which tastes a bit like lobster. The fishing ports of La Coruña and Vigo are enormous, and restaurants up and down the coast will offer you dishes such as turbot sprinkled with a little pimentón and grilled, *merluza con salsa verde* (hake with parsley, peas and clams), simply grilled sardines, and monkfish *a la plancha*, cooked on a flat griddle, often with olive oil and caramelized garlic, and served just with boiled potatoes. It's also a profoundly agricultural area. The top restaurants regard well-aged Galician beef as the best by far. Everywhere you go there will be *caldo gallego*, a potato, cabbage and pork soup with white beans and usually flavoured with more pork in the form of chorizo made with pimentón and garlic. The potatoes are fabulous, and their own variety of greens, *grelos*, could almost be a symbol of the Galician nation.

OLIVE-OIL FRIED BABY GREEN PEPPERS

Pimientos de Padrón SERVES 4 AS A TAPAS (GENEROUSLY!)

This is a popular snack in Galicia and all over Spain: small, bite-sized green peppers from the area around the town of Padrón, a few kilometres south-west of Santiago de Compostela. As I mentioned in the introduction, to me the heart of Spanish food is first-class produce, cooked simply. All you do with Padrón peppers is fry them briskly in olive oil then sprinkle them with sea salt flakes. If I see them on a bar menu anywhere in Spain when they are in season, I will order some – they are just so yummy. It's also well known that one in every ten or so is more like a chilli than a pepper, which gives everyone a little frisson of anticipation, and really that's what eating tapas is all about. Sharing.

250g Padrón peppers
2 tbsp olive oil
Sea salt flakes

Wash the peppers in cold water and pat them dry.

Place a large frying pan over a high heat, add the oil and leave it to get smoking hot. Add the peppers, cover, and shake them over the heat for 4–5 minutes until their skins start to blister and turn brown. Take care not to overcook them; they still need to be a little *al dente*. Drain briefly on kitchen paper, transfer to a plate and sprinkle generously with sea salt flakes. Serve straight away, while still hot.

OCTOPUS TWO WAYS: FAIRGROUND-STYLE & GALICIAN-STYLE

Pulpo a la feria & Pulpo a la gallega SERVES 4–6 AS A TAPAS

Pulpo a la feria is the classic way of serving octopus in Galicia, simply boiled then sliced and served on a round pine board sprinkled with sea salt, smoked paprika and olive oil. *Pulpo a la gallega* is the same thing but accompanied by potatoes that have been boiled in the octopus cooking water, then tossed in olive oil and pimentón. Ideally, use a small frozen Spanish octopus, *Octopus vulgaris* (see page 312), weighing about 1kg. If you can only get a larger one, and they won't sell you half, defrost the whole thing in the fridge, cook it and freeze the remaining cooked meat for later use.

1 cleaned frozen octopus
    (see page 312), weighing
    about 1kg, thawed overnight
Coarsely ground rock salt or
    sea salt flakes

FOR PULPO A LA FERIA:
½ tsp *pimentón picante*
    (smoked hot Spanish paprika)
50ml extra virgin olive oil

FOR PULPO A LA GALLEGA:
250g peeled small waxy main-crop
    potatoes, such as Désirée, cut
    into wedges
2 tbsp extra virgin olive oil
½ tsp *pimentón picante*
    (smoked hot Spanish paprika)

Put enough water to easily cover the octopus into a large pan with 1 tablespoon of salt and bring to the boil. Add the octopus and make sure the whole thing is fully submerged. Cover and leave to simmer gently for 45 minutes to 1 hour, by which time it should be tender. To check, push a fine metal skewer into the thickest part of the tentacles up near the head. If it goes in easily, with no resistance, the octopus is cooked.

Carefully remove the octopus from the pan using tongs or 2 forks. Don't remove the pinky-mauve skin as it looks good in contrast to the whiteness of the flesh. When cool enough, cut the tentacles on the diagonal into slices about 5–10mm thick, and the head into similar-sized pieces.

For the *pulpo a la feria*, arrange the octopus on a warmed plate and sprinkle with the pimentón and extra salt, then drizzle over the olive oil.

For the *pulpo a la gallega*, drop the peeled potatoes into the octopus cooking water and simmer for 10 minutes or until tender, then drain well. Heat the olive oil in a large frying pan, add the pimentón, then the potatoes and toss them around for about 20 seconds or so until they are well coated in the red-coloured oil. Serve them alongside the cooked slices of octopus, sprinkled with just a little extra salt but no more pimentón.

MUSSELS in TOMATO VINAIGRETTE

Mejillones con vinagreta de tomate SERVES 4–6 AS A TAPAS

The world's largest mussel beds are in the Rias Bajas, the estuaries along the western Atlantic shores of Galicia, where they are grown on ropes suspended from rafts that from a distance look like mini battleships. Needless to say, mussels feature heavily in the tapas bars of La Coruña and Santiago de Compostela, and indeed in tapas bars all over Spain. I particularly like these, served with sherry vinegar, olive oil, finely chopped peppers and red onions. Probably because of their slight astringency, an ice-cold Galician beer would be the perfect accompaniment.

750g large, rope-grown mussels
1 medium vine-ripened tomato, skinned and roughly chopped
1 tbsp sherry vinegar
3 tbsp extra virgin olive oil
1 tbsp capers, roughly chopped
2 pickled cornichons, finely chopped
1 tbsp finely chopped red onion
1 tbsp finely chopped green pepper
1 tbsp finely chopped red pepper
1 tbsp finely chopped flat-leaf parsley
Salt and freshly ground black pepper

Wash the mussels in plenty of cold water and scrape off any barnacles with a knife. Discard any that don't show signs of closing when squeezed gently, then pull out the tough fibrous beards protruding from between the closed shells.

Heat a large, heavy-based pan over a high heat. Add the mussels and 2 tablespoons of water, cover and shake around for 2–3 minutes or until the mussels have just opened. Drain into a colander and leave until cool enough to handle. Then break away the empty, top half-shell from each mussel, and release the meat in the other shell but leave it in place. Place them side by side on a serving platter.

For the dressing, put the chopped tomato into a mini food processor and whiz until smooth. Add the vinegar, oil and some salt and pepper to taste and whiz briefly once more to combine. Tip into a small bowl and stir in the capers, cornichons, red onion, green pepper, red pepper and parsley. Spoon some of the dressing over each mussel and serve at room temperature.

HADDOCK a la PLANCHA with CARAMELIZED GARLIC

Eglefino a la plancha con ajo SERVES 2

In Cornwall we are lucky enough to get a good supply of small haddock weighing about a pound. These lend themselves to being grilled or fried whole, though when I found this dish in Galicia, the fish had been split down the back, opened out like a kipper then cooked *a la plancha*, on the thick steel plate (a griddle, in other words) the Spanish use to cook most of their fish and seafood. The griddle takes a bit of getting used to, but then it becomes absurdly simple to cook anything on it. In this case, some olive oil was brushed over the hot surface and the fish were fried quickly on both sides then lifted off the hotplate. A small ladleful of garlic, which had been slowly caramelized in olive oil, was poured on the hot surface of the plancha to crisp up and the fish was placed back on top, so the garlic encrusted its flesh. The fish were then lifted onto a plate, with the rest of the golden garlic quickly scraped off the plancha and sprinkled on top before serving. I was drinking a bottle of albariño at the time with Debbie and my son Jack, and it seemed to me a perfect example of the effectiveness of Spanish fish cookery. I've never had a better-tasting piece of fish, ever. Because we don't have planchas at home and not everyone has a ready supply of whole small haddock, I've used fillets for the recipe instead, to make things a bit easier.

4 x 100–125g unskinned fillets
    haddock or hake
2 tbsp olive oil
2 tbsp *Slow-cooked garlic*
    (see page 306)
Salt

Season the fish fillets on both sides with a little salt. Heat a large frying pan over a high heat. Add the olive oil and as soon as it is shimmering hot, add the fish, flesh-side down first, and cook for 2 minutes, until richly golden. Turn the fish over and cook for 1 more minute.

Carefully remove the fish from the pan, remove the pan from the heat and leave it to cool very slightly. If you add the garlic to the pan straight away it will burn.

Return the pan to a medium heat, add the slow-cooked garlic and cook until it is just golden brown. Return the fish fillets to the pan, flesh-side down, and shake around briefly to encourage the garlic to stick to the fish. Remove from the pan once more and serve flesh-side up with any remaining garlic from the pan spooned over.

BAKED SCALLOPS with GUINDILLA PEPPER, CHORIZO and CRISP BREADCRUMBS

Vieras al horno SERVES 4 AS A STARTER

Galicia is the region in Spain for scallops. They are extensively farmed in the Rias Bajas, the rocky western coastal region near the town of Pontevedra. Indeed, the pilgrim routes to the cathedral in Santiago de Compostela are marked out with the symbol of a scallop shell and finally, when you get to the city, the route to the cathedral is marked out with golden scallops embedded in the pavements. I had various baked scallop dishes while I was there but wasn't knocked out by any of them so I've taken the liberty of making up my own. I've made a sauce of roasted red pepper, chorizo and some soaked dried guindilla peppers, which are slightly fiery, testimony to the influence of South America on Galicia. If you can't get hold of scallops in the shell, just use prepared scallops and spoon the sauce into small baking dishes instead.

5 dried guindilla peppers or ½ tsp crushed dried chilli flakes
4 tbsp olive oil
75g finely chopped shallot
4 garlic cloves, finely chopped
65g cooking chorizo sausage, skinned and finely chopped
1 *Roasted red pepper* (see page 307), finely chopped
2 vine-ripened tomatoes, skinned, seeded and chopped
8 prepared large scallops in the shell
60g breadcrumbs, made from crustless day-old white bread
Sea salt

Remove the stalks from the dried peppers, slit them open and remove all the seeds. Soak in hot water for 1 hour. Drain the peppers and scrape the flesh away from the skins with a spoon. Discard the skins.

Preheat the oven to 200°C/gas 6. Heat 3 tablespoons of the olive oil in a frying pan over a medium heat. Add the shallot, garlic and chorizo and cook gently, stirring occasionally, for 5 minutes or until the shallots are soft and sweet. Add the guindilla pepper flesh, roasted red pepper and tomatoes, season to taste with a little salt and simmer for another 3 minutes.

Detach the scallops from their shells and cut them horizontally in half, leaving the coral attached to one slice. Spoon some of the sauce into the bottom of each of the shells. Season the scallop pieces lightly and place 2 slices, slightly overlapping, on top of the sauce.

Mix the breadcrumbs with the remaining olive oil and a pinch of salt and sprinkle over the scallops and partly over the sauce. Place them side by side on a baking tray, and bake on the top shelf of the oven for 8–9 minutes or until the scallops are just cooked through and the breadcrumbs are crisp and golden.

Virgen del Carmen

HECHO POR JOSE RAMON GALLEGO REBOLLAR

GALICIAN BEAN, POTATO and CABBAGE SOUP

Caldo gallego SERVES 6

If you're ever unsure what to choose for a starter in Galicia, go for the caldo, as it's always good. In the genre of comforting soups this is one of the best. A piece of cured pork back fat is often added to the soup to further enrich it. As with the cocido on page 34, it's what Galicia is all about. Well, that and some of the best seafood in the world, of course.

200g dried white beans, such as *alubia planchada,* soaked overnight in cold water
50g pork back fat (optional)
225g streaky bacon, in one piece
2 cooking chorizo sausages
1 fresh ham bone or ham knuckle
2 large (approx. 400g) floury potatoes, such as Maris Piper or King Edwards
150g turnips tops or curly kale, washed and torn into small pieces
Salt

Drain the white beans and put them into a large flameproof casserole or saucepan with 2 litres water. Bring to a simmer over a medium heat. Add the pork back fat if using, the bacon, chorizos and ham bone and simmer for 1 hour or until the beans are tender.

Peel the potatoes and cut them lengthways into quarters then across into small chunks. Remove the ham bone from the beans and discard it, and check the broth for seasoning. Add about ¾ teaspoon of salt if lacking in flavour. Add the potatoes and simmer for a further 8 minutes or until tender.

Lift the pork back fat, bacon and chorizo sausages from the pot. Discard the back fat and cut the bacon and chorizo into bite-sized pieces and set to one side. If the broth is not quite as thick as you would like it, remove a large spoonful or two of the potatoes and beans, mash them roughly and stir them back into the soup. Add the 'greens' to the pot and simmer for a further 10 minutes. They need to be well cooked. Then stir the bacon and chorizo back into the soup and leave to heat through for a minute or two.

Check the seasoning once more, then ladle into 6 large warmed soup plates and serve immediately.

POTATO TORTILLA

Tortilla de patatas SERVES 6

The *tortilla de patatas* at Armando Blanco's La Casa de las Tortillas, in the village of Cacheiras just outside Santiago de Compostela, is nationally famous. The many-roomed restaurant is hung throughout with photos of Armando shaking the hands of almost everyone famous in Spain, including the King and Queen, and from further afield, such as the Pope. What I loved about the restaurant was its ordinariness. I recall sitting eating my tortilla surrounded by a large party of parents and screaming children, with the parents smoking furiously in front of the children and all over the food. A fog of smoke, but who cares when the tortillas are so exquisitely good? Normally tortillas come thick and well cooked, but these are like a really good French omelette, soft and slightly runny in the middle, what the French call '*baveuse*'. Traditionally, Spanish omelettes are made just with eggs, potatoes, olive oil and salt, but they do sometimes add onions too, which I rather like. It's quite hard to achieve a satisfactorily shaped omelette that also allows for a soft centre. The trick is to start with the cooked potatoes, onions and olive oil in the pan, then pour over the whisked and seasoned eggs on the heat and cook while very gently cutting through the ever-thickening egg to allow some of the still runny mixture to sink to the bottom of the pan and set. Only when the surface texture is just slightly sticky do you slide it onto a plate, invert it back into the pan, and cook for a minute or two more. Eat while still warm or at room temperature, but never cold straight from the fridge.

600g evenly sized main-crop potatoes, such as Maris Piper or King Edwards
150ml olive oil, plus 2–3 tbsp if needed
1 medium onion, halved and thinly sliced
12 large free-range eggs
Salt

Peel the potatoes, halve them lengthways and then cut them across into roughly 6–7mm thick slices. Heat the 150ml of olive oil in a shallow 26–28cm reliably non-stick frying pan over a medium heat, add the potatoes and ¾ teaspoon of salt and leave them to cook, stirring every now and then, for about 10 minutes or until very tender but not browned. Spoon onto a plate, leaving behind as much of the oil as you can, and set to one side.

Add the onion and 2 tablespoons more of oil if necessary to the pan and fry for 7 minutes, stirring regularly to avoid caramelizing the onions, until they are soft and sweet. Return the potatoes to the pan and, using a fork, mix together well with the onions, then arrange the ingredients in an even layer over the base of the pan.

Break the eggs into a bowl, season with ¾ teaspoon of salt and whisk together well to slightly aerate them. Pour them over the potatoes and onions and cook over a medium-low heat, lifting the mixture here and there every now and then to allow the loose egg to run underneath, for 6–7 minutes or until almost set but still slightly soft on top.

Release the omelette from the sides of the pan with a knife and carefully slide it out onto a large plate. Brush the base of the pan with a little more oil, then turn the pan over and cover the omelette with it. Holding the pan and the plate together, quickly turn them over again so the omelette is back in the pan, cooked side up. Return it to the heat for just 1 minute then slide once more onto a large warmed plate and serve straight away, with a green lettuce salad, dressed with a little olive oil, red wine vinegar and a pinch of salt.

Galicia

EMPANADA of SEAFOOD with TOMATOES, PEPPERS and PIMENTÓN

Empanada de mariscos MAKES 10–12 PIECES

One of the best places to eat empanada in Santiago de Compostela is the Gato Negro, a tiny and ancient bar tucked away down one of the many side streets that circle the cathedral, which is where this recipe comes from. They make the empanadas in baking trays using a rich, yeasted dough and whatever seafood is to hand – such as octopus, conger eels, mussels or sardines – layered with a rich tomato sauce flavoured with pimentón. What I like about this recipe is that the sauce is rich but quite moist and the rolled-out dough is thin, giving you a pie that is certainly a little delicate to handle but full of flavour. The pimentón in the bread crust gives the pastry a subtle flavour and the finished pie a beautifully rich, amber tint.

625g plain flour
1¼ tsp fast-action dried yeast
1¼ tsp *pimentón dulce* (smoked sweet Spanish paprika)
250ml hand-hot water
120ml olive oil
1 free-range egg, beaten, to glaze
Salt

FOR THE FILLING:
7 tbsp olive oil
2 medium onions, finely chopped
3 garlic cloves, crushed
2 red peppers, seeded and finely chopped
2 tsp *pimentón dulce* (smoked sweet Spanish paprika)
2 x 400g cans chopped tomatoes
500g fish of your choice: coley fillet, freshly filleted sardines, cooked octopus (see page 20), cooked mussel meats (see page 22) or tinned tuna
Freshly ground black pepper

For the dough, sift the flour, yeast and pimentón into a mixing bowl and make a well in the centre. Dissolve 1¼ teaspoons of salt in the hand-hot water, pour into the well along with the oil and gradually mix in the dry ingredients until everything comes together into a dough. Turn out onto a lightly floured surface and knead for 5 minutes until smooth. Return to a clean bowl, cover and leave somewhere warm for 1 hour, while you make the filling.

Heat 6 tablespoons of the olive oil in a large, deep frying pan, add the onions, garlic, red peppers and pimentón and fry together gently for about 25 minutes, stirring now and then, until soft and sweet. Add the tomatoes and continue to cook gently for 35–40 minutes, stirring more frequently as the sauce gets thicker, until the excess moisture has evaporated and it is just starting to catch on the bottom of the pan. Season with ½ teaspoon of salt and leave to cool.

Preheat the oven to 200°C/gas 6. Lightly grease a 3cm deep, 37 x 26cm baking tray with a little lard. Turn out the dough onto a lightly floured surface and knead once more until smooth. Cut in two, one piece slightly larger than the other. Cover the smaller piece and set to one side. Roll out the other piece into a large rectangle and use to line the base and sides of the tin, leaving about 1cm overhanging.

Cut the coley fillet, if using, across into 7–8mm-thick slices, slice the octopus or roughly flake the tuna. Spoon half the tomato sauce into the tin and spread it evenly over the base. Season the fish of your choice and arrange it on top, then cover with the rest of the sauce. Sprinkle over the last tablespoon of olive oil.

Roll out the remaining piece of dough into a rectangle the same size as the top of the tin. Lay it over the filling, brush the edge with beaten egg, then fold over the overhanging edges of dough and press them together well to make a good seal.

Pierce the top of the pie with the tines of a fork, then brush with the beaten egg. Bake for 30 minutes or until richly golden. Leave to rest for 10 minutes before cutting in half lengthways, then across into pieces. Eat warm or at room temperature.

BOILED BACON with CHORIZO, CHICKPEAS, POTATOES and CABBAGE

Cocido gallego SERVES 8

John Barlow, whom I mentioned in the introduction, wrote *Everything but the Squeal: A year of pigging out in Northern Spain*. In one chapter he describes in affectionate detail the ruggedness of the food in Galicia, particularly *cocido*. John is obsessed with it, describing it as the sort of dish you'd either run away from in horror or, like him, dive into with gusto. He took me to the village of Montfero, about 30 minutes west of La Coruña, to a restaurant called Casa Juan. It was cold and pouring with rain, needless to say (it does a lot of that in Galicia), and the surrounding patches of *grelos* – a brassica something like turnip greens – looked a dull, droopy green in the bone-chilling weather. But inside the restaurant there was a beautiful aroma of hot ham and chorizo, and those same *grelos* were now a sharp, appetizing dark green. How can you describe a dish that arrived with half a pig's head on one platter, the teeth glinting through the jaw, and racks of boiled ribs, trotters and pieces of spine together with chorizo, gammon and salted pork shoulder on another platter, with vast bowls of boiled potatoes, chickpeas and boiled *grelos?* Well, this is my version, with not a pig's tooth in sight.

1 x 2kg piece of boned and rolled collar of bacon
600g dried chickpeas
2 medium onions, halved
6 cloves
1 whole garlic bulb, halved
4 fresh bay leaves
½ tsp black peppercorns
500g smoked streaky bacon, in one piece
2 large carrots, each one cut into 4 pieces
2 celery stalks, each one cut into 4 pieces
8 medium (200g) main-crop potatoes, peeled and cut into quarters
8 x 10cm cooking chorizo sausages
1 large Savoy cabbage (approx. 800g), quartered, cored and cut into 2.5cm-thick slices
Salt
Crusty fresh bread and Dijon or English mustard, to serve

Cover the bacon joint with cold water and leave to soak for 8 hours. Cover the chickpeas with cold water and soak alongside the bacon.

Drain the bacon, put it into a large stockpot (one that holds at least 6 litres) and cover by 3cm with cold water. Slowly bring to the boil, skimming off any scum as it rises to the surface. Stud the onion halves with the cloves and add to the pan with the garlic, bay leaves and peppercorns. Cover and simmer as gently as possible for 1 hour.

Drain the chickpeas, add them to the pan, bring back to a simmer and cook for 20 minutes. Then add the piece of streaky bacon to the pan, bring back to a simmer and cook for a further 20 minutes.

Remove the clove-studded onions with a slotted spoon and discard. Add the carrots, celery, potatoes and chorizo sausages and simmer for 15–20 minutes, until tender.

Just before everything is ready, ladle off 300ml of the broth into a separate large saucepan, add the cabbage and ½ teaspoon of salt, cover and simmer vigorously for 5 minutes, stirring once or twice, until tender. Warm a serving platter, 3 serving bowls and a jug.

Lift the collar of bacon, streaky bacon and chorizos out of the broth onto a carving board. Carve the bacon into slices and the chorizos into thick diagonal pieces and arrange on the platter. Transfer the carrots, celery and potatoes with a slotted spoon to one of the bowls. Drain the remaining stock through a colander set over a large clean pan. Tip the chickpeas into the second bowl. Drain the cabbage well and spoon into the third bowl. Reheat the broth and pour into the jug. Serve with bread and with plenty of mustard, which the Spanish don't but it works for me.

GALICIAN HAKE on a BRAISE of POTATOES, GARLIC, TOMATO and ONION

Merluza a la gallega SERVES 4

There is a homely wholesomeness about Galician food, and this is the sort of dish you could imagine also coming from some region of the British Isles, like west Wales, if only we loved hake like the Spanish do. Interestingly, when Debbie and I cooked this for our recipe testing in a blistered and cracked terracotta cazuela and gave it to our deli to sell, it was all gone in about 20 minutes. What I love about this is the thickness and whiteness of a good piece of white fish and the aroma of the garlic and tomato coming from the potato fondue below. Like many of these sorts of dishes, I believe in completely cooking the vegetables first on top of the stove, and then baking the fish on top in the oven. If you don't do this it can end up a bit watery, but this way its flavour is much more rich and concentrated.

4 x 225–250g steaks of white
    fish on the bone, such as hake
    or cod
7 tbsp olive oil
8 garlic cloves, thinly sliced
1 large onion, halved and thinly
    sliced
225g skinned chopped tomatoes,
    fresh or from a can
300ml *Chicken stock*
    (see page 306)
1kg peeled floury potatoes, such
    as Maris Piper or King Edwards
1 tbsp chopped parsley
Salt

Season the fish steaks on both sides with a little salt and set to one side. Heat 4 tablespoons of the olive oil in a 28–30cm terracotta cazuela or a similarly wide, deep, flameproof casserole. Add the garlic and onion and fry gently for 10 minutes or until soft and lightly golden. Add the tomatoes and fry for 3 minutes until starting to break down into a sauce, then stir in the stock and 1 teaspoon of salt and bring to the boil.

Cut the potatoes across into slices 7mm thick and stir them in. Simmer for 15–20 minutes until tender when pierced with the tip of a small, sharp knife. Meanwhile, preheat the oven to 200°C/gas 6.

When the potatoes are tender, heat the remaining 3 tablespoons of olive oil in a large non-stick frying pan. Pat the fish steaks dry on kitchen paper, add them to the pan and fry for 2 minutes on each side until golden brown. Carefully lift them on top of the potatoes, transfer to the oven and bake for 10 minutes, until the fish steaks are cooked through. Remove from the oven, sprinkle over the parsley and serve.

RABBIT with CHESTNUTS

Conejo con castañas SERVES 6

Before the arrival of the potato, the starchy chestnut was an important part of the Galician winter diet, and it is still very much loved in stews like this, as well as roasted or candied and sold as a regional speciality similar to *marrons glacés*. They even have a chestnut festival in Orense, the provincial capital, in October, but then, you name a food in Spain and there's a festival somewhere to celebrate it. I can't understand why rabbit isn't more popular back home, but I guess I stumbled across the truth when I was making a TV series a few years back called *Food Heroes*. I was keen to film in a rabbit farm, until I discovered that I was likely to be regarded as a pet-killer. Then, when my late and much-loved dog Chalky dispatched one in a Peter Rabbit-style garden, I thought my number was up. 'Rick Stein's dog kills pet rabbit,' roared the *Daily Mail*. Debbie, who works with me on these books, also remembers some kindly French neighbours in Normandy once offering to give her nephews two of their rabbits as pets. 'But we're not here all the time,' they said. 'Oh, no problem,' they replied. 'We'll eat these, and you can have two more when you come back.' That says it all really. This dish can be made with chicken if you wish.

2 x 750g farmed rabbits, jointed
  (see page 146)
4 tbsp plain flour
4 tbsp olive oil
1 onion, finely chopped
100g carrots, finely diced
2 garlic cloves, finely chopped
150g thinly sliced serrano ham,
  chopped
A small pinch of saffron strands
4 tbsp brandy
4 tbsp sweet sherry, such as oloroso
200g skinned chopped tomatoes,
  fresh or from a can
300ml *Chicken stock*
  (see page 306)
2 fresh thyme sprigs
400g cooked peeled chestnuts
Salt and freshly ground black
  pepper

Season the rabbit pieces all over then dust them with the flour. Heat 2 tablespoons of the olive oil in a large flameproof casserole over a medium heat, add the rabbit pieces a few at a time, and fry until they are lightly browned all over. Remove each batch to a plate.

Add the remaining oil and the onion, carrot and garlic to the casserole and cook gently for 10 minutes until soft and lightly golden. Add the ham and cook for 1 minute more.

Stir in any remaining flour, followed by the saffron, brandy, sherry, tomatoes and stock and bring to the boil, stirring. Return the rabbit to the casserole and add the thyme sprigs. The rabbit should be just covered with liquid, so add a little more stock if it's not. Bring to a simmer, cover and leave to cook gently for 30 minutes.

Remove the lid and stir in the chestnuts. Simmer for a further 10–15 minutes, uncovered, until the liquid has reduced a little and the rabbit is tender. Adjust the seasoning to taste and serve.

Chapter Two

ASTURIAS &
CANTABRIA

Driving through Asturias and Cantabria, it's never far from your mind that this northern coastline is known as 'Green Spain'. Climatically, these regions, together with Galicia and the *pais vasco* (Basque country), are a different country from the rest of Spain, and when I was filming here it was my misfortune to experience the wettest May for, I believe, 115 years. This rain even fell as snow on my trip to the high Picos mountains to find a cabrales cheese-maker. Arriving in the swirling snow at a tiny village where they make the cheese, then being driven in the cheese-maker's ancient four-wheel-drive up an impossibly rocky track to a cold and dark cave where the cheeses were stored, seemed to me like a scene out of *Lord of the Rings*. Cabrales cheese, which is made from cow, goat and ewe's milk, is stored in these cold damp caves to form the irregular streaks of blue that give it its distinctive, piquant flavour. To drive back to the very attractive coast was a bit of a relief, passing as I did through Oviedo, the capital of Asturias – a delightful city I knew very little about but discovered is a gem. The covered central market, the Mercado El Fontan, is as pretty as, if a little smaller than, the market in Valencia, and apart from having great fish counters, with cod both fresh and salted as *bacalao* – such a feature of Spain in general, no matter how far inland you are – they also had excellent vegetables, cheeses and *embutidos* (charcuterie), such as chorizo and morcilla. But the two products I was particularly looking for were the dried white beans called *fabes de la granja*, which they use for *fabada*, the famous bean and cured pork stew, and their salt pork, which comes in every guise, whether it be tongues, trotters, snouts, tails or heads, the jaws clamped in rubber bands, hoisted up on high like some medieval shop sign.

The cider houses of Oviedo are their equivalent of the tapas bars of Seville, Barcelona and Madrid. There's a street there called Calle Gascona, known as the 'boulevard of cider'. In some the waiters aerate the cider by pouring it from high above their heads; in others, ingenious machines, one shaped like a serpent's head, do the same thing by pumping the cider, whether electrically or by hand, to drop it from on high into the glass. To an outsider it seemed endearingly eccentric to put so much effort into it all. 'Does it really make that much difference?' you ask, and you suspect it's just part of the theatre. If the locals don't finish their small glass quickly, before the slight fizz has disappeared, they tip it onto the floor along with the toothpicks and paper napkins, and go onto to the next glass, or the next bar. There's something so attractive about this ebbing and swelling of crowds, not just through the cider bars of Oviedo, but the pintxos bars of San Sebastian or the tapas bars of Seville too. It's the sharing of the enjoyment that makes it so special. The reason tapas bars don't really work outside Spain is that you need lots of them. Throwing your cider on the floor, banging down your glass and moving on with your friends to the next bar, that's the fun of it. I wouldn't say the cider is all that special, it's just what everyone drinks, and there are lots of cider-makers in both Asturias and Cantabria.

I visited one cider-making company, called Trabanco, about ten miles inland from the fishing port of Gijón, where they store their cider in tanks in the tunnels of an old mine to keep it at a constant temperature. They took us out to lunch afterwards – I'd asked if I could try a good *fabada* – and as the afternoon progressed the cider got more and more important in helping to wash down the enormous amounts of beans and sausage we were presented with. That lunch took me about two days to get over; beans are just so filling.

After that, I was looking forward to some very plain fish cooking again. In Cantabria, in the Barrio de Pescadores in Santander, down near the docks, I was not disappointed. I've relied rather heavily on the dishes I had there in this chapter. In addition they do a rather intriguing dish of monkfish dusted with pimentón and steamed to resemble lobster, sardines grilled over charcoal, and lightly steamed sea urchins too. They also do hot shellfish, cooked *a la plancha* with garlic and olive oil; a great pile of lobster, langoustines, mussels, prawns, clams, razor clams and white crab meat served in the back shell, and *bacalao* in red pepper stew with olive oil and pimentón. And it's worth pointing out that Santander is an attractive city. What I particularly like about those cities along the north coast is that most of them – San Sebastián, Santander, Gijón and La Coruña – just like St Ives, have ocean beaches right at the front, which gives the light a special quality.

OCTOPUS SALAD with SPRING ONIONS and PEPPERS

Pulpo vinagreta SERVES 6 AS A STARTER

I had this as a first course in a very everyday sort of restaurant in the fishing village of Santoña, near Laredo in Cantabria. I love going into somewhere you'd never find in a food guide where the food is simple, local stuff. I also find this sort of restaurant in northern Spain quite charming because they are decorated, or rather over-decorated, in a style that suits the whims of the owners. In this case the owner was obviously a massive fan of hunting. There were pictures of shooting and fishing on every wall, guns everywhere, stuffed heads, and trophies all over the place. This salad made with just a few local ingredients – red and green peppers, spring and red onions, a little garlic and olive oil – seemed entirely appropriate and rather a good way of serving sliced octopus.

450–500g cooked octopus (see page 20)
Half a red onion (approx. 75g)
75g piece (about ½) seeded red pepper
75g piece (about ½) seeded green pepper
1 bunch spring onions, trimmed and thickly sliced on the diagonal
3 tbsp red wine vinegar
120ml extra virgin olive oil
1 garlic clove, very finely chopped
Salt and freshly ground black pepper
Crusty fresh bread, to serve

Cut the octopus into bite-sized pieces: the tentacles into slices about 7–8mm thick, and the head into similar-sized pieces.

Cut the red onion lengthways into arc-shaped slices. Cut the red and green pepper lengthways into slices then across into small chunky pieces. Put the octopus into a large mixing bowl with the red onion, peppers and spring onions.

Whisk the vinegar, oil, garlic, 1 teaspoon of salt and some pepper together in a small bowl, pour over the octopus and vegetables and stir together well. Serve with some crusty fresh bread.

CRISP DEEP-FRIED SQUID

Calamares a la romana SERVES 6 AS A TAPAS

I know I have given recipes for deep-fried squid in some of my previous books, but you can't do a book of Spanish recipes without including deep-fried squid because it is one of the most popular tapas, served all over the country. I think you can always judge a restaurant by the quality of the *calamares*. If they get this right, you can usually be sure that everything that comes after it will be good too. I might be guilty of going on about the rather special flour the Spanish use for deep-frying but, being coarser than normal flour, it does give a much lighter, crisper finish. You don't normally get alioli with this type of squid in tapas bars, but I love it.

350g prepared medium-sized squid
Olive oil or vegetable oil, for deep-frying
Harina de trigo especial para freir, or fine-ground semolina, for dusting
Salt
Alioli (see page 307) and 2 quartered lemons, to serve

Pat the squid dry with kitchen paper, then cut the pouches across into rings and the fins into strips, 1.5cm wide in both cases. Cut each bunch of tentacles in half.

Spread the squid out on a tray and lightly season with salt. Heat some oil for deep-frying to 190°C and tip plenty of flour into a large bowl.

Toss a small handful of squid in the flour, shake off the excess and deep-fry for 1 minute until crisp and lightly golden. Remove with a slotted spoon and drain on a tray lined with kitchen paper. Serve straight away with the alioli for dipping and the lemon for squeezing, then repeat with the remaining squid.

A CANTABRIAN PRAWN COCKTAIL

SERVES 4 AS A STARTER

I've come to the conclusion that the Basques and Cantabrians are inordinately fond of seafood with some sort of mayonnaise-based sauce. There are many different combinations on display in the pintxos bars of San Sebastián, even some made with shredded crab sticks, which are not my cup of tea. This particular dish I had in a tiny restaurant in a little sardine-fishing village called Santoña, near Laredo. I've called it a prawn cocktail because I can't find a better way of describing it, and, as a purist, I feel such cocktails should be served in glasses, but this came on a plate, topped with whole prawns, drizzled with a little good balsamic vinegar and garnished with a pitted green olive. Not exactly a local dish or haute cuisine but irresistible never the less. What I particularly liked was the combination of chopped prawns and white crab meat.

2 little gem lettuce, outer leaves discarded
1 small carrot
200g cooked peeled large prawns
125g handpicked white crab meat
2 vine-ripened tomatoes, skinned, seeded and diced
1 tsp aged balsamic vinegar
A pinch of *pimentón dulce* (smoked sweet Spanish paprika)
4 pitted green olives

FOR THE COCKTAIL DRESSING:
150g *Mayonnaise* (see page 306), made with sunflower oil
1½ tbsp tomato ketchup
3 tbsp double cream
¾ tsp lemon juice
A pinch of salt

For the cocktail dressing, put the mayonnaise, tomato ketchup, double cream, lemon juice and ¾ teaspoon water into a bowl and mix together well until smooth. Season to taste with salt.

Separate the lettuce leaves, wash and dry well. Cut the carrot into 2 shorter pieces and finely shred on a mandolin, or coarsely grate. Finely shred the lettuce leaves, mix with the grated carrot and divide between 4 medium-sized plates.

Set aside 12 of the prawns and cut the remainder across into slices 5mm thick. Stir them into the cocktail dressing with the crab meat and diced tomato and spoon into the centre of the salad leaves. Arrange the whole prawns on top of the salad, drizzle ¼ teaspoon of the balsamic vinegar on each and sprinkle with a tiny pinch of pimentón. Garnish with the green olives and serve.

WHITE BEANS with CLAMS

Fabes con almejas SERVES 4–6

I wonder why we don't have the enormous variety of hearty bean dishes that other countries in Europe have. Dried peas, yes – mushy peas, pease pudding, pea and ham soup – so why not beans? It seems so natural to combine seafood with beans, as they do in Asturias, with some saffron and pimentón, garlic and olive oil. I love the simplicity of this recipe, the flavour of the salty clams shining through the beans with a little hint of chilli in the background. As with all bean dishes, it's difficult to be exact about the amount of liquid needed. It depends on the age, type and therefore absorbency of the beans, as well as how much liquid the clams will release. What you want is a dish with a stew-like consistency, not too dry or too soupy.

6 tbsp olive oil
2 medium onions, finely chopped
2 garlic cloves, crushed
1 tsp *pimentón picante*
    (smoked hot Spanish paprika)
400g dried white beans, such
    as *alubia planchada*,
    soaked overnight in
    plenty of cold water
4 fresh bay leaves
A large pinch of saffron strands
1kg small clams, such as
    carpetshell
100ml dry white wine
2 tbsp chopped flat-leaf parsley
Salt
Crusty fresh bread, to serve

Heat the olive oil in a large flameproof casserole or saucepan. Add the onion, garlic and pimentón and fry gently for 10 minutes until lightly golden. Drain the beans and add them to the pan with 1 litre of fresh cold water. Bring to the boil, skimming off any scum as it rises, add the bay leaves, cover and leave to simmer very gently for 1½ hours.

Uncover the beans, stir in the saffron and 1 teaspoon of salt or to taste and simmer slightly more vigorously for 30 minutes more, until the liquid has reduced and thickened and the beans are tender.

Just before the beans are ready, wash the clams, discarding any that don't show signs of closing when gently squeezed. Heat another large pan over a high heat, add the clams and the wine, cover and cook, shaking the pan every now and then, for 2–3 minutes until all the clams have opened.

Lift the clams out of their cooking liquor with a slotted spoon and stir them into the beans with the parsley and a few tablespoons of the cooking liquid to give the beans a stew-like consistency. Adjust the seasoning to taste, ladle into warmed shallow bowls and serve with the bread.

CLAMS with GARLIC, ANCHOVY, CHILLI and SLOW-COOKED ONIONS

Almejas 'Sarten' SERVES 4 AS A TAPAS OR STARTER

Testimony to the excellence of the restaurants in the Barrio Pescadores in Santander, the fishing docks of the city, is that I have included recipes from two restaurants there, a seafood paella from La Gaviota (see page 58), and this one from the Ristorante Vivero, more or less opposite. Vivero is one of those delightfully unpretentious places, all painted in blue and white, with portholes, coiled ropes and paintings of fishing boats. I went there on the first night after getting off the ferry from Plymouth and it was like falling off a log. You travel to Santander expecting to find some great seafood and fish in a place on the quay, you go to the quay, and the clams and the hake are all good, the wine is albariño and all's well with the world. I couldn't work out the exact ingredients of this when I was eating it, but it's pretty close to what I've written here, except they didn't have parsley in it. But I love my parsley. And just a quick note: for speed, you could also make this using the finely chopped onion confit on page 306. Simply heat a third of the mixture in a pan with the anchovies, and when they have melted, add the garlic and dried chilli, then continue with the recipe.

1kg small clams, such as
    carpetshell
150ml olive oil
25g unsalted butter
4 anchovy fillets in olive oil
2 large onions, finely chopped
3 garlic cloves, finely chopped
½ tsp crushed dried chilli flakes
4 tbsp dry white wine
2 tbsp chopped flat-leaf parsley
Salt and freshly ground black
    pepper

Wash the clams in cold water and discard any that don't show signs of closing when squeezed gently.

Put the olive oil and butter into a large pan with the anchovy fillets and heat gently until the anchovies have 'dissolved'. Stir in the onion and ½ teaspoon of salt and leave to cook very gently for 30 minutes, stirring every now and then, until very soft and sweet but not at all browned. Add the garlic and crushed dried chilli and cook for a further 10 minutes. Season lightly with a little more salt and some black pepper. This can be done ahead of time if you wish.

Just before serving, heat a large pan over a high heat, add the clams and the wine, cover and cook for 2–3 minutes, shaking the pan every now and then, until the clams have just opened.

Lift the clams out of the pan with a slotted spoon and add them to the onion mixture with 5–6 tablespoons of the clam cooking liquor – just enough to make a light sauce with the onions, but not so much that it makes them soupy – and the parsley. Stir together well and serve in warmed shallow bowls, or take to the table on a warmed serving plate everyone can dig into, as for tapas.

BEEF in WHITE WINE, OVIEDO-STYLE

Carne gobernada SERVES 6

This *gobernada* is a speciality of the capital city of Asturias, Oviedo, which is, incidentally, Woody Allen's favourite city in Europe. It is here that they present the prestigious Prince of Asturias awards for notable achievements, of which Woody Allen was a winner in 2002. Other recent winners in the Arts category include Pedro Almodóvar and Bob Dylan. Oviedo is a lovely place and quite unexpected; it has a great market, a fantastic location in the foothills of the Picos mountains and some great cider bars, where the waiters fill your glass with serious panache. On the face of it, this stew looks pretty uninteresting: just onions, carrots, garlic, beef and wine. First of all, it's unusual to have a beef stew made with white wine, which gives it a clean taste, and then there's a large amount of onion and garlic cooked with the beef in olive oil for hours, which ends up producing a well-reduced sauce with a lovely rich texture. As in a number of other dishes in this book, I'm intrigued by the use of bay leaf as the only herb, but that gives it considerable individuality. The Spanish like to serve this stew on top of some freshly made patatas fritas (see page 146), fried, of course, in the best olive oil.

1.5kg chuck or blade steak
7 tbsp olive oil
600g onions, chopped into 1cm pieces
10 garlic cloves, crushed
6 fresh bay leaves
300ml dry white wine
300g small carrots, cut into 5cm lengths
Salt and freshly ground black pepper
Patatas fritas or *Crisp-fried potatoes* (see pages 146 and 198), to serve

Trim the meat of any fat and gristle and cut it into 3cm chunks. Season well with salt and pepper.

Heat 2 tablespoons of the olive oil in a large flameproof casserole and fry the beef in batches until nicely browned. Set aside on a plate.

Add the remaining olive oil and the onions, garlic, bay leaves and ½ teaspoon of salt to the pan and cook very gently over a low heat for 30 minutes until the onions are soft and sweet and golden.

Return the beef to the pan, add the wine, bring to the boil and season with another ½ teaspoon of salt and some freshly ground black pepper. Cover and leave to simmer gently for 2 hours, stirring now and then.

Uncover, add the carrots, re-cover and cook for a further 30 minutes until the wine and meat juices have combined with the onions to make a thick sauce and the meat is meltingly tender. Adjust the seasoning to taste and serve with patatas fritas or sandy-textured fried potatoes.

THE SHELLFISH GATHERERS' OCTOPUS STEW

Pulpo mariscado SERVES 4–6

The appetite of many a Galician or Asturian is apt to make your average British person feel rather inadequate. At the restaurant where I enormously enjoyed this *pulpo mariscado,* the order of dishes for lunch ran as follows: deep-fried *chiperones* (whole baby squid); tripe with belly pork and *zorza,* a chorizo-like minced pork mixture; steamed sea urchins; this stew; *fabada* (see page 70), and finally *flan* (crème caramel). There may have been a tiny element of Spanish hospitality going on here but this was by no means the only Henry VIII-style lunch we encountered during our time in Spain. Nevertheless, the shellfish gatherers' octopus stew, course number four, was magnificent, but I have had to simplify it somewhat as there were so many different species of seafood included. It hasn't suffered for that. The secret is the really robust shellfish stock combined with the flavours of seafood cooked at the very last minute.

FOR THE STOCK:
4 tbsp olive oil
2 medium onions, chopped
2 leeks, cleaned and sliced
3 large carrots, thinly sliced
2 celery stalks, sliced
250g unpeeled North Atlantic
  prawns
1 large fish head, such as cod
2 large beef tomatoes, chopped
150ml dry white wine

FOR THE STEW:
5 tbsp olive oil
2 large onions, chopped
4 garlic cloves, finely chopped
1 green pepper, seeded and
  chopped
450g peeled Charlotte potatoes,
  cut into small chunks
3 tbsp plain flour
150ml dry cider
2 tbsp brandy
1 tbsp tomato purée
450–500g cooked octopus
  (see page 20)
500g mussels, cleaned
500g small clams, such as
  carpetshell, washed
8 large unpeeled cooked crevettes
2 tbsp chopped flat-leaf parsley
Salt
Crusty fresh bread, to serve

For the fish stock, heat the olive oil in a large pan over a medium-high heat. Add the onion, leek, carrot and celery and fry for 5–6 minutes until lightly golden. Add the prawns and fry for 2 minutes more. Add the fish head, tomatoes, wine and 4 litres of water, bring to the boil, lower the heat and leave to simmer for 40 minutes. Strain the stock, return to a clean pan and simmer rapidly until reduced to 1 litre. Set to one side. This can be done in advance.

For the stew, heat the olive oil in a large flameproof casserole. Add the onion, garlic and green pepper and fry gently for 5 minutes. Add the potatoes and continue frying for a further 5 minutes. Stir in the flour and cook for 1 minute, then stir in the cider, brandy, tomato purée and seafood stock. Bring to a boil, lower the heat, add ½ teaspoon of salt and leave to simmer for 10 minutes.

Meanwhile, slice the cooked octopus into bite-sized pieces. Add the mussels, clams and crevettes to the stew, cover and simmer until the mussels and clams have opened. Uncover, stir in the octopus and simmer for 1 minute to heat through. Adjust the seasoning to taste, sprinkle over the parsley and serve with bread.

A SEAFOOD PAELLA
from the COSTA VERDE
Paella de Barrio Pescadores SERVES 6–8

I was in the Barrio Pescadores in Santander. This is a rather unprepossessing area just by the docks, a sort of inner-city housing estate, with two or three large-windowed restaurants and an assortment of charcoal grills and paella burners on the pavement outside them. Their fish restaurants are all really good but I chose La Gaviota (the Seagull), because I'd been told they did very good hake. Somewhat irritatingly, David, the director, noticed they were making a large paella and insisted on filming it. 'Why are we filming a paella in Cantabria,' I asked truculently, 'when Valencia has the best paellas on the planet?' 'Because they look nice,' he said. Reluctantly, I got involved, and I have to say it tasted very nice, and led me to form the opinion that there's an awful lot of pressure about the best paellas. Basically, it's a simple dish if cooked correctly. The only rule I utterly agree with is: never eat a paella at night. They are far too filling. This is as good a seafood paella as you are going to find anywhere. In Spain they add a little yellow food colouring (see page 313) as well as saffron, but it's not essential to this dish.

500g prepared medium-sized
  squid, cut into 3cm pieces
5 tbsp olive oil
3 garlic cloves, finely chopped
150g shallot, finely chopped
1½ red peppers, seeded and
  chopped into 1cm pieces
1½ green peppers, seeded and
  chopped into 1cm pieces
1½ tsp *pimentón picante*
  (smoked hot Spanish paprika)
225g large raw peeled prawns
500g small clams, such as
  carpetshell, washed
600g short-grain paella rice,
  such as Calasparra
1 heaped tsp loosely packed
  saffron strands
1.5 litres *Fish stock* (see page 306)
250g large mussels, cleaned
6–8 cooked langoustines or
  unpeeled cooked crevettes
Salt
Alioli (see page 307), to serve
  (optional)

Dry the squid well on kitchen paper, season with salt and set to one side. Place a 40–50cm paella pan over 2 burners on a medium heat. Add the oil and garlic and, as soon as the garlic begins to sizzle, add the shallot and fry for 5–6 minutes until soft and sweet, turning the pan every few minutes so that everything cooks evenly. You will need to do this throughout the cooking time.

Add the red and green peppers and pimentón, and fry for 5 minutes until the peppers are just softened. Stir in the squid and stir-fry for 3–4 minutes until it becomes white and opaque.

Scatter the prawns and clams around the pan, add the rice and saffron, and stir everything together well. Add the stock and 2½ teaspoons of salt and bring to the boil, stirring briefly to redistribute the ingredients around the pan.

Leave to simmer vigorously for 6 minutes over a medium-high heat, but do not stir it any more, remembering to give the pan a turn every 2 minutes. Then reduce the heat to medium, arrange the mussels and langoustines or crevettes evenly around the pan and push them down slightly into the rice. Leave to cook for a further 14 minutes, again without stirring, by which time all the liquid will have been absorbed and the surface of the rice should be pitted with small holes.

Turn off the heat, cover the pan with a clean tea towel and leave to rest for 5 minutes before serving. Serve warm straight from the pan – with alioli, if, like me, you love it.

1 DE AGOSTO
EN EL PASEO DE SAN ANTONIO

40

festival de

la sardina 2009

Candás

FIESTAS DE SAN FELIX
DEL 30 AL 2 JULIO/AGOSTO

ASTURIAN MONKFISH FRITTERS

Frito de pixin SERVES 4 AS A TAPAS

This dish is sold in the *sidrerias* (cider houses) of Asturias, especially in Gijón, a city with a particular interest for me since the majority of live lobsters from Padstow are sent in a vivarium, a large articulated lorry fitted out with tanks of aerated and pumped seawater, to Spain, and Gijón is one of the ports to receive them. I ordered a couple of plates of monkfish fritters in a cider bar just near the Roman citadel one busy Saturday afternoon. As the afternoon progressed the floor steadily became littered with cocktail sticks and skewers, paper napkins, hand wipes and receipts, stubbed-out cigarettes and olive stones. It's not that the Spanish are messy or that it's unpleasant, it's just what they do. There's a big-screen TV on the wall and during the week it shows Argentinian soaps and at the weekend local bands looking decidedly dishevelled and bolshie, but somehow not quite as bolshie as our own. And these fritters are fantastic; beautifully fresh, clean-tasting monkfish, coated in flour and beaten egg, then fried in olive oil. The egg coating goes very well with the slightly acidic cider, made bubbly by being poured into the glass from a great height before serving.

1 x 400g monkfish fillet,
    trimmed of all membrane
1 garlic clove, very finely chopped
Olive oil, for shallow frying
25g plain flour
2 medium free-range eggs, beaten
Salt

Cut the monkfish fillet across into medallions 1cm thick. Sprinkle the pieces on both sides with the garlic and salt to taste.

Pour 1cm of olive oil into a large non-stick frying pan and place over a medium-high heat. Put the plain flour into one shallow dish and the beaten eggs into another.

Dust the pieces of monkfish a few at a time in the flour, knock off the excess, and then dip into the beaten egg. Add to the hot oil and fry for 2 minutes on each side until crisp and golden. Drain briefly on kitchen paper and serve straight away while still hot.

CRISP LETTUCE, ANCHOVY, EGG and CROUTON SALAD with a CREAMY VINAIGRETTE

SERVES 6

The future of fish stocks is not all bad news. In February, I went to a tinned anchovy producer in the Cantabrian port of Laredo. I was told they were one of the best producers of anchovies in Spain, and that actually means in the world, because even the Italians grudgingly admit that the anchovies from the Cantabrian Sea, salted, hand-filleted and preserved in Spanish olive oil, are the best. However, during my first visit they said they were processing anchovies from Argentina because the local fishery had been closed for four years, but they were confident that later that spring the local ones would be coming in on the boats again. And so it proved to be, and lots of them. It only goes to show that with a bit of care and stock management, four years can change everything in a fishery. These tinned anchovies have what I can only describe as a sweetness that I've never tasted before, and quite rightly the locals rank them up there with truffles and caviar. This isn't a traditional Spanish salad but I do think it draws attention to their superb flavour.

3 x 40g slices white crusty
   bread, cut 1cm thick
1 tbsp olive oil
6 medium free-range eggs
3 little gem lettuce
50g (approx. 12) large anchovy
   fillets in olive oil, drained
   and cut on the diagonal into
   2.5cm pieces

FOR THE DRESSING:
1 small garlic clove, crushed
1 large free-range egg yolk
1 tsp Dijon mustard
2 tbsp lemon juice
½ tsp caster sugar
150ml extra virgin olive oil
Salt and freshly ground
   black pepper

For the croutons, preheat the oven to 180°C/gas 4. Cut the crusts off the bread and tear the remainder into small pieces. Toss them in a bowl with the olive oil. Spread them on a baking tray and bake for 5–7 minutes or until crisp and golden. Remove and leave to cool. Then season lightly with salt.

Meanwhile, put the eggs into a pan of boiling water and hard-boil for 8 minutes. Drain and cover with cold water.

For the dressing, put the garlic, egg yolk, mustard, lemon juice, sugar and some seasoning into a small bowl. Mix together briefly with a hand-held electric whisk, then slowly whisk in the oil to make a smooth dressing.

Discard the outside leaves of the lettuce if necessary and tear the rest into small pieces. Wash and dry well, then spread over the base of 6 medium serving plates. Peel the hard-boiled eggs and cut them into quarters. Arrange 4 pieces over each plate of lettuce leaves with the 4 strips of anchovy fillet and a few croutons. Drizzle 1 tablespoon of dressing over each plate and serve straight away.

CRISP CORNMEAL FLATBREADS with FRIED EGGS and SAUSAGES

Tortas de maíz con huevos y chorizo SERVES 4

I'd heard about these cornmeal *tortas* from Asturias before I even got there. Maize from the New World was taken up very speedily in both Asturias and Galicia because the land was deemed too poor for growing wheat. I finally got to eat the classic combination at the Casa Poli restaurant in Puertas de Vidiago where we had lunch after we had filmed the hake on page 88 in their kitchen. I was much taken with it, the combination of the chewy flatbread with runny fried eggs and fried *gigas*, which is essentially the spicy meat mixture than goes into sausage skins to make chorizo, and which seemed almost Mexican in flavour. So I just had to buy some maize meal, chorizo and eggs and try it in the camper van I was travelling around in. Actually, we had it for lunch, but it would make a great breakfast dish with a *café negro* and maybe a couple of pickled chillies on the side.

125g *masa harina* (see page 311)
165ml hot water
olive oil for shallow frying
300g Spanish sausages, such
    as chorizo or chistorra
4–8 free-range eggs
Salt

Sift the *masa harina* and ½ teaspoon of salt into a mixing bowl and stir in the hot water to make a moist dough. Cover and set aside for 15 minutes. Then divide the dough into 8 evenly sized pieces (35–40g each) and roll them into balls. Working with one ball of dough at a time, roll or press out between 2 sheets of clingfilm into a 12cm disc.

Pour 5mm of olive oil into a frying pan, place over a medium heat and heat to about 170°C. Add one of the *tortas* at a time and fry for 1½–2 minutes on each side until slightly puffed up and golden brown. Keep warm, wrapped in a clean tea towel.

Fry the sausages in a little oil for about 5 minutes. Thicker, 3.5cm chorizos take about 10 minutes on a gentle heat. Slice into thick pieces on the diagonal. Fry the eggs to your liking. I like to use plenty of hot olive oil and spoon it over the eggs to slightly mist over the yolks. Serve with the crisp *tortas*.

ROASTED RABBIT with HOT BACON and CABBAGE SALAD and FONDANT POTATOES

SERVES 4

This recipe was prompted by a very good potato dish I discovered in Cantabria. There it was served with fried hake, and I just thought it would go extremely well with roasted rabbit.

2 farmed rabbits, weighing about 1.25–1.5kg each
3 tbsp olive oil
The leaves from 4 thyme sprigs
Salt and freshly ground black pepper

FOR THE FONDANT POTATOES:
3–5 tbsp olive oil
1 large onion, halved and thinly sliced
2 garlic cloves, thinly sliced
500g floury main-crop potatoes, such as Maris Piper or King Edwards, peeled
2 tsp fresh thyme leaves
180ml *Chicken stock* (see page 306)

FOR THE SAUCE:
150ml *Chicken stock* (see page 306)
100ml oloroso sherry or Madeira
60g chilled unsalted butter, cut into small pieces

FOR THE HOT CABBAGE AND BACON SALAD:
3 tbsp extra virgin olive oil
175g smoked bacon lardons
15g butter
1 small 400g Savoy cabbage, quartered, cored and shredded
3 tbsp sherry vinegar

Preheat the oven to 220°C/gas 7. Joint each rabbit into 8 pieces (see page 146), rub with olive oil and season well. Put the back legs in a roasting tin, sprinkle over some of the thyme leaves and set aside.

For the fondant potatoes, heat the olive oil in a large frying pan over a low heat. Add the onion and garlic, season, and cook for 15–20 minutes, stirring regularly, until the onion is lightly caramelized. Thinly slice the potatoes, on a mandolin if possible, and add them to the pan with the thyme leaves. Fry for 6–8 minutes, turning them over now and then, until lightly golden and almost tender. Transfer to a gratin dish, pour over the stock and bake for 30 minutes or until all the stock has been absorbed and the potatoes are tender.

After the potatoes have been cooking for 10 minutes, put the roasting tin of back legs into the oven and roast for 6 minutes. Add the rest of the rabbit pieces into the tin, sprinkle over the remaining thyme and a little more oil and roast for a further 12–14 minutes until the juices run clear when the thickest parts are pierced with a skewer.

Meanwhile, for the sauce, put the stock and sherry or Madeira into a small pan, bring to the boil and reduce to 3 tablespoons. Remove from the heat and set to one side.

Remove the rabbit from the oven, cover with foil and leave to rest for 5 minutes. For the hot cabbage salad, heat the 3 tablespoons of olive oil in a large pan, add the bacon lardons and fry gently until crisp and golden. Add the butter to the pan and when it has melted, add the shredded cabbage and sherry vinegar and toss over a high heat for 3 minutes until wilted but still slightly crunchy. Season to taste with salt, cover and keep warm.

If the fondant potatoes are not brown on top, place them under a hot grill for 2–3 minutes until they are crisp and caramelized. Bring the sauce reduction back to the boil, gradually whisk in the pieces of chilled butter, then season to taste. I like to serve this at the table with the rabbit on a big plate accompanied by the fondant potatoes, the salad in a bowl and a jug of the sauce.

MADRID-STYLE TRIPE

Callos a la madrileña SERVES 4

I first ate this dish, tripe with chorizo, pork and tomato, in Asturias and was disappointed, but only because I discovered it was from Madrid and I was looking for local dishes. However, it was exceptionally good. Later I found it on menus all over the country. I still cannot understand why so many people have an aversion to tripe, particularly when served like this with the flavours of garlic, chilli and pimentón prominent. To me it has the most satisfyingly tender texture, and I can't help feeling that the taste resides in the same area of flavour as really good buffalo mozzarella. How can it not be a delight? Perhaps it's an acquired taste, like the goaty taste of goat's cheese, which you come to appreciate and love in time.

500g ox tripe
150g piece boneless pork belly
100ml dry white wine
200g skinned chopped tomatoes,
    fresh or from a can
2 medium onions, chopped
6 garlic cloves, thinly sliced
10 fresh gratings of nutmeg
2 cloves
10 black peppercorns
The leaves from 3 sprigs fresh
    thyme
2 fresh bay leaves
2 tbsp olive oil
150g cooking chorizo sausage,
    skinned and chopped
1 tbsp *pimentón picante*
    (smoked hot Spanish paprika)
½ tsp crushed dried chilli flakes
1 tbsp plain flour
A small handful of flat-leaf
    parsley leaves, chopped
Salt
Crusty fresh bread, to serve

Preheat the oven to 140°C/gas 1. Cut the tripe into 3cm squares and put into a small flameproof casserole with the pork belly, wine, tomatoes, half of the chopped onions, the garlic, nutmeg, cloves, peppercorns, thyme, bay leaves and ½ teaspoon of salt. Add 700ml water, bring to the boil, cover with a lid and transfer to the oven. Leave to cook for 1½ hours.

Shortly before the tripe is ready, heat the oil in a medium-sized frying pan, add the remaining onion and chorizo and fry gently until the onion is very soft and just beginning to colour. Add the pimentón and crushed dried chillies and fry for 1 minute. Stir in the flour and cook for another minute. Remove the tripe from the oven and gradually stir 125ml of the cooking liquor into the pan. Bring to the boil, stirring, and leave the sauce to simmer for 3–4 minutes.

Meanwhile, lift the piece of pork belly out of the casserole and cut into pieces similar in size to the tripe. Stir them back into the casserole together with the sauce mixture, re-cover and simmer together for 3–4 minutes. Stir in the parsley, spoon into 4 shallow terracotta serving dishes and serve with plenty of bread for mopping up the juices.

CHICKEN with GARLIC

Pollo al ajillo SERVES 4

This is probably the most popular way of eating chicken in Spain. I'm always a little loath to remove skin from chicken because I enjoy it so much, but it is much better on a whole roasted chicken, where it becomes crisp, than here where the chicken pieces are marinated in crushed garlic, salt and olive oil and the skin becomes an impediment to the flavour of the garlic permeating the flesh. The Spanish way is to eat a chicken sauté like this on the bone with their fingers, but of course feel free to use boneless thighs or breasts if you wish. Either way it's the delicious brown garlicky finish to the chicken and more slices of fried garlic in the sherry-flavoured sauce that makes it so special.

1 x 1.5kg free-range chicken
8 fat garlic cloves
7 tbsp olive oil
200ml dry sherry or white wine
2 fresh bay leaves
Salt and freshly ground black
    pepper

First cut your chicken into small pieces. Slice through the skin joining the legs to the body, and cut through the joint, taking the 'oyster' of flesh on the backbone with them if you can. Cut the legs in half at the joint, cleaver the thighs in half and cut off the bony ends of each drumstick. Then cut off the wings, taking with them a little bit of meat from the bottom of each breast. Cut off the wing tips. Next, cut down either side of the breastbone, and then through the bones on either side of it and open up the bird. Cut horizontally through the bones beneath the breasts to remove them from the carcass and cut each one across into 3 pieces. Skin all the pieces of meat, put them into a large mixing bowl and season with a little salt and pepper.

Crush 4 garlic cloves into the bowl, add 1 tablespoon of the oil and 1 teaspoon of salt, and work the mixture into each piece of chicken with your hands. Cover and leave at room temperature for at least 1 hour.

Heat the remaining oil in a deep, 28cm frying pan over a medium heat. Add the chicken pieces and fry them, turning now and then, for about 20 minutes or until richly golden all over. Set them aside on a plate.

Pour away all but 1 tablespoon or so of the oil from the pan. Thinly slice the remaining garlic cloves. Return the pan to a medium heat, add the garlic and leave it to sizzle until lightly golden. Add the sherry or white wine and bring to the boil, rubbing the base of the pan with a wooden spatula to help release all the caramelized juices. Return the chicken pieces to the pan, add the bay leaves and cover with a lid. Lower the heat slightly and leave to cook gently for 15 minutes, uncovering the pan for the last few minutes to allow the wine to evaporate and almost disappear. I like to serve this with creamy mashed potatoes.

WHITE BEAN STEW
with PORK and SAUSAGES
Fabada asturiana SERVES 4

To me, *fabada* and a glass or two of Asturian cider, poured from a great height into your glass to oxygenate it, is a match made in heaven. In the cider bars of Oviedo, the pouring of cider seems to me to be a perfect local manifestation of macho, the object being to hold the cider bottle above your head and the glass in the other hand as near to the floor as possible, and to pour without looking so that the stream of cider passes close to your chest without splashing onto it. The restaurant where they cooked this for me, Las Peñas in the village of Santurio close to Gijón, was one of those life-affirming places you find from time to time on your travels. Situated right in the Asturian hills, the foothills of the Picos mountains, it was an enormous *sidreria* (cider house) with a massive car park, all the family loquaciously involved in either cooking the *fabada* or serving it and the cider, hordes of locals all cheerful and friendly, and a giant TV screen in the corner, playing Brazilian and Argentinian soaps from day to night. It's the sort of dish for which you need to set aside the rest of the day, and is therefore only to be taken at lunchtime, with the opportunity of a long afternoon of sleepy digestion ahead of you. Nothing else better brings out the flavour of a good smoky chorizo and some locally produced, heavily smoked *morcilla* (blood sausage) or the fatty delicacy of some thick slices of belly pork, and the wondrous *fabes de la Granja*, a long white bean about the size of half your little finger with a creamy, buttery, almost melt-in-the-mouth texture. If you cannot get them, I suggest you use cannellini beans or butter beans instead.

600g dried white beans, such as
    fabes de la Granja, cannellini
    beans or butter beans
100g piece of pork back fat
    (optional)
200g well-smoked, streaky
    bacon, in one piece
4 smoked cooking chorizo
    sausages
25g butter
A large pinch of saffron strands
4 x 75g smoked morcilla or
    300g piece of black pudding
Salt

Put the beans into a large bowl and cover by 8–10cm with cold water. Leave to soak overnight.

The next day, drain the beans and put them into a large flameproof casserole or saucepan. Cover with 1.5 litres cold water and bring to a boil over a medium heat, skimming off the scum as it rises to the surface. Reduce the heat to a simmer, add the pork back fat, if using, cover with a lid and leave to simmer gently for 1 hour, stirring every now and then to make sure nothing is sticking to the base of the pan. If necessary add a little more boiling water, so as to keep the beans just covered at all times.

After the beans have been cooking for 1 hour, add the piece of smoked bacon and push it down well into the beans. Cover and continue to simmer for another 30 minutes.

Now taste the beans and add about 1 teaspoon of salt, the chorizos, butter and saffron to the pan and stir well to mix everything in. Place the morcilla or black pudding on top of the beans and simmer, uncovered and a little more vigorously it if looks too wet, for another 30 minutes or until the beans and the meats are fork-tender and the liquid has reduced to leave a stew-like consistency. Turn off the heat and leave the *fabada* to rest for 10 minutes. Then lift the sausages and meat onto a board and carve the bacon into short, thick slices. Spoon some beans into large warmed soup plates, top with chorizo, morcilla and bacon, ladle a few more beans on top and serve.

MENÚ
ASTURIANO
1º FABADA
O POTE ASTURIANOS
O ENSALADA SETAS
2º TROCEADO BUEY
O TERNERA ASTURIANA
O CACHOPO, JAMÓN, QUESO
O PESCADO

Chapter Three

BASQUE COUNTRY

Arriving in Axpe Marzana, you could have been in an alpine village, with the misty limestone crags towering above you. It was distinctly chilly and there was a scent of woodsmoke in the air. I parked in a little square, the Plaza San Juan, with a pretty church on one side and a pelota court on the other. I know that, because they were whacking balls about like mad things that day. I went into the Asador Etxebarri and upstairs to a beautiful, lofty dining room with a certain austerity about it. I ate carrot soup in a very nice carrot-coloured bowl, followed by a small plate of very salty, lightly smoked butter, which had been rolled in truffle-flavoured dried breadcrumbs. I was in a very receptive mood. I usually am for lunch on a chilly day in a beautiful country, and the delicate smoke with the butter seemed astonishingly sensitive. After that came a small plate of *percebes*. These goose-necked barnacles were very good indeed because they had been slightly undercooked. Then came some poached, lightly smoked oysters on a leaf of laverbread seaweed served with the only foam in the whole meal, again tasting of seaweed. Then came steamed cockles in the shell with the zest of grapefruit. Next, a very lightly poached egg yolk on a delicate olive-oil mashed potato and a great pile of shaved black truffle. Next, a lightly grilled *txistorra* sausage that had been split open lengthways, accompanied by a cornmeal breadstick. Then, nearly the star of the show, a small, thick fillet of very fatty mackerel which had been cooked in smoke but was still very underdone. I still remember the melting quality of that mackerel and the way the smoke emphasized its freshness. Next came a small pile of elvers, very tiny eels, very delicate and almost impossible to get anywhere any more, again with just a scent of smoke about them, and then came what I would call the pay-off. Up to this point the courses had been so tiny that I was charmed and delighted by the fresh, just-cooked flavours of everything. What goes wrong for me in multi-course menus is that I get bored after a while with too many little dishes, but not here. An enormous rib chop of beef, a *chuleta*, arrived, but not any old rib of beef, as I later discovered, but from Galician blond beef cattle, dry-aged for four weeks and cooked over charcoal, salty and smoky and very, very rare. To put it pretentiously, it was like the end of a symphony with drums going and cymbals crashing. And to finish came a perfectly executed Basque cheesecake, which looked like an individual ripe cheese sinking slightly in the centre, with a lick of caramel around the plate. I had to discover more about this food, and met the chef-patron Victor Arguinzoniz, and the head chef Lennox Hastie, who turned out to be from Queensland and whose English made it easier to understand the ethos of the kitchen. Victor was steeped in the ways of the Basque Country and there was nothing he didn't know about wood. It turned out that all the dishes had been cooked over charcoal made by them from various different types of wood, such as holm oak and vine trimmings, so that each dish was smoked by the correct-flavoured charcoal. Even delicate produce like the elvers, oysters and cockles had been cooked on bars that could be moved up and down above the coals with a pulley, some of them in a specially designed mesh pan to allow the smoke to permeate the food to the right degree. To me this lunch said everything about the superlative quality of Basque produce, and I also felt I was in the company of two people who were doing something truly original, but at the same time very satisfying for the slightly old-fashioned customer, like me.

I keep getting asked where I had the best food in Spain. I find that difficult to answer, but I rate Basque cooking very highly. Barbecuing over charcoal, not just meat but even delicate fish like turbot, is very close to my heart, and the pintxos (tapas) bars in the Parte Vieja, the old quarter of San Sebastián, are worth a journey from the UK in their own right. The Basques say that pintxos started a long while before tapas, in the fifteenth century, but the simple idea of moving from one bar to another – known as the *txikiteo* (pronounced 'chikiteo') – is a civilized way of eating and drinking. Calling in for a txakoli, the fresh slightly fizzy white wine, and maybe a plate of salt cod fritters with romesco sauce, or a slice of tortilla or a little tart of *txangurro* (spider crab) with tomato and chilli is pretty close to perfection for any lover of eating and drinking.

CRAB TARTS with GARLIC, TOMATO and TARRAGON

MAKES 12

In the pintxos bars of San Sebastian, *txangurro* ('changurro'), or baked spider crab, turns up in all manner of guises: in small spider-crab shells, scallop shells or ramekins, or as a filling for crepes, puff-pastry cornets and small crisp pastry tartlets like these. I confess to taking a slightly less hard line these days on buying certain pre-made ingredients. You can now buy good ready-made pastry and tartlet cases. Perhaps not as good as my recipe here, but I don't want to insist, because this recipe does require a bit of work even without the pastry-making. I do think it is one of the best baked crab dishes anywhere, one we still sell in the Seafood Restaurant today some fifteen years after I first discovered it on a holiday in St Jean de Luz. If you can't get spider crab, brown crab is nearly as good. And if you don't want to make the crab-shell stock, leave that stage out and fold just the crab meat, from a spider or brown crab, into the spicy tomato sauce. It won't be true txangurro but it will still taste very good.

1 quantity *Rich shortcrust pastry* (see page 307)
2 large cooked spider crabs or 1 large cooked brown crab
5 tbsp olive oil, plus 1 tsp
8 garlic cloves, 4 bruised and 4 finely chopped
200g can chopped tomatoes
60ml white wine
60ml brandy
3 fresh bay leaves
1 large sprig tarragon
1 small bunch flat-leaf parsley
100g shallot, finely chopped
40g finely chopped carrot
¼ tsp crushed dried chilli flakes
225g skinned, seeded and chopped tomatoes, fresh or from a can
25g fresh white breadcrumbs
Salt and freshly ground black pepper

Preheat the oven to 200°C/gas 6. Roll out the pastry very thinly and cut out twelve 9cm discs using a plain pastry cutter. Use these to line lightly greased small tartlet tins that measure 6.5cm across the base. Do this in batches if you don't have enough tins. Line each one with small discs of foil, place on a baking tray and bake blind for 10 minutes or until golden brown. Remove and set to one side.

Remove the white meat from the crabs and set aside. You should have about 225g. Put all the debris except for the back shells in a pan and crush them slightly with the end of a rolling pin. Add 2 tablespoons of oil and the bruised garlic cloves and fry over a high heat for 5 minutes. Add the canned tomatoes, wine, brandy, 200ml water, bay leaves, tarragon and the stalks from the bunch of parsley. Bring to the boil, lower the heat and simmer for 30 minutes, then strain into a bowl or clean pan. Discard everything left in the sieve.

Heat 3 tablespoons of oil in a medium-sized pan over a medium heat. Add the remaining garlic, the shallot, carrot and crushed chilli flakes and cook gently for 10 minutes until very soft, sweet and lightly browned. Add the fresh tomatoes, crab shell stock and a pinch of salt and simmer until the mixture has reduced to a thick sauce. Finely chop the remaining parsley leaves and stir in all but 1 tablespoon with the crab meat and a little more seasoning to taste.

Set the oven temperature to 220°C/gas 7. Spoon the mixture into the pastry cases. Stir the teaspoon of olive oil into the breadcrumbs with the parsley and sprinkle on top. Bake for 5–6 minutes until the topping is crisp and golden. Serve warm.

PIQUILLO PEPPERS STUFFED with SALT COD PURÉE

SERVES 8 AS A TAPAS

This is one of the most common pintxos in the tapas bars of San Sebastián. The peppers either come like this, simply stuffed with a salt cod purée, or turned into a *croquetta*-like fritter, coated in flour, egg and breadcrumbs and deep-fried until crisp and golden. Eating bacalao in the Basque region reminds me of one of my favourite books on food, *Cod* by Mark Kurlansky. In this he points out the enormous importance of cod in world history and the fact that the Basques were the first to exploit the then massive stocks on the eastern seaboard of Canada and America; a sailor was described as saying you just lowered a basket into the sea and pulled them in. Kurlansky points out that the Basques sailed to America hundreds of years before Columbus got there, but didn't see the need to tell anybody. Cod in those days without refrigeration would always have been salted at sea.

2 x 250g jars piquillo peppers
1 quantity *Ajoarriero* (Salt cod
    and potato purée, see page 196;
    made with only 3 tablespoons
    of the cooking liquor)
Extra virgin olive oil

Preheat the oven to 200°C/gas 6. Tip the piquillo peppers out onto a plate and separate them. Working with one pepper at a time, open it up and hold it loosely in one hand. Using a teaspoon, carefully spoon a little of the salt cod purée into each one, packing it in well to give the pepper back its original shape, but taking care not to split them as you do so.

Tightly pack them, open end upwards, in a lightly oiled shallow baking dish, drizzle with a little more oil and bake for 15–20 minutes or until the filling has heated through. Serve hot.

Pimiento
de
Piquillo
1 – 2,50€

CHEESE FRITTERS

Buñuelos de queso SERVES 6 AS A TAPAS

These reminded me a bit of French *gougères* when I had them in San Sebastián, the differences being that they are made with Manchego cheese and flavoured with a generous amount of *pimentón picante*, which gives them a lovely, naturally smoky flavour. Don't deep-fry more than about six at a time in a domestic fat-fryer and have someone standing by to rush them to your guests, as they are so much better eaten immediately, piping hot.

100g butter
150g plain flour
1½ tsp *pimentón picante*
    (smoked hot Spanish paprika)
4 free-range eggs, beaten
100g finely grated Manchego
    cheese
1 tbsp chopped flat-leaf parsley
Olive oil or vegetable oil, for
    deep-frying
Salt and freshly ground black
    pepper

Put the butter and 250ml water into a medium-sized pan and leave over a low heat until the butter has melted. Bring the mixture to the boil and add the flour and pimentón. Take off the heat and beat vigorously until the mixture is smooth and leaves the side of the pan. Return to a very low heat and cook gently for 5 minutes, stirring constantly.

Remove from the heat and leave the mixture to cool slightly before gradually beating in the eggs to make a smooth, glossy paste. Beat in the cheese, parsley, ½ teaspoon of salt and some black pepper to taste. Heat some oil for deep-frying to 180°C.

Drop 5–6 heaped teaspoons of the mixture, about 3–4cm apart, into the hot oil and fry for 4–5 minutes, turning them over in the oil now and then, until puffed up, crisp and golden. Drain on kitchen paper and serve at once.

SAUTÉED WILD MUSHROOMS with EGGS

Setas con huevos SERVES 1 FOR BRUNCH OR LUNCH

I ate this at a pintxos bar-come-restaurant called Bar Ganbarra, situated on the Calle de San Jerónimo in the Parte Vieja of San Sebastián. The display of tapas on the bar was very appetizing, particularly a mountain of wild mushrooms including my favourite, ceps, all in perfect condition. For this the mushrooms were sliced and quickly cooked in olive oil, *a la plancha*, in other words on a searingly hot flat stainless-steel griddle, then served with simply a raw egg yolk in the centre of the plate, sprinkled with a little sea salt. The egg yolk acted as a sauce when broken and mixed with the hot mushroom juices and I was left philosophizing on the fact that the simple things in life are often the most enjoyable.

200g mixed wild mushrooms, such as ceps, trompettes de la mort, pieds de mouton and chanterelles
1 tbsp olive oil
1 large, free-range egg yolk
Sea salt and freshly ground black pepper
Crusty fresh bread, to serve

Clean and trim the mushrooms before using. Simply brush away any stray particles of dirt or undergrowth with a dry pastry brush and, if really necessary, wipe them clean with a damp cloth. Thickly slice the mushrooms only if they are particularly large.

Heat the olive oil in a 25cm frying pan over a high heat. Add the mushrooms, cut-face down if sliced, and leave to cook for 1 minute until they colour slightly. Season lightly, turn them over and cook for 1 minute more, seasoning them again lightly as they cook.

Spoon the mushrooms onto a warm plate and push them slightly towards the rim to create a small space in the centre. Drop in the egg yolk and season it with a little sea salt and black pepper. Serve straight away with crusty bread.

BRAISED PETIT POIS with OLIVE OIL, SPRING ONIONS and WET GARLIC

SERVES 4 AS A STARTER OR VEGETABLE COURSE

I wish more chefs in British restaurants had the courage to serve up a seasonal vegetable dish as a course. Asparagus we do, but what about the first sprouting broccoli of the season with hollandaise sauce, or some baby carrots glazed in butter, sugar and tarragon? I found this in the Basque Country: peas lightly cooked with green garlic, which is garlic picked when still only the size of a spring onion. It would be nice to be able to buy it in Britain, but using spring onions and new season's wet garlic is nearly as good.

4 tbsp olive oil
20g (approx. 4 large cloves) garlic,
    ideally new season's wet garlic,
    thinly sliced
1 bunch spring onions, trimmed
    and cut into 2.5cm lengths
500g shelled petit pois peas,
    ideally new season's fresh,
    but frozen will do
½ tsp caster sugar
Salt

Put the olive oil and sliced garlic into a wide-based pan and cook gently over a low heat for about 1 minute, until softened but not at all coloured. It is very important to cook this dish slowly and gently.

Add the spring onions to the pan and continue to cook gently for 4 minutes until just soft but still holding their shape.

Add the peas, 250ml water, sugar and 1 teaspoon of salt and bring to a simmer. Cook for 1 minute only, then ladle into warmed soup plates and serve.

CRISP-FRIED HAKE in GARLIC OIL with a DRESSED GREEN SALAD

Merluza rebozada con ensalada SERVES 4

The Basque gastronomic societies, called *txokos* ('chokos'), were one of most pressing reasons for a journey to Spain. The idea of these all-male clubs meeting regularly to cook together and probably talk and drink too much was thoroughly attractive to me. The societies started in the mid-1800s and spread like wildfire as industrialization brought prosperity to the cities, so much so that there are more than three hundred in San Sebastián alone. Some are big, like the one I visited, called Gaztelupe, complete with dining room, bar and restaurant-sized kitchen, where a dozen or so members can cook lunch for themselves and friends. Others are much smaller. I had what I can only describe as a rip-roaring lunch. First, I joined in the preparation of this perfectly simple way of cooking hake and an accompanying salad, and then I sat down to enjoy *txistorra*, skinny chorizo sausages, with some thick-crusted bread, followed by boiled white asparagus dressed with a white wine, shallot and parsley vinaigrette, and then this hake dish. The hake exemplified fresh fish cooked simply, but was almost outshone by the Basque ewe's milk cheese, Idiazabal, served with membrillo and some excellent walnuts to finish. We sang, they danced, they played music, and we stumbled out, full of bonhomie and love of Spanish hospitality. And as for the women? They are, they claim, glad to get the men out of the house for a while, for a few hours of welcome peace.

250ml olive oil
6 garlic cloves, roughly sliced
75g plain flour
2 free-range eggs, beaten
8 x 100g pieces skinned hake fillet
Salt

FOR THE GREEN SALAD:
1 soft-leaved lettuce, broken
  into leaves, washed and dried
1 medium onion, halved and
  thinly sliced
2 tsp white wine vinegar
3 tbsp extra virgin olive oil

Put the olive oil and garlic into a large, deep frying pan. The oil needs to be about ½ cm deep. Place the pan over a medium heat and leave until the garlic turns golden brown. Remove the pan from the heat and quickly remove the garlic with a slotted spoon and discard.

Put the flour into one shallow dish and the beaten eggs into another. Place the lettuce leaves for the salad in a shallow serving bowl and scatter over the onion slices. Whisk the vinegar and oil together with a pinch of salt.

Place the pan of garlic-infused oil back over a medium heat. Season the pieces of hake on both sides with salt and then dip half the pieces first into the flour and then the beaten egg. Put them into the hot oil and cook for about 5 minutes, turning them over halfway, until cooked through. Drain briefly on kitchen paper and transfer to a warmed serving plate. Keep warm while you cook the remainder.

Drizzle the dressing over the lettuce and onions, toss together briefly and serve with the crisp-fried hake.

HAKE with CLAMS, ASPARAGUS, PEAS and PARSLEY

Merluza a la koxkera SERVES 4

Juan Mari Arzak is, together with his daughter Elena, responsible for the next most famous and highly awarded restaurant in Spain after El Bulli, Arzak. El Bulli is closing down for good, so if you wish to appreciate the enormous complexity of a Spanish Michelin 3-star restaurant – where I had 15 different dishes at lunch and there must have been about 40 chefs cooking it – Arzak is a must. In addition to that, Juan Mari and Elena completely understand traditional Basque cooking and you can also order a meal of entirely Basque dishes. Juan Mari listed for me the five most important classic dishes: *bacalao a la vizcaína* (salt cod in a dried red pepper sauce), *chipirones en su tinta* (baby squid in black ink sauce), *kokotxas al pil pil* (hake cheeks in garlic sauce), *pastel de krabarroka* (rascasse mousse) and *merluza con salsa verde* (hake in green sauce). The only difference between *merluza con salsa verde* and *merluza a la koxkera*, this recipe, is the addition of asparagus, normally white, though I've used green, as it's hard to get fresh white asparagus in the UK. Apparently, to be called *koxkero*, a true Basque, you have to have been born in the Calle 31 de Agosto in San Sebastián, which is where some of the best pintxos bars are – even harder than a cockney being born within the sound of Bow Bells because it's rather a short little street.

4 x 175–200g pieces skinned hake fillet, cut 2–2.5cm thick
200g asparagus tips, each about 8cm long
250g peas, fresh or frozen
Plain flour, for dusting, plus 1 tbsp
6 tbsp olive oil
4 garlic cloves, finely chopped
100g finely chopped shallot
175ml dry white wine
100ml *Fish stock* (see page 306)
250g small clams, such as carpetshell, washed
1 tbsp chopped flat-leaf parsley
Salt

Season the pieces of hake generously on both sides with salt and set aside for 10–15 minutes. Meanwhile, drop the asparagus tips into a pan of well-salted water and cook for 2 minutes until just tender. Add the peas, bring back to the boil, drain and refresh under running cold water. Leave to drain.

Dust the hake steaks in flour and shake off the excess. Heat 4 tablespoons of the olive oil in a large frying pan over a medium-high heat. Add the hake and fry for 2–3 minutes on each side until golden brown on the outside but not quite cooked through. Lift out onto a plate and set to one side; wipe the pan clean.

Add the remaining 2 tablespoons of oil and the garlic and shallots to the pan and fry over a medium heat for 3 minutes or until soft and lightly golden. Stir in the tablespoon of flour, then gradually stir in the wine and stock to make a smooth sauce. Bring to a simmer, return the hake to the pan and cook for 1 minute. Add the clams, cover and cook for 2–3 minutes until all the clams have opened and the fish is cooked through.

Uncover and scatter over the asparagus tips, peas and parsley. Simmer for a minute or two more until the vegetables have heated through. Taste the sauce, adjust the seasoning to taste, and serve.

CUTTLEFISH in a RICH SQUID INK SAUCE

Chocos en su tinta SERVES 4

I was in half a mind not to include this recipe in the book, because stewing cuttlefish with garlic, tomato, white wine, olive oil and its own ink ends up in a deep black dish, which is the equivalent of going to one of those restaurants where you are served your food in darkness and have the slightly dubious pleasure of trying to work out what you're eating. However, this was the first 'foreign' dish I ate as an eight-year-old. I might have been trying to show off to my parents, but I do remember being quite impressed that it didn't taste fishy, and in fact it's very good because the ink imparts just a subtle, sweet flavour of the sea. I ate it back then while on holiday in the Cantabrian fishing port of Laredo, but when I went there recently I found that our hotel, the Carlos V, had long gone and the place is now a campsite.

1kg uncleaned cuttlefish
150ml *Fish stock* (see page 306)
4 tbsp olive oil
1 large onion, finely chopped
3 garlic cloves, crushed
200g skinned chopped tomatoes, fresh or from a can
2 fresh bay leaves
150ml white wine
1 tbsp chopped flat-leaf parsley
Salt and freshly ground black pepper

To prepare the cuttlefish, first cut off the tentacles just in front of the eyes. Remove the beak-like mouth from the centre of the tentacles and throw it away, then pull the skin off the tentacles and set them to one side. Cut the head sections from the body and discard, then pull off the fins and pull the skin off these. Cut the body sections open from the top to bottom along the dark-coloured back and remove and discard the cuttlebones. Remove the entrails and locate the ink pouches, which are small pearly white pouches, in amongst them. Carefully remove them without bursting them and set to one side. Discard the rest and then wash out the bodies well and pull off the skin. Leave the tentacles whole and cut the bodies and wings across into strips 1.5–2cm wide.

Drop the reserved ink sacs into the fish stock, carefully slit them open with a small knife and rinse them out in the stock to remove as much of the ink as you can. Remove the little sacs and discard.

Heat half the oil in a large frying pan over a high heat, add half the prepared cuttlefish and some seasoning and sauté for 1 minute until lightly golden. Remove with a slotted spoon, set aside and repeat with the remainder.

Add the onion and garlic and leave to cook gently, stirring now and then, for 5 minutes until soft but not browned. Add the tomatoes, bay leaves, wine, inky stock and some seasoning and bring to a gentle simmer. Add ½ teaspoon of salt and the cuttlefish, part cover and simmer for 45 minutes. Then uncover the pan, increase the heat slightly and leave to simmer a little more vigorously until the sauce has reduced and thickened and the cuttlefish is tender. Adjust the seasoning to taste, sprinkle with the parsley and serve.

A SMALL STEW of MUSSELS, CLAMS, PRAWNS and HOME-SALTED COD with POTATOES, LEEKS and ALIOLI

SERVES 4

The idea for this dish came from the classic Basque soup called *purrusalda*, of leeks, potatoes and bacalao, *puerros* being the name for leeks, and *saldos* meaning well-balanced. I made this and found it remarkably similar to fish stews I've made in the past, from the Charente and Brittany coast in France. I had a conversation with someone in Australia recently about my books, where he referred jokingly to my 'parsley period' and said that all my dishes had loads of parsley in them. I fear I'm now in my 'alioli period', as I couldn't resist stirring some into this stew and adding a pinch of saffron to give it a nice subtle yellow colour.

200g piece of *Home-salted fresh cod* (see page 307)
300g shell-on North Atlantic prawns, thawed if frozen
500g fresh mussels, cleaned (see page 22)
500g small clams such as carpetshell, washed
900ml *Fish stock* (see page 306)
½ tsp loosely packed saffron strands
1 tsp lemon juice
600g floury main-crop potatoes, such as Maris Piper or King Edwards
2 leeks, trimmed and washed (to leave you with about 450g)
3 tbsp oil
3 garlic cloves, thinly sliced
10 tbsp (about 130g) *Alioli* (see page 307)
2 tbsp chopped flat-leaf parsley
Salt and freshly ground black pepper

If you haven't already done so, cover the home-salted cod with cold water and leave to soak for 1 hour.

Peel the prawns, reserving the heads and shells. Heat a large pan over a high heat, add the mussels and clams and a splash of the fish stock, cover and cook, shaking the pan every now and then, for 2–3 minutes or until their shells have opened. Tip into a colander set over a bowl to collect the cooking liquid and leave to cool slightly. Remove the meats from the shells and set aside with the prawns.

Put the remaining fish stock, all but the last tablespoon or two of the mussel and clam cooking liquor, the saffron, lemon juice, the prawn heads and shells into a pan and simmer until reduced to 600ml. Strain and set aside.

Peel the potatoes and cut into 1.5cm cubes. Put in well-salted boiling water and simmer for about 8 minutes or until just tender. Drain and set aside.

Thinly slice the leeks. Heat the oil in a large pan over a medium heat, add the garlic, and as soon as it starts to sizzle, add the leeks and a small splash of the reduced fish stock. Cover and cook gently for 6 minutes until soft but still holding their shape.

Drain the salted cod and put into a pan with cold water to cover. Bring to the boil and simmer for 5 minutes. Lift out onto a plate, cool a little then break the fish into large flakes, discarding the skin and any bones. Cover and keep warm.

Put the alioli into a bowl, add a good splash of the warm stock and stir until smooth. Add the remaining stock to the leeks and bring to a simmer. Stir in the potatoes, prawns, mussels, clams and flakes of salt cod and warm through gently for just 1–2 minutes. Stir in the alioli mixture, chopped parsley and seasoning to taste and leave until hot enough to be just uncomfortable to your little finger and slightly thickened – but take care not to let the soup boil or the mixture will split. Serve straight away.

CHARCOAL-GRILLED MONKFISH with a BASQUE VINAIGRETTE

Rape a la parilla SERVES 2

The cooking of fish on the north coast of Spain is characterized by the simplicity of the dishes. If you order a *centolla* (spider crab) or a couple of *necora* (swimming crabs), they'll come simply boiled in seawater with not even a slice of lemon as an accompaniment. The locals feel that anything this good requires nothing more. Even when you get to the Basque coast simplicity rules, but here some of the best fish cooking comes from the *asadores,* restaurants that specialize in cooking fish over charcoal. The grill is called a *parilla* and the grill chef a *parillero.* What they do might appear easy but that's deceptive; their skill is considerable and they are paid more than run-of-the-mill chefs. They specialize in cooking fish *a la espalda,* 'on the back'. The fish, such as sole or their much-prized turbot, is held in a long-handled wire clamp and cooked on grill bars raised and lowered by the turning of a wheel. The *parillero* at the Asador Mayflower in Getaria brushes all his fish with a mixture of olive oil, lemon juice, vinegar and salt. Most of the grilled fish are then taken into the kitchen to be filleted and dressed before being brought to the table. Traditionally you don't get anything on the side, but I ordered a green salad and some chips. The only thing to add to what for me was perfection was a bottle of chilled Txakoli, the slightly sparkling Basque wine.

1 x 350–400g skinned monkfish tail, trimmed of all membrane
2 tbsp olive oil
1 large garlic clove, thinly sliced
A pinch of crushed dried chilli flakes
1 tsp white wine vinegar
1 tsp finely chopped parsley
Salt and freshly ground black pepper

FOR THE BARBECUING MARINADE:
2 tbsp olive oil
1 tbsp lemon juice
1 tbsp white wine vinegar

Light the barbecue (see page 314) to high. For the barbecuing marinade, mix the olive oil, lemon juice and vinegar together in a small bowl with ½ teaspoon of salt.

Brush the monkfish lightly with the marinade and barbecue for about 7 minutes on each side, brushing with more of the marinade every now and then, until just cooked through. Lift the fish onto a board and separate the 2 fillets from each side of the bone. Transfer to a warmed serving platter, cover and keep warm.

Put the olive oil, garlic and chilli flakes into a small pan and heat over a high heat until the garlic is turning golden. Remove from the heat and stir in the vinegar, parsley and ¼ teaspoon of salt. Drizzle this mixture over the fish and serve.

POT-ROASTED CHICKEN with CHORIZO, LEEKS and CIDER

SERVES 4

I have to confess this is not entirely a local dish, but it *could* be. What I wanted was a recipe for a pot roast, as it produces such succulence in a good free-range bird. And I'm very fond of chorizo cooked in cider, a popular tapas along the northern coast of Spain, cider being as important in the Basque Country as it is in Asturias and Cantabria. So I came up with this. It's very good with mash.

1 x 1.75kg free-range chicken
2 tbsp olive oil
2 cooking chorizo sausages, sliced
50g butter
700g leeks, cleaned and sliced
4 garlic cloves, thinly sliced
300g baby carrots, trimmed
    and peeled or scraped clean
The leaves from 2 large thyme
    sprigs
2 fresh bay leaves
200ml dry cider
Salt and freshly ground black
    pepper

Preheat the oven to 160°C/gas 3. Season the chicken inside and out with salt and pepper. Heat the olive oil in a flameproof casserole dish large enough to take the chicken. Brown the chicken on all sides until nicely golden then lift onto a plate and set to one side.

Lower the heat and add the chorizo, butter, leeks, garlic, carrots, thyme and bay leaves. Cover and cook gently for 5 minutes until the leeks have softened.

Uncover the casserole and place the chicken on top of the vegetables. Pour over the cider, re-cover and cook in the oven for 1 hour. Then uncover once more, increase the oven temperature to 200°C/gas 6 and continue to cook for another 20 minutes to brown the skin.

Remove the casserole from the oven, lift the chicken onto a carving board, cover with foil and set aside. Skim the excess fat from the surface of the vegetables and cooking juices, then place over a medium heat and simmer vigorously for 5 minutes to reduce the liquid and concentrate the flavours a little. Season to taste with more salt if necessary.

Cut the string off the chicken. To carve, cut off the legs and cut each one in half at the joint. Carve the breast away in slices. Using a slotted spoon, put the chorizo and vegetable mixture into the centre of 4 warmed plates with chicken on top. Spoon over the cooking juices and serve.

BEEF RIB CHOP with SPICY POTATOES and GRILLED RED PEPPERS

Chuletón con patatas picantes y pimientos asados SERVES 2

I wonder if the *Pais Vasco* is not responsible for the barbecue, now the most popular form of cooking in the States, Australia, New Zealand, and even across the road from my cottage in England, when the smell of sausages permeates my sitting room on a still, humid night. It appears that the idea of grilling beef over glowing embers in this region of Spain originated with the charcoal burners who cooked their meals over their own product, but whether it's true or not, the Basques have tremendous *parrilladas* (barbecues) and the equipment for raising and lowering meat or fish over the hot coals is very sophisticated. My enthusiasm for cooking a whole forerib of beef on the bone comes from a fabulous dinner I had at Roxario's *sidreria* (cider house), in the town of Astigarraga just outside San Sebastián, where smoky steak, some delicious Basque cider, and an incredibly busy and atmospheric dining room are a must for anyone who likes their beef rugged.

3 large red peppers
1 large, chined forerib of beef on
    the bone (it should be about
    5cm thick and will probably
    weigh about 1.3kg)
2 tbsp extra virgin olive oil
Sherry vinegar
Sea salt and freshly ground
    black pepper

FOR THE POTATOES:
450g new potatoes, scrubbed
    clean but not peeled
1 tsp crushed sea salt flakes
A pinch of crushed dried chillies
½ tsp *pimentón picante*
    (smoked hot Spanish paprika)

Light the barbecue (see page 314) to high. Grill the red peppers for 15–20 minutes, turning them every now and then, until the skins are charred black. Leave to cool, remove and discard the stalks, seeds and skin and cut the flesh into strips.

Cook the potatoes in well-salted water for 20 minutes or until tender. Drain well, transfer to a large frying pan and place over a medium-low heat. Sprinkle the potatoes with the crushed sea salt flakes and leave to cook for 20 minutes, tossing the potatoes around now and then, until their skins dry up and shrivel, become coated in the salt and just start to turn a very light golden brown.

Meanwhile, season the rib chop on both sides with salt and pepper. Cook it on the barbecue for 5 minutes on each side for rare, 6½ minutes for medium-rare, or until the temperature in the centre of the meat reaches 55°C. Remove, cover and leave to rest for 5–10 minutes.

Meanwhile, heat the olive oil in a small frying pan, add the pepper strips and a pinch of salt, and leave them to fry gently over a medium-low heat for a couple of minutes.

To serve, cut the beef away from the bone and slice the meat across into 1cm-thick slices. Sprinkle the potatoes with the crushed dried chillies and the pimentón and toss together well, and sprinkle the peppers with a few drops of sherry vinegar to taste. You want them very slightly piquant. Serve the beef with the potatoes and peppers on the side.

Chapter Four

RIOJA &
NAVARRA

When I was travelling to Santiago de Compostela along the pilgrim route, seeing many pilgrims, quite a few with tracksuits and telescopic walking sticks, I remembered the words that start the prologue of Chaucer's *Canterbury Tales*: 'When in April the sweet showers fall'. After a few lines of glorious description of spring, he writes, 'then folk do long to go on pilgrimages', and there I found myself in spring in the rain with the same sort of excitement about a long journey as those pilgrims. But the rain followed me from Galicia through Asturias and Cantabria all the way to San Sebastián in the Basque Country and on up into the foothills of the Pyrenees through Pamplona and into the Salazar valley in Navarra, close to the French border. Here we filmed two ladies in their eighties and their nephew cooking a suckling pig in the traditional manner. I haven't included the recipe because sadly it's almost impossible to get suckling pig in this country, but I have included the lamb *chilindrón* they also cooked. It's a stew made with red peppers, chilli and pimentón and is almost as hot as a curry. I was charmed by their house, unchanged for probably fifty years. It was a fearfully cold day with icy rain, and we filmed in their tiny, extractor-free kitchen that soon filled with smoke. Throughout the house were laces and crucifixes, icons of Jesus and Mary, prayers in frames, heavy walnut furniture and ornate chandeliers. Though solid, it also had a delicious frailty about it, a memory of an age when everyone went to church. Laurence, their nephew, who had lived in England, said he used to come back every summer just for the atmosphere of the house and his delightful aunts, Maria Petra and Maria Carmen. Outside, we filmed a bakery van parking by a bridge across the river delivering warm crusty bread. Back in the house, we sat down for lunch. The two aunts enjoyed a full glass of Rioja with the rest of us. Lola, Laurence's wife, was from Andalucía and spoke longingly about the heat and gaiety of that warm region while we froze, but the wine cheered us all up. Towards the end of lunch, one of the aunts recited a poem by the Basque poet Gabriel Aresti:

> I shall defend the house of my father
> Against wolves
> Against drought
> Against usury
> Against the law

The significance of this, they told me, was that in the Basque Country it is the people who belong to the house, not the house that belongs to the people. In a very old Basque house like theirs, a *caserío* with its heavy stone walls, wide and low with a gently sloping terracotta-tiled roof, I could well understand the sentiment.

I was hoping that this would be the day when the weather changed and the sun came out over the green mountains, but it never did. But that's the essence of a journey, I suppose: ever anticipating something better, wishing one's life away. Finally, though, on leaving Pamplona, having eaten *rabo de torro* (braised oxtail) and drunk beer in Hemingway's favourite bar, and heading towards Rioja, the sun came out and green Spain was behind me. And Rioja was Spain as I had expected it. Vast open country with hills in the far distance, but unlike La Mancha, green with endless rows of neatly trimmed vines. Passing through I spotted famous names such as Viña Tondonia, Ygay, Imperial, Rioja Alta and Faustino. After several days of Riojan food such as *bacalao riojana*, *pisto* and *croquettas*, and a glorious afternoon spent cooking *chuletillas,* spring lamb chops, over vine prunings, I had a much deeper understanding of Rioja wine. That always happens to me when I visit a wine-growing area. To me, it's why fish straight off the boats in Padstow tastes better than in a fish restaurant in London. After Rioja, I swung back into Navarra again on my way to Catalonia, but this time it was a flat, hot Navarra on the banks of the Ebro river where some of the best vegetables in the whole country come from: white asparagus, young peas and broad beans, tiny globe artichokes, cardoons, borage grown as a vegetable, garlic grown like spring onions and new potatoes that seemed particularly sweet.

SERRANO HAM and CHICKEN CROQUETTES

Las croquetas del Echaurren SERVES 8/MAKES ABOUT 24

As every local cook will tell you, nothing is ever wasted in the Spanish kitchen, and no recipe better typifies this admirable philosophy than croquetas. Since we started to sell jamón ibérico de bellota, sliced from the bone, in my restaurant in Padstow, we've been putting the trimmings into croquetas, which we give as a little 'bar snack'. These crisp mouthfuls with their silky smooth centres tasting of cured ham and chicken are a delight in Spain, but the filling needs to be light and airy, which means serving them as soon as they are cooked. It also means making the béchamel filling as light as you dare while still allowing you to roll them into a gobstopper and then a cork-shape prior to flour-, egg- and breadcrumbing. Finally, cook them for no more than 2 minutes, until just a light golden brown. Once you've mastered the basic béchamel, or, more correctly, panada, for these, you can flavour them with pretty much what you like: chopped prawns, flaked cooked bacalao or home-salted cod, mushrooms, especially wild such as ceps, or grated well-flavoured cheese.

85g butter
50g good quality thinly sliced Spanish air-dried ham, roughly chopped
115g flour, plus 75g extra for coating
500ml full-cream milk
75g cooked chicken breast meat, chopped
1 hard-boiled egg, peeled and finely chopped
2 free-range eggs, beaten
200g fresh white breadcrumbs, made from crustless day-old bread left to dry out overnight
Vegetable oil for deep-frying
Salt

Melt the butter in a medium saucepan over a medium heat, add the ham and leave to cook gently for a minute or two to soften. Stir in 115g of the flour and cook for 1 minute, then very gradually stir in the milk, a little at a time, beating really well between each addition so that the mixture becomes silky smooth. Increase the heat slightly, bring to the boil, and leave to cook gently, whisking constantly, for 5 minutes, to cook out the flour.

Stir in the chicken and 1 teaspoon of salt or to taste, then stir in the hard-boiled egg. Scrape the mixture into a bowl, press a sheet of clingfilm onto the surface, and chill in the fridge, for at least 6 hours but ideally overnight, until really firm.

For the croquettes, shape 1½ tablespoons of the chilled mixture between lightly floured palms into balls and then cork-shaped barrels. You should make about 24. Refrigerate again for 30 minutes.

Heat some oil for deep-frying to 190°C. Put the remaining 75g of flour, egg and breadcrumbs into 3 separate, shallow trays or bowls. Take the croquetas from the fridge and dip them 4 or 5 at a time into the flour, then the beaten egg and then the breadcrumbs, then lower them into the hot oil and cook for not quite 2 minutes until crisp and lightly golden. You can tell when they are done because as they cook, the béchamel mixture starts to melt inside and the croquetas start to make a different noise in the fryer. Lift out onto plenty of kitchen paper and drain briefly. Serve while they are still hot.

RUSSIAN SALAD
with MELBA TOASTS

Ensaladilla rusa SERVES 4 AS A TAPAS OR STARTER

As someone who as a teenager working in the Station Hotel at Paddington made approximately three kilos of Russian salad and two litres of mayonnaise every day, I shouldn't feel too kindly towards it, but I do. Even then I was keen to cook the vegetables separately in well-salted water, and not for too long, and to make sure that the mayonnaise was piquant with mustard and vinegar. I hadn't really come face to face with it again until recently, when I discovered there was a renaissance in Spain. They love putting vegetables with lots of mayonnaise, and seafood too. I think it's all down to the cooking of the vegetables and not going mad with the mayo. They often serve it with a slice or two of melba toast and sometimes with a pile of freshly cooked crabmeat. I'm planning to serve it as a starter for Christmas lunch.

500g waxy new potatoes, such
     as Charlotte, scraped clean
     or peeled
200g peeled carrots, halved
     lengthways
150g fine green beans, topped
     and tailed
125g fine asparagus tips
100g fresh or frozen peas
50g pitted green olives
1 bunch spring onions, trimmed
200g *Mayonnaise* (see page 306)
2 tsp lemon juice
1 small white 'tin' loaf
Salt

Bring 2 pans of well-salted water to the boil. Add the potatoes to one pan and simmer until tender – about 15–20 minutes depending on their size, then drain and leave to cool. Add the carrots to the second pan and simmer for 10–12 minutes until just tender. Remove with a slotted spoon and drop into a large bowl of iced water. Add the green beans to the pan and cook for 5 minutes, remove and add to the bowl of iced water with the carrots. Add the asparagus tips and cook for 2 minutes. Remove and refresh in the cold water. Add the peas and just bring back to the boil for frozen, or cook for 1–2 minutes for fresh. Drain and add to the bowl of cold water.

Drain the refreshed vegetables and dry well on a clean tea towel. Cut the potatoes into 6–8mm dice and cut the carrots, beans and asparagus tips into similar-sized pieces. Finely chop the olives and very thinly slice the spring onions.

Mix the mayonnaise with the lemon juice and ¼ teaspoon of salt or to taste in a large bowl. Add all the cooked vegetables and gently stir together.

For the melba toasts, preheat the grill to medium-high. Slice the loaf of bread 1cm thick and toast on both sides until lightly golden. Cut off the crusts and then slice through the soft bread between the 2 crisp faces and separate. Cut lengthways into wide fingers and grill once more, on the untoasted side, for a few seconds until golden brown. Leave to cool and serve with the Russian salad.

EGGS SCRAMBLED with BRAISED SUMMER VEGETABLES

Pisto riojano SERVES 4 AS A STARTER OR LIGHT LUNCH

A *pisto* is a slow braise of mixed summer vegetables, commonly peppers, onions, courgettes and tomatoes, with eggs sometimes lightly scrambled into the mixture at the end of cooking, and, as with all things simple, it's often difficult to get right. It's very similar to piperade, which comes from the Basque region of France. This is from the hotel Echaurren in Ezcaray, where the chef Francis Paniego explained to me that it's all down to cooking the vegetables very gently and without any water – water, he said, was the arch enemy of a *pisto*. By lightly seasoning each batch of vegetables with a little salt as they get added to the pan, enough liquid is extracted from them by the process of osmosis to allow them to steam and cook without losing flavour. He took immense care in not overcooking the egg too and serving the dish when the egg was what the French call *baveuse*, almost runny but not quite.

100g small waxy potatoes,
    such as Charlotte
2 small green peppers
175g courgettes
3 tbsp olive oil
1 medium onion, chopped
2 garlic cloves, finely chopped
4 tbsp *Tomato sauce*
    (see page 306)
200g vine-ripened tomatoes,
    skinned, seeded and diced
½ tsp caster sugar
3 large eggs, beaten
2 tbsp chopped flat-leaf parsley
Salt and freshly ground black
    pepper
Crusty fresh bread, to serve

Peel the potatoes and cut them into 7–8mm dice. Remove the stalk and seeds from the green peppers and top and tail the courgettes and cut them into the same size pieces.

Heat the olive oil in a medium-sized, deep-sided, non-stick frying pan over a medium heat. Add the potatoes and sauté them for 5 minutes until soft and very lightly browned. Lift out with a slotted spoon onto a plate and set aside.

Add the onion, garlic, green peppers and ¼ teaspoon of salt and cook gently for 3 minutes. Add the courgettes, sprinkle with another ¼ teaspoon of salt, cover and cook gently for 5 minutes.

Uncover the pan and stir in the reserved fried potatoes, tomato sauce, fresh tomatoes and sugar and simmer, uncovered, for 3–4 minutes until the sauce has reduced and slightly thickened.

Stir the beaten eggs and chopped parsley into the mixture and cook over a medium-low heat, stirring with a fork, for about 1 minute until the eggs are softly scrambled. Spoon into small warmed dishes and serve with crusty fresh bread.

LITTLE GEM LETTUCE and SPRING VEGETABLE SALAD in a LEMON VINAIGRETTE

SERVES 4 AS A STARTER

Navarra is a region of distinct terrains. To the north is the rugged, hilly land of the foothills and the high Pyrenees, the sort of place where Belloc wrote of 'the fleas that tease in the high Pyrenees and the wine that tasted of tar' – though it certainly doesn't any more – and to the south lie the flat, enormously fertile plains of the river Ebro. Tudela, the main town of this region, is particularly famous for its small, sweet lettuces, which are very similar to our little gems and are often served up in salads such as this, inspired by the very best of the sweet young vegetables from the region.

4 little gem lettuces
280g jar chargrilled artichoke
   hearts in olive oil
300g shelled baby broad beans
150g fine asparagus tips
150g shelled baby peas

FOR THE DRESSING:
2 tbsp freshly squeezed then
   strained lemon juice
6 tbsp extra virgin olive oil
¼ tsp caster sugar
1 small garlic clove, very finely
   chopped
The white part of 2 spring
   onions, very thinly sliced
Salt

Remove the large, outer leaves of each lettuce and use for another salad. Separate the remaining leaves, wash thoroughly and dry well. Cut the larger ones in half lengthways, seal in a plastic bag and chill in the fridge for at least 1 hour.

Pour off the oil from the jar of artichoke hearts, cut them in half and leave them to drain on kitchen paper. Bring a pan of well-salted water to the boil. Add the broad beans, cook for 1 minute, then remove with a slotted spoon and drop into a bowl of iced water. Add the asparagus tips, cook for 2 minutes, then remove with a slotted spoon and add to the iced water. Add the peas to the pan, leave for 1 minute, then drain and refresh in the iced water. Drain all the vegetables well and dry on kitchen paper.

Slip the broad beans out of their skins. Remove the lettuce leaves from the fridge and scatter them over the base of a shallow serving platter. Scatter over the artichokes, broad beans, asparagus tips and peas.

For the dressing, whisk the lemon juice, olive oil, sugar, garlic and salt to taste in a small bowl. Stir in the spring onions, drizzle over the salad and serve straight away.

A STEW of MIXED SUMMER VEGETABLES

Menestra SERVES 6 AS A STARTER

Tudela in Navarra is the centre of one of the best vegetable-producing areas in Spain. I was taken to a high spot in the town to look over the River Ebro and its surrounding allotments, or *huertas*. Not just vegetable gardens, they were also works of art, dotted with beautiful old lodges. My companions were an enterprising market gardener called Floren Domezain Semanes and his, I have to say, gorgeous wife, Mercedes. He cooked us this *menestra*, a stew of summer vegetables, in which the star was the artichokes that turned the dish emerald green. This happens to artichokes if there's enough magnesium in the local water, he explained. I really liked Floren; he was very on the ball. He was making a good living from selling, amongst other things, very early peas and broad beans, the peas no bigger than a seed pearl – and of about the same value by the time they got to the kitchens of such restaurants as El Bulli and Arzak.

4 large globe artichokes
The juice of ½ lemon
200g Swiss chard
250g bunch fine asparagus spears
100g fine green beans, topped and tailed
4 tbsp olive oil
1 onion, halved and thinly sliced
1 garlic clove, thinly sliced
25g plain flour
½ tsp caster sugar
350g shelled peas, ideally fresh
Salt

First, prepare the artichoke bases. Using a serrated carving knife or a bread knife, cut the stems off the artichokes close to the bases and discard. Now cut off the leafy top half and then, using a smaller knife, slice the tough outer leaves away from the base, working round the artichoke as you do so, until you reveal the pale inner leaves. Slice these away from the base along with the hairy choke in the centre. Finish off scraping away any strands of the choke with a teaspoon. Drop the round bases into a small bowl of water acidulated with the lemon juice to prevent them going black.

Prepare the rest of the vegetables. Strip the green leaves from the stalks of the Swiss chard, cut the stalks into 5cm pieces and tear the leaves into medium pieces. Snap the woody ends off the asparagus spears and cut them across into three, and cut the beans in half.

Bring 1.5 litres water to the boil in a large pan with 1 tablespoon of salt. Add the artichoke bases and cook for 10 minutes or until tender. Lift out with a slotted spoon and leave to cool before cutting each one across into 4 thick slices. Add the green beans to the same water and cook for 5 minutes. Lift them out into a colander and refresh under cold running water. Add the asparagus and Swiss chard stems to the water, cook for 3 minutes, then lift out into the colander and again refresh with cold water. Reserve the cooking water.

Heat the olive oil in a cazuela, shallow flameproof casserole, or another wide shallow pan over a medium heat. Add the onion and garlic and cook for 10 minutes or until soft but not browned, then stir in the flour. Gradually stir in 600ml of the vegetable cooking water and the sugar, bring to the boil, stirring, lower the heat and simmer for 2–3 minutes.

Stir the peas and Swiss chard leaves into the sauce and cook for 2–3 minutes. Then stir in all the cooked vegetables and simmer for 5 minutes until the peas are tender. Season to taste and serve.

BARBECUED LAMB CUTLETS with ALI⦿LI

Chuletillas con alioli SERVES 4

High on my list of top ten food-experiences-to-have-before-you-die – a list that includes a fish stew cooked by fishermen on their boat somewhere in the Mediterranean, a whole pig stuffed with an aromatic spice paste, roasted over coffee wood and basted with coconut oil in Indonesia, chicken and pumpkin cooked in a hangi pit in New Zealand, and cod and chips fried in beef dripping on the Yorkshire coast – would be *chuletillas*, extremely thin, milk-fed-lamb chops cooked over a fire made from vine trimmings in a vineyard somewhere in Spain. So when I finally got to the village of Briones in Rioja to meet Miguel Merino, it seemed entirely natural to enjoy a glass or two of his excellent red wine while he prepared exactly that dish. He bought along a couple of his chums, one clearly quite a trendy photographer who turned up with his very pretty daughter in an old Jaguar; what style, I thought, except that it wouldn't start when he went to leave. We can't get milk-fed lamb in the UK, but our early spring lamb would be perfect. They are generally served on their own to be eaten with your fingers. I don't know whether it's correct but I've included a bowl of alioli in which to dip them, which seemed very good to me.

16–20 spring-lamb cutlets, cut as thinly as the bones will allow
A little olive oil
A handful of soft, not woody, thyme sprigs, chopped
Salt and freshly ground black pepper
1 quantity of *Alioli* (see page 307), to serve

Place the lamb cutlets in a single layer on a large baking tray and rub with a little oil, then sprinkle on each side with the thyme leaves and some salt and pepper.

Light the barbecue (see page 314) to high, then place the cutlets side by side in a grilling rack, if you have one, and clamp it shut. This just makes it easier and quicker to turn them, also ensuring they don't overcook. If using a frying pan, choose the largest one you have so you can fit in at least half the cutlets in one layer. Heat the pan over a high heat, then add 1 teaspoon of oil.

Cook the cutlets for 2–3 minutes on each side until the fat is crisp and golden but the flesh is still moist and juicy inside. Remove and serve straight away, with the alioli for dipping.

SLOW-BRAISED LAMB with FRESH and DRIED RED PEPPERS

Cordero al chilindrón SERVES 6

The valley of the river Ebro, flowing from Navarra through Aragon to the west, is known not only for its wonderful vegetables but also as the *zona de chilindrones*, everyday stews of chicken or lamb braised with lots of dried and fresh red peppers together with tomatoes, onion, garlic and serrano ham. This dish is also a celebration of *pimentón picante*, so much so that my chilindrón here could almost be described as the Spanish equivalent of a curry. By that I mean I like it to be really quite spicy; serve with rice or couscous if you wish.

2 dried choricero peppers
1.5kg well-trimmed boneless
    lamb shoulder
4 tbsp olive oil
2 medium onions, chopped
4 garlic cloves, sliced
1 tbsp *pimentón picante*
    (smoked hot Spanish paprika)
100g sliced serrano ham,
    chopped into small pieces
450g skinned chopped tomatoes,
    fresh or from a can
250ml dry white wine
The leaves from 4 fresh thyme
    sprigs
4 fresh bay leaves
2 large *Roasted red peppers*
    (see page 307)
1 tbsp chopped flat-leaf parsley
Salt

Remove the stalks from the dried peppers, slit them open and remove the seeds. Soak in hot water for 1 hour.

Cut the lamb into 3–4cm chunks and season all over with some salt. Heat 2 tablespoons of the olive oil in a large, flameproof casserole, add half the lamb and fry over a medium-high heat until nicely browned all over. Spoon out onto a plate and repeat with the rest of the lamb.

Add the remaining olive oil, the onions, garlic and pimentón to the casserole and fry over a medium heat for 10 minutes until soft and lightly golden. Add the ham and cook for a further 2 minutes.

Drain the soaked peppers and scrape the flesh away from the skin. Discard the skin. Stir the flesh into the casserole with the lamb, tomatoes and white wine and leave to bubble for a few minutes until the wine has reduced by about half. The lamb will make its own juice during cooking so don't be tempted to add any other liquid. Add the thyme, bay leaves and ½ teaspoon of salt, cover with a tight-fitting lid and leave to cook very gently over a low heat for 2 hours, or until the lamb is meltingly tender.

Remove the stalks, skin and seeds from the roasted red peppers and cut the flesh into thin strips. Uncover the lamb and remove and discard the bay leaves. Stir in the roasted red peppers and adjust the seasoning to taste, adding more pimentón if it's not spicy enough for you. Simmer briefly for 5 minutes, then sprinkle with the parsley and serve.

ROASTED PARTRIDGE
with CHORIZO, CABBAGE
and WHITE BEANS

SERVES 4

Partridge is typically paired with cabbage and white beans in the northern regions of Spain, in the dish commonly known as *perdices con col*, but this was one of those dishes that altered somewhat in filming. First of all, the two ladies who were helping said it was common to cook the white beans with a cured ham bone to give them extra flavour, whereas I'd originally intended simply to simmer them. I also didn't like the idea of stewing the partridge with the cabbage for a long time, so instead I roasted the birds with slices of chorizo to give them some colour and flavour, then used the roasting juices and the chorizo, together with some garlic, onion, serrano ham, bay leaf and red wine, to flavour the cabbage, which I only cooked for a few minutes. This was one of those occasions when I felt I was tramping over hallowed ground but Isabel and Vanessa said my recipe was good.

100g dried white beans, such as *alubia planchada*, soaked overnight
A cured ham bone, if you have one to hand (optional)
4 oven-ready partridges
2 tbsp olive oil
100g cooking chorizo sausage, skinned and coarsely chopped
1 small Savoy cabbage, weighing about 600g
2 garlic cloves, finely chopped
1 medium onion, finely chopped
4 fresh bay leaves
100g thinly sliced serrano ham, cut across into strips
100ml red wine
100ml *Chicken stock* (see page 306)
Salt and freshly ground black pepper

Drain the beans and put them into a pan with 800ml fresh cold water. Add the ham bone, if using, bring to the boil, cover and leave to simmer very gently for 2 hours, stirring the beans every now and then, and seasoning with 1 teaspoon of salt towards the end. Discard the bone, re-cover and set aside. This can be done in advance.

Preheat the oven to 230°C/gas 8. Season the cavities of the partridges with salt and pepper.

Heat the olive oil in a large flameproof roasting tin. Add the chopped chorizo and fry gently for 2 minutes. Lift the chorizo out onto a plate with a slotted spoon, leaving behind the oil. Add the partridge to the tin and turn them over a few times in the chorizo-flavoured oil, then season all over. Turn breast-side up, transfer to the oven and roast for 15 minutes, then lower the temperature to 180°C/gas 4 and roast for 10 minutes more. Meanwhile, remove the outer leaves from the cabbage and quarter, core and shred the rest.

Remove the partridge from the oven and lift them onto a plate. Cover tightly with foil, turn off the oven and slide them back inside to keep warm, leaving the door ajar. Place the roasting tin directly over a medium heat, add the garlic, onion and bay leaves and fry gently for 5 minutes. Add the ham and fried chorizo and cook gently for 2 minutes, then add the cabbage and seasoning and stir-fry for 2 minutes until it just begins to wilt. Add the red wine and chicken stock and cook for 10 minutes, turning the mixture over regularly, until the cabbage is just tender. Meanwhile, gently reheat the beans.

When the cabbage is tender, using a slotted spoon, remove the white beans from any remaining liquid and add them to the cabbage. Stir together and adjust the seasoning if necessary. Lift the partridge onto warmed serving plates, spoon some of the cabbage and beans alongside, and serve.

OXTAIL and RED WINE STEW from PAMPLONA

Rabo de torro de Pamplona SERVES 6

It looks like bullfighting might be on the way out in Spain. It is now banned in Catalonia. Were this to happen, I think Pamplona would be the last to give it up, so important is the bullring and bull-running to their culture, and so excellent is the beef from the bulls, readily available at the local butchers' and markets when the fights are in season. Oxtail stew has long been the signature dish at the Gran Hotel La Perla. and before that at the famous Las Pocholas restaurant, which was run by – and named for – the nine unmarried Guerendiain sisters during the 1940s, and was popular with the rich and famous of the day. Two of them, Josefina and Conchita, are still alive, now in their eighties and nineties, and I went to see them one day in their elegant apartment by Plaza de Castillo. They were both a delight. Restaurateurs have an enormous amount in common at whatever age, and even though long-retired these two women were still full of humour and sociability. The dish was cooked for me by the chef at the hotel, Alex Mugica, and I ate it in a magisterial dining room with a couple of glasses of full-bodied Navarra wine, watched over at my table by the heads of two fighting bulls. Excellent with steamed potatoes and broccoli florets, scattered with the chopped parsley.

2kg oxtail, cut across into
    5cm-thick pieces
50g plain flour, seasoned
4 tbsp olive oil
4 garlic cloves, sliced
2 medium onions, chopped
200g carrots, sliced
175g leeks, thickly sliced
4 tbsp brandy
500ml red wine
500ml browned *Beef stock*
    (see page 306)
A bouquet garni of bay leaves,
    parsley stalks and thyme sprigs
1 tbsp chopped flat-leaf parsley
Salt and freshly ground black
    pepper

Trim the oxtail pieces of excess fat and season well on both sides with salt and pepper. Toss the pieces in the seasoned flour and knock off the excess; keep the remaining seasoned flour. Heat 2 tablespoons of the olive oil in a large flameproof casserole over a medium-high heat, add half the oxtail pieces and fry until nicely browned all over. Lift them onto a plate and repeat with the remaining oxtail.

Add the remaining oil to the pan with the garlic, onions, carrots and leeks and fry for 10 minutes or until nicely browned.

Pour over the brandy and set it alight. When the flames have died down, stir in the remaining seasoned flour, then gradually stir in the red wine and bring to the boil, stirring. Simmer for 3 minutes, then stir in the oxtail pieces, the beef stock, bouquet garni, ½ teaspoon of salt and plenty of black pepper. Cover and simmer gently for 2½–3 hours, until the oxtail is really tender but not falling apart. Remove from the heat, leave to cool, then cover and chill overnight.

The next day, scrape the layer of fat off the top of the casserole and discard. Gently reheat the casserole, then lift out the pieces of oxtail into a bowl. Pass the sauce through a fine sieve into a clean pan, pressing out as much of the sauce as you can with the back of a ladle. Discard what's left in the sieve. Return to the heat and simmer vigorously for 5–10 minutes until the sauce has reduced and is well flavoured. Return the oxtail, season to taste and simmer for 5 minutes to heat through. Serve sprinkled with the chopped parsley.

SALT COD in a DRIED RED PEPPER SAUCE

Bacalao a la riojana SERVES 4

The town of La Guardia, which looks out over the Rioja river, is famous for its long, pointed, scarlet red peppers, known locally as 'goat's horn peppers', which in late September are left to dry in the sun on pretty much every balcony in the town. So it's not surprising that these peppers, fresh or dried, find their way into many of the regional dishes, *a la riojana*, incidentally, meaning a dish made with red peppers, not wine. It's difficult to get these peppers outside of Spain, but dried choricero peppers (see page 312), are the perfect substitute. This was made for me in the town of Ezcaray in Rioja, at the hotel El Echaurren, by Marisa Sánchez. The large kitchen there is interesting: at one end is the restaurant serving dishes like this, where Marisa holds court, while at the other end her son Francis cooks Michelin-starred food. Indicative, I think, of the close connection between the new and traditional Spanish cooking. Francis, obviously well taught by his mother, can also turn out superb classic Riojan dishes like the croquetas on page 104 and the *pisto* on page 108.

4 x 150g thick, square, boneless
    pieces of *Bacalao* (salt cod;
    see page 313)
5 large dried choricero peppers
2 large red peppers
1 green pepper
6 tbsp olive oil
2 large onions, chopped
2 garlic cloves, crushed
1 tsp *pimentón dulce* (smoked
    sweet Spanish paprika)
6 tbsp *Tomato sauce*
    (see page 306)
2 tsp sherry vinegar
Salt

Soak the bacalao in 3–4 litres of water in the fridge for 24–48 hours, depending on thickness. Change the water when it tastes salty, normally at least twice.

Preheat the oven to 220°C/gas 7. Remove the stalks from the dried peppers, open up and remove the seeds. Soak in hot water for 1 hour, then scrape the soft flesh from the skins. Roast the red and green peppers for 20–25 minutes, turning them over halfway through. Leave to cool, then remove the stalks, seeds and skin and cut the flesh into strips 1cm wide.

Heat 4 tablespoons of the oil in a large frying pan over a medium heat, add the onions and garlic and fry gently for 30 minutes, stirring now and then, until soft and sweet but not browned.

Stir the pimentón into the onions and cook for 2 minutes. Stir in the dried pepper pulp and the tomato sauce and simmer for 5 minutes more. Blend in a food processor until smooth, return to the pan, stir in the vinegar and season to taste with salt. Keep warm. Heat the remaining 2 tablespoons of oil in a small frying pan, add the roasted pepper strips, season with a little salt and fry gently, stirring every now and then, for a few minutes. Keep hot.

Put the bacalao into a wide shallow pan, skin-side up, and cover with 1 litre of water. Bring to the boil, lower the heat and leave to poach gently for 5–6 minutes or until just cooked through. Carefully remove from the water with a fish slice onto a plate and remove the skin from each piece. Stir enough of the poaching liquor (approximately 400ml) into the tomato and red pepper sauce to give it a good consistency and bring it back to a gentle simmer.

Transfer the fish to warmed plates and spoon some sauce over. Pile roasted pepper strips on top of each steak and serve.

PAN-FRIED TROUT
with CRISP HAM

Trucha con jamón SERVES 2

One of my favourite Ernest Hemingway books is *Fiesta: The Sun Also Rises*, so to go to Pamplona for the first time and sit where Hemingway himself used to sit outside the Café Iruña on the Plaza del Castillo with a coffee and some churros, thinking of bull-running and bullfighting, was especially meaningful. Then a trip up the Salazar valley alongside a trout river in the foothills of the Pyrenees meant that bit extra for me because Hemingway loved the valley. This fabulous dish combines a trout from the river with the lovely cured ham of Spain, but I'm afraid you'll have to use farmed rainbow trout even if you get to Navarra, because most trout fishing is currently banned to help preserve stocks. I've started frying the trout in a pan for this recipe and then transferred them to an oven, which means you can get a perfectly golden crust and don't run the risk of burning it while waiting for the fish to cook right through. I earnestly recommend you invest in a thermal probe for dishes like this; if you have one, the fish will be perfectly soft and moist and ready to eat when the temperature at the centre reaches about 58°C. The perfect accompaniments to this would be boiled potatoes and a lightly dressed little gem lettuce salad.

4 tbsp olive oil
6 small, thin slices of air-dried ham, such as serrano
2 x 300–350g rainbow trout, cleaned
50g plain flour, for coating
1 fat garlic clove, finely chopped
20–25g knob of butter
Juice ½ lemon
A small handful of flat-leaf parsley leaves, chopped
Salt

Preheat the oven to 200°C/gas 6. Heat the oil in a heavy-based frying pan over a medium heat. Add 4 of the slices of ham and fry for a few seconds on each side until the fat has rendered out and therefore flavoured the oil, and the ham is crisp and lightly golden. Remove to a plate. Finely chop the remaining 2 ham slices and set aside.

Season the belly cavity of each fish with a little salt, then place 2 slices of the crisp ham inside each one. Season the outside of the fish, then dust them in the flour, knocking off the excess.

Return the pan to a medium heat and add the fish. Fry for 2 minutes on each side until golden brown, then carefully transfer to a lightly oiled baking dish and bake for 5 minutes. Set the frying pan to one side.

Remove the trout from the oven, cover loosely with foil and leave somewhere warm to cook on for a further 3–4 minutes. Return the frying pan to the heat, add the chopped ham and fry briefly over a high heat until starting to become golden and crispy. Turn down the heat, add the garlic and butter to the pan and continue frying until the butter is nut-brown and the garlic is starting to colour. Add the lemon juice and parsley, spoon the mixture over the trout and serve.

Chapter Five

CATALONIA

Catalonia to me is a little fishing village with a gnarly fisherman painting his boat in bright blue paint for the coming season. It's Dalí's twisted paintings, like 'The Persistence of Memory' with a background that is still recognizably the rocky limestone coast around Cadaqués. It's a very built-up coastline that manages to be a lot more upmarket than some further south. It's wonderful Barcelona, with its magnificently eccentric church, La Sagrada Família, still uncompleted after 130 years. This and the other buildings built by the architect Antoni Gaudí have given the city an Art Nouveau identity as clear as the Métro in Paris. The reality, however, is that much of the region is the familiar big country of most of Spain.

So it was that I came to the town Lleida from Navarra to celebrate a favourite food of the Catalans: snails. During the long weekend of this snail festival, they got through some 12 tons of them, most locally reared but some from as far away as Morocco and South America. I don't know about you, but I find something immensely reassuring about a people who are willing to spend a whole weekend eating nothing but snails and drinking large amounts of red wine. You sit at long trestle tables eating copious quantities of snails with tomato, garlic and pimentón, or grilled over charcoal to be dipped into alioli, hot with garlic. There's a bewildering number of groups of friends, each with their own personal colours and each with a raucous band trying to outdo the others with the loudness and intensity of their music and dancing. I grew increasingly enthusiastic about the way the almost bland taste of snails goes so well with smoky pimentón, serrano ham, garlic, red wine and tomatoes.

But it was for the coast that I was really headed, north of Barcelona. I remembered staying for some time in a youth hostel in Arenys de Mar and wanted to see how it had changed in the last forty-odd years. I booked into a hotel at the back of the town. Clearly built for early package holidays, the rooms were tiny, as were the balconies from which you could see the sea a long way away, and I felt nostalgic for the simpler pleasures of a life on the Costa Brava around the time when we won the World Cup. Nearby was a restaurant famous throughout Catalonia for its faithful production of local dishes. The two sisters who ran it, Paquita and Lolita, were intimidating in the same way as the late Rose Gray and Ruth Rogers at the River Cafe.

In other words, they had clarity of vision about the importance of cooking simple food without male ego and peacock plumage. I once had a conversation with a famous American chef, Mark Miller, who said if you blindfolded him and took him into any restaurant he would be able to tell if a woman was cooking there by the down-to-earth style of the food. When I arrived with the film crew, about twelve locals were settling down to a Catalan breakfast of *langosta con patatas* (spiny lobster with potatoes), braised tiny peas with leeks, *fricandó* of veal, *pan con tomate*, chargrilled meaty sausages with beans and potatoes and a tortilla of artichokes. This may not have been their normal breakfast, they may have been doing it just for us, but it didn't matter. I was impressed with the sophistication and variety of Catalan cuisine. My feeling was that it's almost an extension of the cooking of Provence. Not surprising, when you consider that the Catalans were originally called Francos by other Spaniards, and are more receptive to French ideas than the rest of the country. Their cuisine is as important to them as their language, spoken by more than nine million people in Catalonia, Valencia and the Balearic islands as well as the city of Alghero in Sardinia, Roussillon over the border in France and in significant numbers in Aragón and Murcia. All testament to the historical importance of a people whose rule in the thirteenth century encompassed parts of Sicily and Greece.

The element of their cuisine that is particularly special is the mixing of seafood and produce from the rocky mountainous terrain – what they call *mar i muntanya*. Dishes like the Cuttlefish with Meatballs and Peas on page 134 are common everywhere in northern Catalonia. But above all it's the thought of a lunch in the pine-scented hills of rabbit cooked over a wood fire with alioli, followed by a dinner, in somewhere like the fishing village of Palamós, of large deep red prawns in the shell, sautéed in olive oil with garlic and parsley, where you suck the juice out of their shells to enjoy every morsel, that sums *mar i muntanya* up for me.

TOMATOES and BREAD

Pan con tomate SERVES 4

Bread is hugely important to the Spanish. Go into any traditional Spanish home and there's a special drawer in a dresser for bread, both the new loaf of the day and the old bits. Stale bread is no less important than fresh because there are so many uses for it: as a thickening for soups such as gazpacho (see page 260), or for toasting, rubbing with garlic and putting in the bottom of a bowl of soup like the one from La Mancha on page 205. It's used fried with garlic and nuts for making a picada, a paste for thickening stews, but most famously for grating tomatoes and garlic which is then eaten with lashings of olive oil and a little salt. In Catalan dialect this is known as *pa amb tomàquet,* and it's a symbol of Catalan nationality – just like in Majorca, where it's similarly important, and known as *pa amb oli.* Try it with some good sourdough and some really ripe vine-grown tomatoes in the height of summer and serve it instead of plain bread or as a tapas. There's something elementally satisfying about it.

1 loaf day-old, crusty
    white bread
2 fat garlic cloves, halved
4 really ripe, large slicing
    or beef tomatoes
The best extra virgin olive
    oil you can buy
Sea salt flakes

Cut the bread into 1cm-thick slices. Toast them, under the grill or in a toaster, until dry and only just starting to colour, then rub the cut face of the garlic over the slightly abrasive surface. Halve the tomato horizontally and then rub, cut-face down, over the bread, soaking the bread with the tomato flesh. Discard the skin. Sprinkle the tomato-soaked bread with sea salt, drizzle generously with olive oil and serve.

ROASTED VEGETABLE SALAD

Escalivada SERVES 4, AS A STARTER

Occasionally people refer to *escalivada* as a Spanish version of ratatouille, since it's made with aubergines, peppers and onions, but it's not the same. Here the overriding flavour comes from the smoky taste of vegetables that were traditionally left to roast in the hot embers of a wood fire, though today it's more likely to be done over a charcoal grill or even under a hot grill as a last resort. The vegetables are left until they are charred black on the outside but tender on the inside. They are then split open and the soft flesh peeled away from the skin. The flesh is torn into long strips and seasoned with salt, and I find it's best if they are then left for a while to absorb the seasoning. Just before serving, everything is scattered with finely chopped garlic and drizzled with a few drops of vinegar and some good olive oil. I like to serve it on some slices of grilled rustic bread with anchovy fillets and black olives.

2 x 200g (approx.) aubergines
3 large red peppers
2 large onions, left unpeeled
1 fat garlic clove, very finely
    chopped
A little red wine vinegar
Some good extra virgin olive oil
4 large or 8 smaller slices rustic
    white bread
8 anchovy fillets
8 black olives
Sea salt flakes

Light the barbecue (see page 314) or preheat the grill to high.

Pierce the aubergines near the stalk end with a fork to prevent them from bursting, then barbecue or grill for 30 minutes, turning them regularly, until their skins are black, the insides feel soft and they smell 'smoky'. Halve the onions and barbecue or grill with the peppers, turning them regularly. The peppers will take 15–20 minutes and the onions about 25–30 minutes.

When all the vegetables are cooked, leave them to cool then peel away the blackened skins, discarding the stalks and seeds from the peppers.

Pull the aubergines and peppers into long thin strips and break the onions into pieces. Arrange them on a large serving plate and sprinkle with ½ teaspoon of salt.

Just before serving, sprinkle the garlic, a few drops of vinegar and some olive oil over the vegetables. Barbecue or griddle the slices of bread until nicely browned on both sides. Pile some of the vegetables onto each slice and garnish with the anchovy fillets and black olives. Serve straight away while the bread is still crunchy.

CUTTLEFISH with MEATBALLS and PEAS

Sepia amb albóndigas y guisantes SERVES 6 AS A STARTER

I wish we weren't saddled with the idea of surf and turf. It's so vulgar, while something like *mar i muntanya* – dishes that combine meat or sometimes chicken, rabbit and even snails with lobster or prawns, cuttlefish or squid – are anything but. Traditionally it was a way of eking out expensive meat or chicken with dirt-cheap seafood, but now of course the reverse is true, which is why I've used mostly cuttlefish. a seafood that is still very good value for money. I find that minced chicken and pork meatballs and the cuttlefish go well together. Do use squid if you can't find cuttlefish. This dish isn't always garnished with prawns but I love the colour they add.

6 tbsp olive oil
2 garlic cloves, finely chopped
1 medium onion, finely chopped
90ml dry white wine
1 large vine-ripened or beef
    tomato (about 200g), halved
2 tsp tomato purée
15g slice crustless white bread
1½ tbsp milk
2 tbsp chopped flat-leaf parsley
225g minced chicken
225g minced pork
A little freshly grated nutmeg
6 large shell-on raw prawns
375g cleaned cuttlefish, cut into
    2cm-wide strips
150ml *Chicken stock*
    (see page 306) or water
100g shelled peas, fresh or frozen
Salt and freshly ground black
    pepper
Crusty fresh bread, to serve

FOR THE PICADA:
2 tbsp olive oil
2 fat garlic cloves, peeled but
    left whole
10g slice crustless white bread
10g toasted blanched almonds
1 small vine-ripened or beef
    tomato, halved
1 tsp flat-leaf parsley leaves

Grate the halved tomatoes for the tomato sauce and the picada, pressing the fleshy, cut face of the tomato against the grater. (As you grate each tomato half, the skin will flatten out and be left behind.) Discard the skin.

For the picada, heat the olive oil in a small frying pan over a medium heat. Add the garlic cloves and slice of bread and fry, turning over now and then, until golden brown. Lift out with a slotted spoon and add to the bowl of a mini food processor with the almonds, tomato, parsley and 1 tablespoon cold water. Blend to a paste and set aside.

Put 2 tablespoons of the oil, half the garlic and the onion into a saucepan and fry for 10 minutes until soft, sweet and lightly golden. Add the wine, grated tomato and tomato purée and simmer, stirring occasionally, for 6–7 minutes until reduced and thickened.

For the meatballs, tear the bread into a small bowl, sprinkle with the milk and leave until soft. Break up the bread with your fingers and add the remaining chopped garlic, the parsley, minced chicken and pork, nutmeg and ½ teaspoon each of salt and black pepper. Mix together well and shape into 2.5–3cm balls.

Heat 2 tablespoons of oil, add the meatballs and fry for 3 minutes, shaking the pan every now and then, until golden brown. Set aside on a plate. Discard any oil left in the pan.

Heat another tablespoon of oil in the pan, add the prawns and fry for 1 minute on each side until just cooked through. Set aside on a plate. Add another tablespoon of oil to the pan, then the cuttlefish and stir-fry for 2 minutes or until it is nicely caramelized and just cooked through. Set aside with the prawns.

Add the tomato sauce to the pan, stir in the picada and simmer for 2 minutes. Reduce the heat to medium, stir in the stock or water and bring to the boil, stirring. Add the peas, meatballs and cuttlefish and season to taste with salt and pepper. Scatter over the prawns and simmer for 5 minutes until any remaining liquid has reduced and everything has heated through. Serve with crusty fresh bread.

FRESH BROAD BEANS
with BLACK SAUSAGE
and GARLIC SHOOTS

Faves a la catalana SERVES 6 AS A STARTER

Antonio Miers was the drum player in Los Mustang. They were as big in Spain as the Beatles were in Britain, and indeed many of their early songs were Beatles covers. Antonio cooked this dish for me in his kitchen in Blanes north of Barcelona, because these days he's a cook – not to mention an antiques dealer who also happens to own a garden centre. He remembers his frenetic youth with detached amusement, recalling their breakthrough concert. I believe it was on a beach near Cadaqués, when they were billed as Spain's first amplified band. He remembered the amplifiers and speakers being not much bigger than shoeboxes and their repertoire was somewhat limited: Gene Vincent's 'Be-Bop-A-Lula', followed by Ray Charles's 'What I Say', then 'Be-Bop-A-Lula' a bit louder, then a couple of others. He's a special cook, very much taken with his local Catalan cooking, and this dish of *faves a la catalana* is considered to be one of the three most important dishes in Catalonia. Traditionally it's made with *butifarra negra*, Spanish blood sausages, and fresh garlic shoots, both of which are hard to come by here in the UK, but the dish works adequately well with our black pudding, bulb garlic and some fat salad onions.

225g rindless streaky bacon
   or pancetta, in one piece
2–3 salad onions or 12 spring
   onions
100ml olive oil
20g garlic, finely chopped
625g shelled fresh broad beans
2 fresh bay leaves
1 small handful mint leaves,
   chopped
2 tbsp anis, such as Pernod
225ml *Chicken stock*
   (see page 306)
2 Spanish *butifarra negra*
   sausages or 150g black pudding
Salt
Crusty fresh bread, to serve

Cut the bacon or pancetta into 7mm-thick slices, then again into small dice. Trim the salad or spring onions, cut the white parts in half, then across into thick slices, and thinly slice the green.

Gently heat the olive oil in a cazuela or shallow flameproof casserole over a medium heat. Add the diced pancetta and fry until lightly golden. Add the white part of the salad or spring onions and the garlic and fry until the onion is soft.

Add the broad beans and cook gently for 2–3 minutes. Add the bay leaves, mint, Pernod, chicken stock and a little salt to taste. Add the butifarra sausage or black pudding and push down into the beans, then cover and leave to simmer for 4 minutes. Uncover and continue to simmer until the liquid has reduced and almost disappeared.

Lift out the butifarra sausage or black pudding and place on a board. Stir the green part of the onions into the pan and cook for a minute until just wilted. Thickly slice the black sausage, lay them on top of the beans and serve straight away with the obligatory crusty fresh bread.

SIZZLING PRAWNS
with GARLIC, CHILLI
and OLIVE OIL

Gambas al ajillo SERVES 4 AS A TAPAS OR STARTER

These prawns, also known in some places as *gambas pil-pil*, are a popular tapas or first course all over Spain. They are traditionally cooked and served in shallow 15cm terracotta dishes called cazuelitas, which are taken directly to the table covered with a thick slice of rustic white bread, not only to stop the oil from spitting but for dipping into the delicious garlic and chilli flavours. I serve the same dish in our pub just outside Padstow, the Cornish Arms. There I use little dried piri-piri chillies, which come from Africa, because the dish originated in Portuguese Mozambique. They are fiendishly hot but are the absolute correct chillies to use, if you can get them.

750g raw unpeeled prawns
8 garlic cloves
5g flat-leaf parsley leaves
300ml olive oil
2 tsp crushed dried chilli flakes
    or 4 small dried piri-piri chillies
Salt
Crusty fresh bread, to serve

Peel the prawns, leaving the last tail segment in place.

Put the garlic and parsley leaves onto a chopping board, sprinkle with ½ teaspoon of salt and chop together into a coarse mixture.

Pour the oil into a large, deep frying pan and place over a low heat. As soon as it is hot, add the chilli flakes or whole dried chillies and the garlic and parsley mixture and cook gently, stirring, for 2–3 minutes until the garlic is sizzling and fragrant.

Increase the heat to medium, add the prawns and cook for 2–3 minutes, stirring, until just cooked through. Season with a little more salt to taste and serve with slices of crusty bread.

TORTILLA of BLACK PUDDING, WHITE BEANS and GARLIC

Tortilla catalana SERVES 4 AS A TAPAS OR LUNCH

This is another very popular rural dish from the Catalan region, one made regularly at home, especially at lunchtime as it can be put together quickly with readily available ingredients, which was exactly why I knocked one up in my camper van one day while we were on the road. Cooking meals en route like this proved to be rather more tricky than you might think. It's one thing for a little family to park up somewhere and cook something simple, quite another when you've got two crew vehicles turning up with a TV camera, a noisy director and the constant changing of the orientation of the van to catch the sun and pleasant backgrounds. This always invites curiosity from onlookers, in this case a rather drunken man from the farmhouse nearby who asked our researcher if she'd like to go back to his house with him and take off her clothes. Talk about health and safety at work. I don't think that one was in our manual. Blood sausages such as *butifarra negra* or morcilla are not easy to come by in the UK but a good quality spicy black pudding would be ideal.

2 x 75–80g Spanish butifarra negra or morcilla, or 150g black pudding
4–5 tbsp olive oil
100g bacon lardons, cut into small dice
1 bunch spring onions, trimmed and cut into 2.5cm pieces
1 garlic clove, finely chopped
175g cooked dried white beans (see page 117)
6 large free-range eggs
Salt and freshly ground black pepper

Halve the blood sausage lengthways, remove the skin and thickly slice. If the blood sausage is particularly thick, such as those illustrated here, slice lengthways into quarters first. Heat 3 tablespoons of olive oil in a frying pan that measures about 18cm across the base and 25cm across the top, over a medium-high heat. Add the bacon, and cook, stirring, for 4 minutes until lightly golden.

Add the spring onion and garlic and fry for 2 minutes until soft but not coloured. Add the blood sausage and fry for 1 minute, taking care not to break it up too much, then add the cooked white beans and cook for 2–3 minutes until they have heated through. Pull the pan off the heat and leave the mixture to cool slightly.

Crack the eggs into a bowl, season with ½ teaspoon of salt and some black pepper and beat together with a fork. Stir in the bean and sausage mixture. Return the pan to a medium-low heat, add another tablespoon of oil and, when it is hot, pour in the contents of the bowl and leave to cook for 15–20 minutes until it is lightly golden brown underneath and almost set on top.

Cover the top of the pan with a large lid or inverted plate, turn the two over together (using a tea towel as the pan will be hot), return the emptied pan to the heat with a final drizzle of oil and slide the omelette back in, cooked side up. Leave for 2 minutes until just cooked through. Slide back on the plate and serve, cut into wedges.

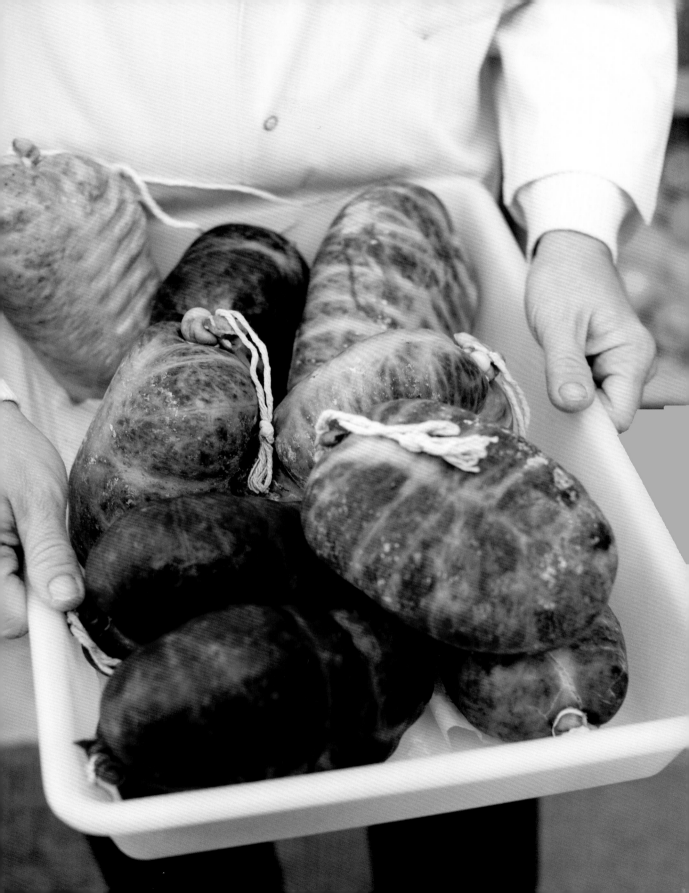

CATALAN NOODLES
with SEAFOOD

Fideua de mariscos SERVES 6

Before I made the trip to Catalonia for this book, I have to confess I had no idea what *fideua* was, and when I was told it was a paella pan of pasta cooked in fish stock I thought I was in for a bit of worthy Catalan cooking. That was, until I tasted it. It is a sort of pasta-version of paella without all the bits, and what makes it special is the initial browning of the dry pasta in a tiny bit of olive oil and then the quality of the stock. The other extraordinary thing was that, when my 'new best friend' in Catalonia cooked it, he finished off the dish by covering it in newspaper, which seemed to make all the little pasta strands, as he put it, 'point up towards heaven'. Next to *suquet de peix*, *fideua* is probably the most passionately discussed dish in all of Catalonia. When I ate it with Rafa and his restaurateur chums at a beach shack where they regularly meet to cook and talk about food, the *fideua* was served together with several other dishes, very much like an Australian barbecue where everyone helps themselves to whatever they fancy. You can find many types of commercially produced *fideua* noodles, but Rafa used fine spaghettini-like pasta, which is easy to break up into small pieces. He served this dotted with freshly made alioli.

4 tbsp olive oil
2 fat garlic cloves, sliced
300g *fideua* no. 2 noodles
    (see page 311) or fine long
    pasta, broken into 2.5cm pieces
175g cleaned fresh medium-sized
    squid, sliced
175g raw peeled prawns
Salt
1 quantity of *Alioli* (see page 307),
    to serve

FOR THE ROCKFISH STOCK:
80ml olive oil
1 large onion, sliced
4 garlic cloves, chopped
¼ tsp freshly grated nutmeg
500ml tomato passata
½ tsp freshly ground white pepper
1.5kg mixed whole fish such as
    gurnard, whiting, grey mullet,
    gutted and thickly sliced
Salt and freshly ground white
    pepper

For the stock, heat the oil in a large pan over a medium heat. Add the onion and garlic and sweat gently for 5–6 minutes. Add the nutmeg, tomato passata, ½ teaspoon of white pepper, 2 litres of water and 2 teaspoons of salt and bring to the boil. Add the fish together with the heads and simmer, part-covered, for 2 hours. Pass through a fine sieve into a clean pan and set aside.

Place a large *paellera* or frying pan of about 38cm over 2 burners on a medium-low heat. Add the oil and garlic and as soon as the garlic starts to sizzle and turn golden, scoop it out and set aside. Add the noodles and leave them to fry, stirring constantly, until they are a light golden brown. Take care not to let them become too dark because this can make the finished dish bitter.

Stir in 1 litre of the rockfish stock (freeze any remainder to use another time), 1 teaspoon of salt and the fried garlic and bring up to the boil, stirring gently to release any noodles stuck to the base of the pan. Reduce the heat to a simmer and cook gently for about 9 minutes, turning the pan regularly so that it cooks evenly, by which time all the liquid should have disappeared. Remove from the heat, cover with an opened-out newspaper and leave to rest for 4 minutes.

Meanwhile, add 2 tablespoons of oil to another large frying pan, add the squid and prawns, and stir-fry over a high heat for 1–1½ minutes, until nicely caramelized and just cooked through. Season with a little salt and spoon onto a warmed serving plate.

Uncover the fideua and dot the surface with teaspoonfuls of the alioli. Serve straight away with the seafood and remaining alioli.

RAFA'S FISH STEW
with ROMESCO SAUCE

Romesco de peix SERVES 4

Is this poetic fancy, I wonder? Rafa Cantero Rodriguez says the flavour of Catalan fish varies according to exactly which part of the Mediterranean shoreline it comes from, because it is affected by the fresh water running into the sea at that point. In north Catalonia, where he is from, the snow that falls on the mountains melts and seeps through the rocks, picking up minerals as it runs to the coast, and this cold mountain water gives the fish along here its own unique flavour. I don't know, but once somebody is telling you something like this about the beautifully fresh monkfish and gurnard they are preparing in front of you, you are captivated. We are all driven by our emotional responses, and I was sure that his *romesco de peix* was going to be legendary, especially after he'd cooked his tomatoes and garlic over charcoal, and added the liver from the monkfish along with some local almonds, some bread crisp-fried in olive oil, juicy garlic and some parsley. And so it was.

1 x 500g prepared monkfish tail, trimmed of all membrane
500g gurnard fillets, pin-boned
4 tbsp plain flour
2 tbsp olive oil
150ml *Romesco sauce* (see page 307)
50ml dry white wine
600ml *Fish stock* (see page 306)
1 tbsp chopped flat-leaf parsley
Salt and freshly ground black pepper
Crusty fresh bread, to serve

Cut the monkfish tail across through the bone into steaks about 2cm thick. Cut the gurnard fillets slightly on the diagonal into pieces 3cm wide. Season the fish lightly on both sides with salt and pepper.

Put the flour on a plate and use to coat the pieces of fish well, knocking off the excess. Heat the olive oil in a shallow flameproof casserole or large deep frying pan in which the fish will fit comfortably in one layer. Add the pieces of fish and fry over a medium heat for 1 minute on each side until lightly golden. Lift onto a plate.

Add the romesco sauce to the remaining oil left in the pan and fry very gently for 1 minute. Stir in the wine and bring to the boil, then add the fish stock and simmer for 7–8 minutes until reduced by half and to cook out the raw taste of the wine.

Return the fish to the pan, spoon over some of the sauce and leave to simmer for 4 minutes until the fish is just cooked through. Season the sauce to taste, stir in the parsley and serve with bread for mopping up the juices.

BARBECUED RABBIT with a TOMATO, PICKLED CHILLI and CAULIFLOWER SALAD

SERVES 4

This is the dish that started my quest to find out all about Spanish food. Years ago a friend of mine, Mark Knight Adams, told me of childhood holidays at Cadaqués in Catalonia, and two particular restaurants his parents used to take him to. One was a bar on the beach at Cala Montjoi where the German owner did food and had a French bulldog, so he called the place El Bulli, and the other was Pont de Molins in the foothills of the Pyrenees, where he remembered an old mill by a chalky mountain stream. Here they cooked rabbit over apple wood and served it with alioli, the best chips he'd ever tasted and a gorgeously simple tomato salad. For me it conjured up a world of honest, rustic, robust food, almost like my memory of the best bits of Hemingway's *For Whom The Bell Tolls*. Once you've got an image in your mind, you have to go and find out if it's true, and on the whole I have to say it is. I found the restaurant by the stream a bit less romantic than the image, because it was now rather big and busy, but the grilled smoky rabbit complete with kidneys and the chips were fabulous. The salad comes from the Hispania restaurant in Arenys del Mar, a bit more sophisticated than the one I had at the mill, but with its pickled chillies and cauliflower it goes well with the rabbit. The pickle makes enough for about 4 meals, so keep leftovers in the fridge for next time.

2 x 1.5kg farmed rabbits
120ml olive oil
Leaves from 2 x 10cm sprigs
   rosemary, finely chopped
Leaves from 4 large thyme
   sprigs, chopped
1 large lemon, halved
Salt and freshly ground black
   pepper

FOR THE TOMATO,
   PICKLED CHILLI AND
   CAULIFLOWER SALAD:
300g cauliflower (about ½)
4 medium-hot green chillies
30g fine salt
400ml white wine vinegar
1 tbsp caster sugar
5 x 250g beef tomatoes, skinned
   and seeded
1 tbsp sherry vinegar
2½ tbsp extra virgin olive oil
1 bunch small white salad onions
Sea salt flakes

FOR THE PATATAS FRITAS:
550g peeled floury potatoes
600ml olive oil, for deep-frying

The day before, pickle the cauliflower and green chillies for the salad. Break the cauliflower into roughly 3cm florets and cut them lengthways into slices 5mm thick. Quarter the chillies lengthways. Toss them with the salt and leave overnight.

The next day, rinse the vegetables well. Bring the white wine vinegar and sugar to the boil in a small pan, add the cauliflower and chillies and bring back to the boil for just 1 minute so they remain slightly crunchy. Remove with a slotted spoon to a bowl and leave both the vinegar and vegetables to cool. Then spoon the vegetables into a small plastic container, pour the vinegar back over, cover with a lid and refrigerate.

Next, joint the rabbits. Cut off the heads and discard. Cut off the front legs and cut off and discard the bony ends. Cut off the hind legs, trim away the belly flap from the body section with scissors and cut each saddle across into 3 pieces, leaving the kidneys in place. Season well all over with salt and pepper. Mix the olive oil with the rosemary and thyme leaves and set to one side to infuse.

Light the barbecue to high (see page 314). For the patatas fritas, cut the potatoes lengthways into slices 8mm thick, then lengthways again into chips 8mm thick. Heat olive oil for deep-frying to 120°C. Drop half the chips into the oil and leave to cook for about 5 minutes until they are tender when pierced with the tip of a knife but have not taken on any colour. Lift them out and leave to drain until you are ready to finish them off. Continue to part-cook the rest of the chips.

Catalonia

Brush the rabbit pieces with the herb oil and barbecue over a high heat for 6 minutes on each side, brushing with more of the herb oil and squeezing over a little lemon juice every now and then, until they are golden brown and cooked through.

To make the tomato salad, cut the tomatoes roughly into chunks, then finely chop 200g of them into a pulp, scoop it into a bowl and stir in 1 teaspoon of the sherry vinegar, 1 teaspoon of the olive oil and salt to taste. Toss the remainder with salt to taste and scatter them over the base of a shallow serving plate. Trim away the green tops from the salad onions and cut the white part into thin wedges through the root end. Lift approximately 75g of the pickled cauliflower and 3 pieces of green chilli out of the vinegar and leave to drain, then cut the chillies across into thin slices. Scatter the pickled cauliflower, chillies and the salad onions over the tomatoes and spoon over the tomato pulp dressing. Sprinkle over the remaining sherry vinegar, olive oil and some sea salt flakes and set to one side.

A few minutes before the rabbit is ready, heat the oil to 170°C. Drop the chips back into the hot oil in batches and fry for 2 minutes until crisp and golden. Drain on kitchen paper, sprinkle with a little salt and serve with the barbecued rabbit and the salad.

BRAISED ROSE VEAL
with WILD MUSHROOMS

Fricandó de ternera SERVES 4

It's heartening that what we call rose veal is becoming more and more popular in Britain. Not all supermarkets have caught on to it yet, but let's hope they will. In Spain, *ternera*, which is never more than a year old, is much commoner in restaurants than beef, both in braises like this and grilled. I find this dish, with the combination of veal and some wild mushrooms such as girolles and trompettes, particularly special, but I've put some dried porcini in too, to lift the mushroom flavour. You can also get very good results with thin slices of braising steak such as chuck or blade. Serve with mash, of course, if you wish.

25g dried porcini mushrooms
4 x 175g slices rose veal or beef
    blade steak, chuck steak
    or boneless shoulder,
    cut 1cm thick
2 tbsp plain flour
5 tbsp olive oil
1 large onion, finely chopped
125g finely chopped carrot
4 garlic cloves, finely chopped
150g vine-ripened tomatoes,
    skinned and chopped
150ml dry white wine
250ml light *Beef stock*
    (see page 306)
The leaves from 2 sprigs
    fresh thyme
A small handful of flat-leaf
    parsley leaves, chopped
25g butter
500g mixed wild mushrooms
    (such as grey chanterelles,
    opposite), well cleaned
    and sliced if large
Salt and freshly ground
    black pepper

Put the porcini into a small bowl, cover with 150ml boiling-hot water and soak for 30 minutes. Meanwhile, season the slices of meat well on both sides with salt and pepper, then dust with the flour.

Heat 2 tablespoons of the olive oil in a flameproof casserole. Add the slices of meat and fry briefly until just beginning to brown, then lift them onto a plate and set to one side.

Add the remaining oil to the casserole with the onion and carrot and fry gently for 15 minutes until soft and golden brown. Meanwhile, drain the porcini, reserving the soaking liquid, and finely chop. Add the porcini to the onions and carrots with half the chopped garlic and fry for a further 5 minutes.

Add the tomatoes and fry for 2–3 minutes until they have broken down, then add the wine and leave to boil for a few minutes, rubbing the base of the casserole to loosen any caramelized juices, until it has reduced by half. Add the stock, mushroom soaking liquor, veal or beef slices and thyme and bring to a simmer. Cover and cook gently until the sauce has reduced and thickened and the meat is meltingly tender: 1–1½ hours for the veal, 2½ hours for the beef.

Meanwhile, put the remaining chopped garlic and the parsley into a mini food processor or mortar with ½ teaspoon of salt and grind into a paste. When the meat is tender, melt the butter in a large frying pan, add the mushrooms and seasoning and fry briskly for 2–3 minutes until tender. Uncover the casserole and stir in the mushrooms and the garlic and parsley paste. Simmer for a further 5 minutes, adjust the seasoning, re-cover and leave to rest for 5 minutes before serving.

BARBECUED YOUNG LEEKS
with ROASTED GARLIC, TOMATO
and ALMOND SAUCE

Calçots con salbitxada SERVES 12

One of the frustrating parts of my journey through Spain was never quite being in the right place at the right time. We filmed a magnificent Easter procession in Oviedo in Asturias complete with solemn drum-beating and a crew of burly men staggering under the weight of the weeping Madonna, but the best ones are in Seville. We missed the Tomatina, the tomato-throwing festival, and the only bull running we could find was in Tronchón in Valencia, where they only had one small bull. Perhaps the worst thing for me was to miss the calçot season in Catalonia. Next to cooking *chuletón* (ribs of beef) or whole turbot over charcoal, the celebration of barbecuing a large type of spring onion in the open air in January and February was something I would have loved to film. The ceremony of peeling off the blackened outer layers, dipping the onions in a sauce made with pounded almonds, tomatoes, garlic, chilli, olive oil and red wine vinegar, holding them aloft and dropping them into your mouth is very convivial and you end up astonishingly messy. I've tried this on my barbecue at home in November using young leeks. Purists would say you've got to have calçots but the leeks seemed damned good to me. I have, however, seen calçots on sale in Borough Market in London, if you happen to be passing . . .

50 young leeks, no more than
   2.5cm thick

FOR THE SALBITXADA
   SAUCE:
4 vine-ripened tomatoes
2 bulbs of garlic, broken into
   cloves but left unpeeled
150g blanched almonds
½ tsp crushed dried chilli flakes
1 tbsp red wine vinegar
120ml olive oil
Salt

For the salbitxada, preheat the oven to 200°C/gas 6. Roast the tomatoes for 20 minutes, the garlic cloves for 30 minutes until soft, and the almonds for 6–8 minutes until golden brown. Leave to cool, then skin the tomatoes and squeeze the soft garlic flesh from the skins. Put the roasted almonds into a food processor and coarsely grind. Add the tomatoes, garlic and chilli flakes and grind into a thick paste. Add the vinegar then, with the motor still running, gradually add the olive oil as if making mayonnaise. The sauce should now be thick but liquid enough for dipping and coating the leeks. Season to taste with salt.

Light the barbecue (see page 314) to high. Slit open the green part of each leek down to the centre but not all the way through and wash away mud from between the leaves.

Place the leeks in one layer on the barbecue and cook for 15–20 minutes, turning regularly, until they are charred black on the outside and feel very soft and squishy in the centre. Lift onto a newspaper, roll up and leave to steam for 5 minutes.

Unwrap the leeks and arrange on a serving platter. Place this and the bowl of sauce in the centre of the table, and instruct your guests to first peel away the smoke-blackened outer layers of each leek, dip the white end into the sauce, tip their heads back, open their mouths wide and eat their way up to the greener leaves. These they can discard. Finger bowls and paper napkins are not very Spanish but might be a good idea.

CLAMS with a GARLIC and NUT PICADA

Almejas de Palamós SERVES 4

What would I say were the most important elements of Spanish cuisine? Pimentón? Chorizo? Saffron? Paella rice? Jamón? Olive oil? Salt cod? Yes, these are all very important, but my latest enthusiasm is for the picada, which is when nuts, such as almonds, hazelnuts or pine nuts, and bread or fried bread, garlic, olive oil and sometimes herbs are pounded together in a mortar and stirred into a dish at the end to thicken the sauce and flavour it. This dish of clams, where they use triangular tellerines but also palourdes, called *almejas*, is simply the clams steamed open in a hot pan with a picada thrown in at the last minute. It comes from Palamós on the Catalan coast north of Barcelona, famous also for some of the best prawns in the Mediterranean.

1kg small clams, such as
   carpetshell

FOR THE PICADA:
30g pine nuts
30g blanched almonds
4 tbsp olive oil
25g slice crustless white bread
4 garlic cloves
Leaves from 4 small sprigs
   flat-leaf parsley

For the picada, heat a frying pan and dry-roast the pine nuts for 1 minute, the almonds for 2 minutes. Leave to cool. Meanwhile, fry the bread in 2 tablespoons of the olive oil for 1 minute on each side until crisp and golden brown. Leave to cool.

Break the fried bread into the bowl of a mini food processor, add the nuts and grind them together quite finely. The mixture at this stage needs to be like coarse sand. Add the garlic and parsley with the remaining 2 tablespoons of oil and grind together into a thick paste.

Wash the clams in plenty of cold water and discard any that don't show signs of closing when squeezed gently. Place a large pan which has a lid over a high heat and, as soon as it is hot, add the clams and 4 tablespoons of water, cover and cook for 1–2 minutes, shaking the pan every now and then, until the clams have just opened.

Remove the pan from the heat, uncover and slightly tilt it so that you can pull the clams slightly away from the cooking liquor. Stir the picada into the cooking juices to thicken it, then stir the mixture back through the clams. Serve straight away.

VEAL, PORK, SERRANO HAM and PORCINI MUSHROOM CANNELLONI

Canalons de ternera, cerdo, jamón y boletus SERVES 6–8

Catalan cooking is much more like that of Provence and northern Italy than Spain. The presence of cannelloni therefore needs no further explanation. But the Catalans have developed them into a very important local speciality, and these with minced chicken or veal and pork flavoured with serrano ham, porcini mushrooms and nutmeg are the sort of cannelloni that, as a child, I would dream about having.

25g dried porcini mushrooms
30g butter
1 medium onion, finely chopped
2 garlic cloves, finely chopped
225g minced veal or chicken
225g minced pork
100g thinly sliced serrano ham
25g plain flour
300ml full-cream milk
1 tbsp chopped flat-leaf parsley
a little freshly grated nutmeg
16 small sheets fresh egg lasagne
100g coarsely grated Manchego
    cheese
Salt and freshly ground black
    pepper

FOR THE
    BÉCHAMEL SAUCE:
1 small onion, halved
6 cloves
4 fresh bay leaves
1.2 litres full-cream milk
80g butter
80g plain flour

Cover the dried mushrooms with boiling water and leave to soak for 30 minutes. Then drain well and finely chop.

For the béchamel sauce, stud the onion with the cloves and put into a pan with the bay leaves and milk. Bring to the boil and set aside to cool.

For the filling, melt the butter in a medium pan, add the onion and garlic, and fry gently for 10 minutes, until soft and sweet but not browned. Add the porcini, minced veal and pork and fry for 3–4 minutes, breaking up any lumps with a spoon as the meat browns.

Put the serrano ham into a food processor and process briefly using the pulse button until finely chopped. Add to the pork and veal and cook for 2–3 minutes. Stir in the flour, cook for 1 minute, then gradually stir in the milk. Bring to the boil, stirring, lower the heat and simmer for 5 minutes, stirring frequently. Stir in the parsley, nutmeg and salt and pepper to taste. Set aside.

Bring 4.5 litres water to the boil in a large pan with 8 teaspoons of salt. Trim down or halve the sheets of lasagne if necessary so they measure about 10 x 15cm. Drop them into the water, turn off the heat and leave them to soak for 5 minutes. Drain, rinse briefly in cold water, then quickly separate before they stick together again.

Spoon 2½ tablespoons of the filling along one short edge of each pasta sheet and roll it up. Lay the canalons side by side and seam-side down in a buttered shallow baking dish in which they fit snugly.

Preheat the oven to 200°C/gas 6. Strain the infused milk into a jug and discard the onion and bay leaves. Melt the butter in a pan, stir in the flour and cook gently for 1 minute. Gradually stir in the milk and simmer for 5 minutes, stirring now and then, until smooth and thick. Season to taste with salt. Pour the sauce evenly over the canalons and sprinkle with the Manchego cheese. Bake for 30 minutes or until golden brown and bubbling.

A CATALAN FISH, LOBSTER and POTATO STEW

Suquet de langosta y peix SERVES 6

Suquet is Catalonia's most famous fish stew, and is basically, like so many fish stews, such as bouillabaisse, cotriade and cacciuccio, a fisherman's boil-up of whatever fish is left over from the day's catch. But like bouillabaisse it has become prestigious, made with expensive ingredients like lobster and John Dory. An important tip in making suquet came from the two Rexach sisters, Paquita and Lolita, who run the Restaurant Hispania in Arenys del Mar. 'Be mean with the water and generous with the fire', they say, meaning cook it quickly and make sure there's only a small amount of very well-flavoured sauce at the end. When Paquita made a suquet for me, she did it with the stomach of a sea cucumber, which you're not going to get at your local supermarket, so I've made it with lobster and I'm using the soft tomalley in the head to help thicken and flavour it. There's a fair bit of work in making this because I want you to use all the meat in the head and legs of the lobster, and to use all the shell to provide extra flavour to the stock. I think it's a great shame the way we throw away lobster, prawn and crab shells, and even fish heads, when there is so much flavour to be garnered from these when making a simple stock.

1 x 750g cooked lobster
8 tbsp olive oil
800ml *Fish stock* (see page 306)
6 fat garlic cloves, 4 whole and
    2 finely chopped
1 kg firm white fish fillet, such
    as monkfish, gurnard, sea bass,
    gilthead bream or John Dory
2 tbsp plain flour
2 medium onions, finely chopped
A good pinch of crushed dried
    chillies
750g vine-ripened or beef
    tomatoes, halved
450g peeled waxy potatoes, such
    as Charlotte, thickly sliced
30g toasted blanched almonds
30g toasted pine nuts
1 tbsp chopped flat-leaf parsley
Salt
Crusty fresh bread, to serve

First of all, prepare the lobster. Remove the legs and claws and cut the body in half, lengthways. Cut the claws into pieces at each joint and crack the shell of each piece with the blade of a large knife. Remove and discard the stomach sac, situated in the head part just behind the eyes, and the intestinal tract (or 'poo-shoot' in Australia), which looks like a dark vein running down the tail meat. Separate the head sections from the tail and remove the tail meat from the shells. Cut each piece of tail meat into 4 even-sized pieces. Remove any red coral and grey-green tomalley from the head section, scrape all the white curd-like material out of the shells with a teaspoon, and set these aside for making the picada. Using a lobster pick, remove as much meat as possible from the head and legs, then chop up all the shell from the legs, head and tail section.

Heat 2 tablespoons of oil in a large pan, add the pieces of lobster shell and fry for 3 minutes. Add the fish stock, bring to the boil, cover and simmer for 10 minutes. Drain through a colander set over a bowl and discard the shells. You should be left with about 700ml.

Heat another 2 tablespoons of the oil in a cazuela, 30cm shallow flameproof casserole or large deep sauté pan over a medium heat, add the whole garlic cloves and cook gently without browning them too much until they are tender. Remove with a slotted spoon and set aside.

Remove any membrane from the monkfish fillet, if using, or pin bones from the fish fillets, then cut into neat 5cm pieces. Season on both sides with a little salt and dust with flour. Return the pan to a medium heat, add the pieces of fish a few at a time and fry for 2 minutes on each side until lightly golden. Lift out onto a plate and set aside.

Add another 4 tablespoons of oil to the pan, add the onions, chopped garlic and chilli flakes and fry gently over a medium heat for 10 minutes or until soft, sweet and just beginning to colour. Meanwhile, grate the halved tomatoes, pressing the fleshy, cut face of the tomato against the grater. (As you grate each tomato half, the skin will flatten out and be left behind.) Discard the skin. Add the grated tomatoes to the pan and cook until they have broken down to make a thick sauce. Stir in the potatoes, lobster-shell stock and another 1½ teaspoons of salt and simmer for 8–9 minutes or until the potatoes are almost tender. You want the potatoes to be almost, but still 4–5 minutes away from being fully cooked.

Add the fish, the pieces of lobster and any meat you have picked from the head and legs to the pan, turn over once to cover in the sauce, then leave to simmer for 2 minutes. Meanwhile, for the picada, put the fried garlic cloves, reserved lobster tomalley, coral and curd-like material into the bowl of a mini food processor with the toasted almonds and pine nuts and grind into a thick paste. You might need to add a tablespoon or two of the sauce to get the mixture moving.

Stir the picada and chopped parsley into the stew and leave to cook for a further 2–3 minutes until the sauce has thickened. Adjust the seasoning if necessary and serve.

MERCÈ'S DUCK with PEARS

Pato con peras SERVES 4

Outside the Moorish-influenced areas of Spain, I didn't come across much fruit in meat dishes, but this traditional Catalan dish is the exception. I find the combination of a roasted duck with some pears cooked in the accompanying sauce very satisfying, particularly when the sauce had been thickened with a picada of toasted and ground dried choricero peppers, hazelnuts, fried garlic and parsley. I discovered this dish at a small cookery school called El Folló just outside of Tagamanent, run by Mercè Brunés and her husband. When I walked into her kitchen it was a bit like I imagined Chez Panisse would be. There were baskets of mushrooms, rounds of homemade bread, bunches of herbs, hams and dried peppers hanging from the ceiling, and an air of seriousness about good food and good cooking. That, and a glorious view over the Catalan hills of the Parc Natural del Montseny.

1 x 2kg oven-ready duck
3 tbsp olive oil
100g finely chopped onion
100g finely chopped carrot
100g finely chopped celery
200g skinned chopped tomatoes, fresh or from a can
180ml dry white wine
600ml *Chicken stock* (see page 306)
4 small firm pears, such as conference, stalks removed
2 tsp sherry vinegar
Salt

FOR THE PICADA:
1 dried choricero pepper
1 tbsp olive oil
3 garlic cloves, peeled but kept whole
65g toasted hazelnuts
10g parsley leaves

Preheat the oven to 180°C/gas 4. Season the duck inside and out with salt, place on a rack in a roasting tin and roast for 1 hour until there is no trace of blood in the juices, pouring the oil out of the tin into a small bowl every 15 minutes or so.

For the picada, pull the stalk out of the choricero pepper and shake out the seeds. Add the pepper to a small frying pan and dry-fry for 4–5 minutes until it has darkened slightly. Leave to cool, then grind to a powder in a spice grinder. Heat the oil in the frying pan, add the garlic cloves and fry gently until richly golden brown. Put the hazelnuts into a mini food processor and grind to a powder. Add the choricero pepper powder, fried garlic and parsley and grind to a sandy texture. Set 1 tablespoon aside for sprinkling over the dish.

Lift the duck onto a carving board and leave to cool slightly. Heat the oil in a large shallow sauté pan. Add the onion, carrot, celery and ½ teaspoon of salt and fry gently for 7–8 minutes until soft and sweet. Add the tomatoes and cook for 5 minutes.

Pour the excess fat away from the roasting tin, place it directly over a medium heat and add the wine. Bring to the boil, strain onto the vegetables, add the stock and bring to a gentle simmer.

Peel the pears, cut them in half lengthways and remove the cores with a melon baller or teaspoon. Add to the sauce, cover and simmer for 10 minutes or until just tender, turning over halfway through.

Meanwhile, joint the duck. Cut off the legs and cut each one in half at the joint. Slice the breasts away from the ribcage in one piece and cut each one across into 2 pieces.

Take the pears out of the sauce. Add 4–5 tablespoons of sauce and the sherry vinegar to the picada mixture and blend to a smooth paste. Stir into the sauce and season to taste with salt. Add the duck and return the pears to the sauce, part-cover and simmer for 5 minutes or until they have heated through and the sauce has reduced and thickened slightly. Uncover, scatter over the reserved dry picada mix and serve.

SOUPY RICE with CHICKEN, PEPPERS, FENNEL and PEAS

Arroz caldoso con pollo y guisantes SERVES 4

I think you could best describe an *arroz caldoso* as a rice casserole. With such large rice-growing areas on the Mediterranean coast, it's not surprising there are many rice dishes in Spain. This is a wet dish, rather like *risi e bisi* in Italy, an everyday kind of dish cooked in a saucepan. It is regularly served in Spanish homes, leaving paella to be cooked outside almost exclusively by men, the Spanish equivalent of the boys looking after the beer and the barbie. The only consistent part in these dishes is rice and a really first-class stock. In this case I've added chicken, onion, garlic, red and green peppers, tomatoes, saffron, fennel seeds and peas, but they are as often made with rabbit and partridge, or meaty seafood like monkfish, squid and prawns. You'll see that the recipe for *arroz meldoso* on page 176 is similarly a wet rice casserole, but much more robustly flavoured with chilli and pimentón. This one is more delicate and easy to do, and makes good use of a whole chicken in one dish.

1.5kg chicken, cut into 12 pieces, on the bone
4 tbsp olive oil
4 garlic cloves, 2 whole and 2 finely chopped
1 medium onion, chopped
1 red pepper, seeded and cut into small dice
1 green pepper, seeded and cut into small dice
1 tsp fennel seeds, lightly crushed
¼ tsp *pimentón dulce* (smoked sweet Spanish paprika)
175g skinned chopped tomatoes, fresh or from a can
1.2 litres *Chicken stock* (see page 306)
A pinch of saffron strands
300g short-grain paella rice, such as Calasparra
3 fresh bay leaves
2 tbsp flat-leaf parsley leaves
200g shelled peas, fresh or frozen
Salt

Skin the chicken pieces and season all over with salt. Heat 2 tablespoons of the olive oil in a large flameproof casserole or saucepan, add half the chicken and fry over a medium heat until nicely golden brown all over. Lift onto a plate and set to one side. Heat the remaining olive oil in the pan and fry the rest of the chicken in the same way. Set aside.

Add the whole garlic cloves to the pan and fry briefly until golden, then remove with a slotted spoon onto a plate and set aside. Add the onion, red and green pepper, chopped garlic, fennel seeds and pimentón and fry for 5–6 minutes until the onions and peppers have softened. Stir in the tomato and cook for 2–3 minutes.

Return the chicken pieces to the pan, pour over the stock, add the saffron and 1½ teaspoons of salt and bring to the boil. Stir in the rice and bay leaves and leave to simmer vigorously for 6 minutes, stirring every now and then to make sure it's not sticking to the base of the pan. Lower the heat to medium and leave to simmer more gently for 12 minutes, briefly stirring now and then.

Meanwhile, put the fried garlic cloves into a mini food processor or mortar with the parsley leaves and grind to a paste. Stir this into the rice with the peas and simmer for 2 more minutes, by which time the rice should be completely tender and the sauce thicker but still liquid. Remove from the heat, remove and discard the bay leaves, adjust the seasoning to taste and serve.

SPINACH with PINE NUTS and RAISINS

Espinacas con pasas y piñónes SERVES 4 AS A SIDE DISH

Raisins and pine nuts are almost a fingerprint for North African or Moorish cuisine.
This is popular all along the Mediterranean coastline, especially in Catalonia, and
makes the perfect side dish for rabbit, lamb and chicken.

50g raisins
50g pine nuts
500g leaf spinach
4 tbsp olive oil
2 garlic cloves, finely chopped
1 tsp sherry vinegar
Salt

Put the raisins into a small bowl, cover with hot water and leave
to plump up for 10–15 minutes. Meanwhile, toast the pine nuts
in a dry frying pan until golden brown. Tip onto a plate and set
to one side. Wash the spinach well, dry and tear into pieces if the
leaves are large.

Put 2 tablespoons of the olive oil into a large saucepan or deep
frying pan and place over a medium-high heat. Add the spinach,
a large handful at a time, and leave it to wilt down slightly before
adding the next, until it is all in the pan. Cook for about 1 minute
until it has all wilted, then tip it into a colander and gently press
out the excess liquid.

Put the remaining 2 tablespoons of olive oil and the garlic
into the pan and return it to the heat. As soon as the garlic starts
to sizzle and change colour, stir in the spinach, drained raisins,
pine nuts, sherry vinegar and some salt to taste. Briefly toss over
a high heat until heated through, then spoon into a warmed
shallow dish and serve.

Chapter Six

VALENCIA

About a year ago my brother John sent me a YouTube clip of the Mercado Central in Valencia. It was a busy morning and there are shots of butchers' stalls, vegetable and fish counters, and *embutidos* stalls with reddy-brown chorizos hanging in front. Suddenly one of the stallholders starts singing an aria from *La Traviata*, 'Parigi, O Cara': 'Let's leave Paris, my darling, and we'll spend our life together. You will be rewarded for your suffering and your health will bloom again.' Then another stallholder joins in, then a couple of shoppers, and the music is coming through the tannoy system. Some of the public start smiling in recognition, others look totally bewildered, but then two of the singers walk into the circle in the middle of the market, one singing as Alfredo and one as Violetta, and the shoppers all gather around. When it finishes, there is rapturous applause. It's rather moving. I was filming a programme about food and Italian opera of the nineteenth century at the time and making much of Verdi's love of cooking. I mentioned it to David, the director, and predictably he said, 'Yeah, fine, but wrong country' – but when we finally got to the mercado and saw that it was possibly one of the most beautiful markets in the world, the full impact of that music, and that beautiful produce, was apparent.

I would say the market alone is reason enough to go to Valencia, but as it happens it's a beautiful city. Not only is it the home of paella and a myriad other rice dishes, and the curious but refreshing drink made out of tiger nuts called horchata, but it's also famous for its oranges, represented not only in the *flan de naranja*, orange and caramel creams, but also in the famous Valencian salad of oranges, salt cod, onions and black olives. The coastal plains either side of the city are incredibly fertile, growing an enormous variety of vegetables, among them, of course, beans. The three varieties that you find in a true paella are the dried white *garrofó*, the fresh flat, wide, green *ferraura* and the *tavella*. Fruits include white-fleshed peaches, kumquats, white-fleshed plums and medlars, grapes ripened on the vines in paper bags, and almonds and other nuts.

But my journey wasn't all about food. A particular schoolboy pleasure for me was to try to discover where the legendary, almost Arthurian, character El Cid had operated, not only in reality but also where they had made the film with Charlton Heston and Sophia Loren. We discovered the castle on the beach at Peñiscola where at the end of the film, the Cid, dead but still strapped to his horse Babieca, had appeared to gallop through the castle gates along the beach, scattering the black-cloaked Arabs who were terrified that he was still apparently leading his army. The film ended with the words, 'Thus the Cid rode out of the gates of history into legend.'

Earlier I had been to the town of Morella, a classic medieval fortified hill town with a castle at the top, which El Cid actually had stormed and taken. Indeed, for much of his military career El Cid, or Rodrigo Díaz, had been working for the Moors, but he became the symbol of a Christian warrior. Amazing how reality never quite does it for people. The countryside surrounding Morella is famous for the hunting of partridge and truffles and I spent a thoroughly enjoyable morning out with a shooting party bagging birds and pickling them, which is the favoured way of preserving them. At the time I thought I would prefer my partridge roasted, but I realized that preserved partridge done with olive oil and vinegar becomes rather an attractive addition to a salad, and the recipe for quail on page 200 follows these principles.

ORANGE, SALT COD, ONION and BLACK OLIVE SALAD

SERVES 4 AS A STARTER

I can think of no dish more celebratory of the colours and flavours of southern Spain than this. Oranges, salt cod and black olives all in a clean, fresh-tasting salad where the firm saltiness of the fish contrasts so satisfyingly with the refreshing sweetness of the oranges and the faint bitterness of the black olives. It's a great winter salad because at this time the oranges are at their best.

500g *Bacalao* (salt cod, see page 313)
3 large oranges
½ small red onion, thinly sliced into rings
24 good quality cured black olives, pitted
2 tbsp chopped flat-leaf parsley
1 hard-boiled egg, peeled and roughly chopped into small pieces

FOR THE DRESSING:
2 tbsp sherry vinegar
2 tbsp red or white wine vinegar
3 tbsp freshly squeezed orange juice (from segmenting the oranges)
8 tbsp extra virgin olive oil
Salt and freshly ground black pepper

Soak the bacalao in 3–4 litres of water in the fridge for 24–48 hours, depending on thickness. Change the water when it tastes salty, normally at least twice.

Put the piece of soaked salt cod into a pan of cold water, bring up to the boil, then cover and turn off the heat. Leave to sit for 10 minutes, then lift carefully onto a plate and leave to cool. Break into flakes, discarding the skin and any bones, cover and set to one side.

To segment the oranges, take a thin slice off the top and bottom of each one and stand it on a chopping board. Cutting from the top down to the bottom, carefully slice away all the skin and white pith. Then holding the orange in one hand and a knife in the other, and working over a bowl to catch all the juices, slice either side of each segment, as close to the dividing membrane as you can, and drop each one onto a plate. Set aside with the cod.

Whisk the ingredients together for the dressing with ½ teaspoon of salt in a small bowl. Put the flaked salt cod, orange segments, onion rings and olives into a mixing bowl and pour over the dressing. Add the parsley and toss together gently. Leave for 5 minutes then adjust the seasoning to taste. Lift the salad out of the excess dressing onto serving plates, garnish with the hard-boiled egg and serve at room temperature.

SQUID with ONIONS

Calamares con cebolla SERVES 4 AS A TAPAS OR STARTER

Though I have come across squid with onion in Spain, the idea for this recipe comes from Frank Camorra's book, *MoVida Rustica*. It's a fabulous book, designed so that it almost feels like it's set in Spain, although both he and his restaurant are in Australia. In the recipe he suggests using small squid and frying them in a little very hot olive oil, then pushing the tentacles back into the body pouch and serving them on a bed of the onions. The onions are cooked very gently for two hours so they have a soft, luscious sweetness about them. I've merely added a few shards of fresh bay leaf, a herb the Spanish are inordinately fond of.

2 fat garlic cloves
1 tbsp chopped flat-leaf parsley
4–5 tbsp olive oil
500g cleaned small squid, with
 pouches ideally 7–8cm long
200g *Slow-cooked onion confit*
 (see page 306)
Sea salt flakes
Lemon wedges, to serve (optional)

Put the garlic cloves onto a board, sprinkle with ½ teaspoon of sea salt flakes and crush into a smooth paste under the blade of a large cook's knife. Scrape the paste into a bowl, add half the parsley, 3 tablespoons of the olive oil and the prepared squid and mix together well, getting some of the mixture down inside the pouches. Cover and refrigerate for at least 1 hour.

Shortly before you are ready to cook, spoon the onion confit into a pan and season to taste with salt. Warm through over a gentle heat until piping hot.

Heat 1 tablespoon of the olive oil in a large frying pan, add half the squid pouches, season with a little more salt and leave them to caramelize on one side for 1 minute. Turn them over, season lightly once more and cook for another minute, then spoon onto a plate. Repeat with the remaining squid pouches. Add a little more oil to the frying pan, if necessary, and the tentacles, season with salt and stir-fry for 1 minute. Remove from the pan and stuff the tentacles inside the pouches.

Spoon onion confit into the centre of 4 medium-sized plates and arrange the squid on top. Scatter with the remaining parsley and serve straight away.

RICE with MONKFISH, SAFFRON and RED PEPPERS

Arroz de rape, azafrán y pimientos SERVES 6

There are many 'dry' rice dishes, or *arroces secos*, in the Valencia region, other than paella: there's rice with cuttlefish and vegetables (*arroz moreno de sepia y verdures*), rice with squid ink (*arroz negro*), and rice with fish on the side (*arroz a banda*), a recipe for which I included in two of my previous books, *Food Heroes, Another Helping* and *Coast to Coast*. I saw this one on the menu at the Casa Salvador in the town of Cullera – situated at the mouth of Rio Júcar, a 40-minute drive south of Valencia – while we were filming another rice dish, a moist one called an *arroz meloso* (see page 176). I didn't have time to get the recipe off them, but I reckon it would be pretty much as I've written it here, and anyway, even though I say so myself, it's bloody good.

4 tablespoons olive oil

75g finely chopped shallot

1 small head of garlic, cloves separated, peeled and finely chopped

½ tsp *pimentón dulce* (smoked sweet Spanish paprika), plus extra for seasoning the fish

A pinch of crushed dried chillies

200g vine ripened or beef tomatoes, halved

1 litre *Fish stock* (see page 306)

½ tsp loosely packed saffron strands

400g short-grain paella rice, such as Calasparra

1 large *Roasted red pepper* (see page 307) or 3 jarred pimientos

500g monkfish fillet, trimmed of all membrane then cut across into 1cm-thick slices

1 quantity *Alioli* (see page 307), to serve

Salt

Grate the halved tomatoes, pressing the fleshy, cut face of the tomato against the grater. (As you grate each tomato half, the skin will flatten out and be left behind.) Discard the skin. Heat 2 tablespoons of the olive oil in a 28–30cm cazuela or shallow flameproof casserole, add the shallot and fry gently for 10 minutes or until soft and sweet but not browned. Add the garlic, pimentón and chillies and fry for 2 minutes more, then stir in the tomatoes and cook until they have broken down into a sauce.

Stir in the fish stock, saffron and 1½ teaspoons of salt and bring to the boil, stirring. Sprinkle in the rice, stir once, then leave to simmer vigorously over a medium-high heat for 6 minutes.

Meanwhile, cut the roasted red pepper or jarred pimientos into 1cm-wide strips, removing and discarding any skin or seeds. Sprinkle them over the top of the rice and shake the pan briefly so they sink into the mixture a little. Lower the heat and leave to simmer gently for another 12 minutes. At the end of this time almost all the liquid should be absorbed and the rice will be pitted with small holes.

Shortly before the rice is ready, pat the monkfish pieces dry on kitchen paper and season well with salt and a little pimentón. Heat the remaining 2 tablespoons of oil in a non-stick frying pan. Add the monkfish slices a few at a time and fry over a high heat for 1 minute on either side until very lightly coloured and almost cooked through.

Lay the pieces of fish on top of the rice, turn off the heat and cover the cazuela or casserole with a clean tea towel, opened-out newspaper or lid. Leave to rest for 5 minutes, during which time the monkfish will finish cooking through. Serve warm with the alioli.

RICE STEW with MONKFISH, LANGOUSTINES and WILD MUSHROOMS

Arroz meldosa con rape, gambas y setas SERVES 6–8

Casa Salvador is perhaps the most famous rice restaurant in the region of Valencia. Salvador Gascon's family arrived there in 1955 and gradually built up an enviable reputation for dishes from the Albufera: rice, snails, frogs, crayfish, as well as chicken, rabbit and all types of seafood from the Mediterranean. Salvador has also written at least two books exclusively devoted to paella, meldoso, caldoso, arroz and arrosejat. This meldoso, made with monkfish, prawns and mushrooms, arrives at your table a deep rusty red from the pimentón, ñora peppers, tomato, saffron and fried red gurnard in the stock. It was one of those very special moments, sitting on his terrace looking out over one of the many rivers that connect with the vast lagoon that is the Albufera, where everything I was eating was probably grown or caught no more than ten miles from where I was sitting.

2 dried ñora peppers
150ml olive oil
12–16 large unpeeled raw prawns
1kg monkfish fillet, trimmed of all membrane then cut across into slices 1cm thick
6 garlic cloves, thinly sliced
150g trimmed salad onions, cut into small pieces
450g mixed wild or chestnut mushrooms, cleaned
300ml skinned chopped tomatoes, fresh or from a can
2 tsp *pimentón dulce* (smoked sweet Spanish paprika)
½ tsp cumin powder
The leaves from 2 sprigs fresh thyme
2 litres *Rockfish stock* (see page 142)
500g short-grain paella rice, such as Calasparra
1 tsp saffron strands
Salt

Remove the stalks from the dried peppers, slit them open and remove the seeds. Soak in hot water for 1 hour. Season the slices of monkfish on both sides with salt.

Drain the soaked peppers and scrape the flesh away from the skin. Discard the skins, finely chop the flesh, scoop it into a bowl and put to one side.

Heat half the olive oil in a large flameproof casserole or saucepan. Fry the prawns for 1–2 minutes until just pink. Remove to a plate and set aside. Add the monkfish slices a few at a time and fry for 1–2 minutes until lightly golden on both sides. Lift onto a plate and set aside with the prawns.

Add the remaining oil, garlic and onion to the pan and fry gently for 4 minutes. Add the mushrooms, season with salt and fry for 2 minutes, then add the tomatoes and ñora pepper flesh and fry for 2 minutes more. Stir in the pimentón, cumin and thyme leaves and fry for 2 minutes, then stir in the stock and 2 teaspoons salt. Bring to the boil, stir in the rice and saffron and leave to simmer vigorously for 6 minutes, stirring now and then to release any rice that may have stuck to the pan. Lower the heat to medium and leave to simmer more gently, briefly stirring now and then, for another 10 minutes.

Stir the monkfish into the rice and arrange the prawns on top. Simmer for 4 minutes until both the monkfish and the prawns have cooked through. Ladle into warmed dishes and serve.

GILTHEAD BREAM
BAKED in a SALT CRUST

Dorada a la sal SERVES 2

All up and down the Mediterranean coast of Spain, I found people who swore that the fish of their stretch of coastline had a unique and pronounced sweetness because of the special salts and minerals in the water there. I want to believe this is true but I fear that a seawater fish, created to resist the effect of osmosis, makes this impossible. Nevertheless, it's a lovely idea, and the production of so much sea salt in southern Spain, particularly around Alicante, would guarantee the emergence of a dish such as this, where fish is baked in a salt crust. Grey mullet and gilthead bream are the two most popular fish cooked in this way, but it works equally well with other meaty fish such as sea bass, snapper, turbot or porgy, whole sardines and large shell-on prawns too. The mixture of salt and egg white sets into a rock-hard crust around the fish, sealing in all the moisture and flavour of the sea and producing fish that is amazingly tender and perfectly cooked. It's important to leave the scales on the fish, however, as this prevents too much of the salt penetrating the fish while it's cooking. Though I've given a precise cooking time in the recipe, it's one of those occasions where a thermal probe is very useful. They are so cheap now, I think every kitchen should have one. I find the piquant salpicón enhances the soft sweetness of any fish cooked in this way. Boiled potatoes are good served alongside.

2 x 425–450g gilthead or
    black sea bream
6 sprigs fresh thyme
4 fresh bay leaves
4 slices lemon
A small bunch flat-leaf parsley
2kg coarse sea salt
2 egg whites
Salt and freshly ground
    black pepper

FOR THE SALPICÓN:
6 tbsp extra virgin olive oil
4 tsp sherry vinegar
1 tbsp nonpareilles capers
3 cornichons, finely chopped
1 tbsp very finely chopped shallot
4 tbsp *Roasted red pepper*
    (see page 307), or jarred
    pimientos, finely chopped
1 tbsp chopped flat-leaf parsley
½ tsp sugar
½ tsp salt

Preheat the oven to 200°C/gas 6. Wash the fish and gut them, then pat them dry, but do not scale them or trim away their fins. Sprinkle a little seasoning into the abdominal cavity and then push in the fresh herbs and lemon slices.

Mix the salt with the egg whites and spread a 1.5cm-thick layer over the base of a large baking dish. Put the fish on top, about 5cm apart, and then cover with the remaining salt, making sure there are no holes or gaps. The top layer should be at least 1cm thick.

Bake the fish for 20 minutes, then remove from the oven. If you have a probe, carefully push it through the crust, guessing where the thickest part of the fish will be. It should register about 58°C.

Meanwhile, mix the ingredients for the salpicon together in a bowl.

To serve, carefully crack the crust with the back of a large knife and lift it away from the top of the fish, so that you can lift them out onto a board or another serving platter. Make a shallow cut through the skin around the edge of the fish close to the backbone and belly, then make a little cut across the tail end. Trap the skin at the tail end between the tines of a large fork and roll it back along the fish to expose the flesh. Lift away the top two fillets, turn the fish over and repeat on the other side, or simply lift away the bones and lift the bottom two fillets away from the skin. Serve with the salpicon.

PRAWNS and POTATOES in GARLIC and PIMENTÓN SAUCE

All-i-pebre de gambas SERVES 6–8

All-i-pebre means 'garlic and pepper', in this case red pepper (*pimentón*) and chilli. It's the name given to a famous dish from the Albufera region just outside Valencia, where it is made with the eel fished from the lagoon. So well known is the dish that its name doesn't even need to mention the eel. Time was when I would happily write a recipe for eel, not really thinking about where anybody could get it from. Sadly reality has dented my optimism and I have to say that eel is hard to get hold of. You can get it by mail order – and to be authentic it should be cut across the bone, as for jellied eels – but all-i-pebre can be made with freshwater crayfish, too, which abound in the rice fields and marshes of the area, and large prawns, and also occasionally fish such as monkfish or John Dory, though I've tried it with monkfish and I don't think it works. You need something with a more robust flavour, such as the fattiness of an eel or, as here, the sweetness of a prawn.

1kg large unpeeled raw prawns
500g small evenly sized waxy
    potatoes, such as Charlotte
1 dried guindilla pepper or ½ tsp
    crushed dried chilli flakes
120ml olive oil
2 garlic cloves, very thinly sliced
1 tbsp *pimentón picante*
    (smoked hot Spanish paprika)
500ml *Fish stock* (see page 306)
Salt
Crusty fresh bread, to serve

Peel the prawns, leaving the last tail segment in place. Peel the potatoes and cut across into slices 1cm thick. Drop them into a pan of cold, well-salted water, bring to the boil and simmer for 5 minutes until barely tender when pierced with the tip of a small, sharp knife. Drain and set aside.

Remove the stalk and seeds from the guindilla pepper and thinly slice it across. Put the oil, garlic and guindilla pepper or dried chilli flakes into a large wide shallow pan or deep frying pan and place over a medium heat. Leave the garlic and pepper to sizzle gently for 3 minutes until lightly coloured, then stir in the pimentón and sizzle for a few seconds more. Add the fish stock and ¾ teaspoon of salt and bring to the boil, stirring. Add the part-cooked potatoes and simmer a little more vigorously over a medium-high heat for about 10–15 minutes until the potatoes are tender and the sauce has reduced and concentrated in flavour.

Add the prawns and simmer for 3 minutes or until just cooked through. Adjust the seasoning to taste, spoon into 1 large or 2 smaller terracotta cazuelas and serve with plenty of bread for mopping up the juices.

BRAISED GUINEA FOWL
with WHITE BEANS

Gallina de guinea con judías estofadas SERVES 4

I would almost call this a Spanish cassoulet, the difference being, as is so often the case with a lot of Spanish food, that there are no hard and fast rules for how to make it. It can equally well be made with partridge or pheasant as guinea fowl. But I think it's true to say that the birds and the beans are always cooked separately and then simmered together briefly at the end. What makes it especially Spanish is the almost ever-present pimentón and saffron.

6 tbsp olive oil
2 medium onions, finely chopped
400g dried white beans, soaked
    overnight in plenty of cold
    water
4 fresh bay leaves
1 x 1.25–1.5kg guinea fowl,
    jointed into 8
100g smoked bacon lardons,
    diced
3 garlic cloves, crushed
4 cloves
½ tsp *pimentón dulce* (smoked
    sweet Spanish paprika)
100g skinned chopped tomato,
    fresh or from a can
A small pinch of saffron strands
200ml *Chicken stock*
    (see page 306)
Salt and freshly ground black
    pepper

Heat 2 tablespoons of the olive oil in a large, flameproof casserole or saucepan. Add half the chopped onion and fry gently for 10 minutes, stirring now and then, until soft and sweet and just beginning to brown. Drain the beans and add them to the pan with the bay leaves and 1 litre of cold water. Bring to the boil, lower the heat, cover and leave to simmer gently for 1½ hours, checking from time to time that they have not stuck to the base of the pan and are still just covered with water. If not, add a little more. After 1½ hours add ½ teaspoon of salt, re-cover or part-cover depending on how much liquid is left (you want this to have reduced to almost nothing by the times the beans are done), and cook for another ½ hour until they are tender.

Meanwhile, heat another 2 tablespoons of oil over a medium heat in another flameproof casserole or large saucepan, for which you have a tight-fitting lid. Season the guinea fowl pieces, add them to the pan, brown them well on all sides then lift out onto a plate.

Add the remaining 2 tablespoons of oil to the pan with the bacon and fry for a few minutes until crisp and lightly golden. Add the remaining onion and fry gently for 10 minutes until soft, sweet and lightly browned. Add the garlic, cloves and pimentón and fry for 2 minutes more.

Add the tomatoes and fry for 2 minutes, then return the guinea fowl pieces to the pan, add the saffron and pour over the stock. Cover with a tight-fitting lid and leave to braise very gently for 30 minutes. When the guinea is tender you should be left with about 350ml of liquid. If there seems to be more, uncover and simmer a little more vigorously for a few minutes until reduced to this amount.

Spoon the beans into the casserole with the guinea fowl and stir together well. Simmer together, uncovered, for 15–20 minutes until the liquid has reduced and the beans have thickened it to give a nice stew-like consistency. Adjust the seasoning to taste, cover and leave to rest off the heat for 5–10 minutes before serving.

CLASSIC SPANISH MIXED SALAD

Ensalada mixta SERVES 4

I like the way a mixed salad in Spain is served. You tend to order one or two communally if you're in a group, in addition to whatever first courses you like, such as jamon or steamed clams or *caldo* (soup). Then there's enough salad left to act as a side dish for hake *a la plancha* or a grilled *chuletón* of beef. The Spanish sprinkle this salad with a little oil, vinegar and some seasoning at the table rather than making a vinaigrette, but the dressing I've given below will give you the flavour you are looking for. I've put in the ingredients I like but other common ingredients are sweetcorn kernels, cooked button mushrooms, cooked sliced carrots, grated raw carrot, cooked peas, cooked green beans, boiled small potatoes or small pickled gherkins.

1 head of crunchy lettuce, such as little gem, romaine or continental
2 medium vine-ripened tomatoes, cut into wedges or sliced
4 spring onions or salad onions, trimmed and thinly sliced
8 spears canned or jarred asparagus, drained
1 x 200g can or jar of tuna in olive oil, drained and flaked
1 tbsp red wine vinegar
4 tbsp extra virgin olive oil
2 hard-boiled eggs, quartered
16 green olives
Salt

Remove and discard the outer leaves of the lettuce if necessary. Break the remainder into approximately 7cm pieces, wash and dry well, in a salad spinner if you have one.

Spread the leaves over 4 medium-sized plates and arrange the tomatoes, onion and asparagus on top. Scatter the flaked tuna over the centre of each plate. Whisk the red wine vinegar and olive oil together with salt to taste and drizzle over the salads. Garnish with the hard-boiled eggs and green olives, and serve.

BARBECUED MUSHROOMS with GARLIC and EXTRA VIRGIN OLIVE OIL

SERVES 4

Life in filming land seems at times to be a bit like *Alice Through the Looking Glass* – everything is back to front. When you plan to film on a beach somewhere, it rains, and when you are filming in a small, hot, dark kitchen, it's a gloriously sunny day outside. When you want somewhere quiet outside in which to do a piece to camera, along come the crows and a helicopter, and when you are out in late September looking for mushrooms, you do so after a period of three weeks without rain, which has stopped them from growing. Consequently, when I went out mushrooming with serious mycologist Demetrio in the Alt Maestrat near Valencia, the only mushrooms we found were *Lactarius deliciosus*, the saffron milk cap. For almost anyone but Demetrio, they would have been impossible to see, since a small displacement of the pine needles on the forest floor was the only evidence they were there. But he picked a basket full and we then drove for an hour to the town of Benasal, with the director complaining all the way, as he often does, about the amount of filming time being used up to get there. Demetrio's friends grilled them over a wood fire in the municipal park and served them for lunch with some grilled chistorra sausages and smoky morcilla. James and Alex, who do the photography and design for the book, had more luck on their fungus foray. They met a Spanish family who had just picked the beautiful basket of mushrooms shown here.

8 firm cup-shaped mushrooms, such as Portobello, field or ceps, about 10cm across
Extra virgin olive oil, for brushing
4 garlic cloves, very finely chopped
Salt and freshly ground black pepper

Light the barbecue (see page 314) to high. Wipe the mushrooms clean with a damp cloth if necessary and remove the stems. Save these for another dish if you wish. Brush the gill sides generously with oil and season well with salt and pepper.

Place the mushrooms gill-side down on the barbecue and cook for 2 minutes. Now brush the tops with oil, season well and turn them over. Sprinkle the garlic over, working it into the gills a little, and cook for another 3 minutes. Flip over once more, gill-side down, and cook briefly for about a minute, by which time they should be tender and ready to serve.

CHICKEN and RABBIT PAELLA with WHITE and GREEN BEANS, TOMATO, PIMENTÓN and SAFFRON

Paella valenciana SERVES 6–8

The Valencians take the making of paella seriously, but this shouldn't obscure the fact that it is an easy-to-make, everyday dish, albeit for a large number of people. I was attracted to this recipe because it contains no seafood. I find that seafood paella in the wrong hands suffers from overcooking (though see the recipe on page 58 for a simple seafood paella from Cantabria). What I love about this dish is the flavour of good stock in the rice, backed by tomato and pimentón and the lovely textures of the rabbit, the green beans and, surprisingly, the white judión beans. I say surprisingly because you would think a large dish of rice with beans in it would be too much, but it works spectacularly. The Spanish often use a powdered yellow food colouring, known locally as *colorante*, to add an extra burst of yellow to their rice dishes (see page 313), but the saffron quantity used here is adequate. Just a quick note about cooking in a paella pan on a domestic hob. Because the pans are so large, I have found the best way is to position it over 2 medium burners and to turn the pan an eighth of a turn every 2–3 minutes, so everything cooks evenly. It works a treat.

125g large dried white beans, such as Spanish garrafon or judión or butter beans, soaked overnight
250g flat green beans, such as runner beans, cut into 5cm pieces
1 x 750g farmed rabbit, jointed (see page 146)
2 boned chicken thighs, skinned
5 tbsp olive oil
125g shallot, finely chopped
3 garlic cloves, finely chopped
1 tsp *pimentón dulce* (smoked sweet Spanish paprika)
225g large, vine-ripened or beef tomatoes, halved
1.5 litres *Chicken stock* (see page 306) or rabbit stock
2 tsp loosely packed saffron strands
The leaves from 2 x 15cm sprigs fresh rosemary
600g short-grain paella rice, such as Calasparra
Salt and freshly ground black pepper

Drain the soaked beans, put them in a pan with plenty of cold water, bring to a simmer and cook gently for 1½ hours or until tender. Drain and set aside. Blanch the green beans in boiling salted water for 2 minutes. Drain and refresh. Set aside with white beans.

Cut each front leg of the rabbit in 2 and each hind leg into 4. Cut the saddle into 8 pieces. Cut each chicken thigh into 3. Season with salt and pepper. Place a 40–50cm paella pan over 2 burners on a medium heat. Add 3 tablespoons of the oil, the rabbit and chicken pieces and leave them to brown slowly, turning them over now and then, for 12–15 minutes until cooked through.

Remove the meat from the pan, add 2 tablespoons of oil and the shallot, garlic and pimentón and fry for 5–6 minutes until the shallot is soft. Meanwhile, grate the halved tomatoes, pressing the fleshy, cut face of the tomato against the grater. (As you grate each tomato half, the skin will flatten out and be left behind.) Discard the skin. Add the tomatoes and fry for 4 minutes then stir in the white and green beans.

Add the stock, saffron, rosemary leaves and 2½ teaspoons of salt to the pan and bring to the boil. Sprinkle in the rice and lightly stir so the ingredients are evenly distributed. Scatter the pieces of rabbit and chicken evenly around the pan, then give it a good shake so they bed down into the rice. Simmer vigorously for 6 minutes over a medium-high heat, but do not stir it any more. Reduce the heat to medium and leave to cook for 14 minutes more, again without stirring, by which time all the liquid will be absorbed and the rice pitted with small holes. Turn off the heat, cover with a clean tea towel or unfolded newspaper and leave for 5 minutes before serving. Serve straight from the pan.

PORK in ALMOND SAUCE

Carne en salsa de almendras SERVES 4

Filming at Matilde Perrero's *casa rural*, a house-come-restaurant specializing in home cooking, was a bit tricky. We had been allowed to look around her kitchen, which was as neat and tidy and organized as she was. Her food was exquisite, particularly this slow braise of pork in a sauce flavoured with a little pimentón, garlic and almonds, but at the last minute she told us it was off, quite simply because she was going to be too busy cooking for the local fiesta featuring bulls with flaming horns careering through the town. She was a delightful woman, sort of like your favourite granny, and a very good cook. Serve this dish on its own, as the Spanish do, or with some boiled potatoes or steamed rice and a green vegetable.

5 tbsp olive oil
8 garlic cloves, 4 chopped
    and 4 left whole
15g slice crustless white bread
1kg piece of rindless free-range
    shoulder of pork
Plain flour, for dusting
1 large onion, finely chopped
½ tsp *pimentón dulce* (smoked
    sweet Spanish paprika)
Leaves from 1 large sprig
    fresh thyme
2 fresh bay leaves
200ml dry white wine
200ml *Chicken stock*
    (see page 306)
75g toasted blanched almonds
1 tbsp flat-leaf parsley leaves
Salt and freshly ground
    black pepper

Heat 2 tablespoons of the olive oil in a large cazuela or shallow flameproof casserole. Add the whole garlic and the slice of bread and fry over a medium-high heat for 2 minutes, turning once, until golden brown. Lift out and leave to drain and cool.

Cut the pork across into 2.5cm-thick slices and then into 75–100g pieces. You want them to be quite large. Season the pieces of pork well, then dust in the flour. Add another 2 tablespoons of oil to the pan and, when hot, add the pieces of meat and fry briefly to seal but only very lightly colour. Remove to a plate and set to one side.

Add the remaining tablespoon of oil to the pan with the onion, chopped garlic, pimentón, thyme and bay leaves and cook gently for about 10 minutes until the onions are soft and sweet but not browned. Add the wine and stock and bring to the boil, rubbing the base of the pan to release any bits and pieces. Return the pork to the pan, lower the heat and season with some salt and pepper. Cover and simmer gently for 1½ hours or until the meat is meltingly tender.

Spoon about 16 tablespoons of the sauce into a liquidizer or food processor and add the fried bread, fried garlic cloves, almonds and parsley leaves and blend to a smooth paste. Stir the picada back into the pan, adjust the seasoning to taste, cover and cook for a further 5 minutes or until the sauce has nicely thickened, then serve.

Chapter Seven

CASTILLA LA MANCHA

There's something quite majestic about driving across the plains of Spain. In his excellent book *The Spaniards*, John Hooper points out that, apart from the relatively narrow coastal strips, the whole of Spain is upland, known as the *meseta*. 'It varies in altitude from 2,000 to 3,000 feet as one craggy mountain range succeeds another. This gives to it one of its most distinctive characteristics – the almost painful brightness of the light. Not only is Spain a land of huge expanses, but one where you can as often as not see to the furthest limits of those expanses.' It's like driving through cowboy country and it has a similar effect on the mind.

I don't think I'd go there for a holiday, but Castilla-La Mancha has probably made more of an impression on me than any other region, and that's because it is an area that is so much how one would romantically imagine Spain to be. After all, *castilla* (Castile) means land of castles, and windmills and fortresses are the famous symbols of the whole region. La Mancha means 'bone dry', coming from the Arabic word *manxa*, meaning parched earth, and many times in the area I couldn't help thinking about the impossible climate in the prairies, far too hot in the summer, and rain and mud and snow in the winter, with very little in between. No wonder for a while in the 1960s and 1970s they made westerns in Spain.

Places like this are majestic but monotonous. In a way, it's a land equivalent of going to sea. There's not actually much to see, but that increases the power of the imagination. I remember travelling for some hours from our base in the rather nondescript town of Alcázar de San Juan, the last part of the trip being off the tarmac along dusty metalled roads, to visit a couple of shepherds with a large flock of *cordero manchego*, one of the oldest native sheep breeds in Spain and long adapted to the tough terrain and harsh climate. The first thing I noticed when I got there was that the farmhouse next to the sheep pens was virtually ruined; the roof was collapsing in and the sheds were all decrepit. It looked like a scene from *No Country For Old Men*. A couple of ruined cars and a tractor with no wheels, a few 44-gallon drums rusting away in a corner, some tattered plastic sacks flapping in the wind, but the two shepherds, lean and gnarled, were cheerful and friendly as they herded their sheep with the aid of a dog nipping less than playfully at the sheep's ankles. 'English dog,' they told us. 'Collie.' And their skill at milking, and the varied tone of the whistles to the dog as they took the flock up over a hill at the back of the sheds, gave me an intense feeling of the serious artisan quality of the Manchego cheese that would be made from the milk.

The landscape is one unforgettable part of La Mancha. For me, Cervantes' Don Quixote is another. In my recipe for *pisto manchego* on page 210, I wrote that so real is the world over which the impoverished old knight rode on his skeletal horse, it's hard to believe the inn, La Venta, where Quixote was knighted by the landlord, never existed. I ate the same food there that appears in the novel, not only the *pisto manchego* but also the *duelos y quebrantos*, 'sorrow and sadness', which is scrambled eggs with kidneys, bacon and lamb's brains. It might sound grim but it's actually very good. There were also lots of dishes containing lentils and chickpeas, as in the novel. Indeed, at one stage, I ate a dish of lentils with chorizo with an amiable bunch of Romanian grape pickers in some old stone and terracotta-tiled sheds at one of the vineyards belonging to Bodegas y Viñedos Castiblanque, an innovative company located in the small town of Peral. I also consumed rather a lot of their excellent Baldor tempranillo at lunch, so much so that I was filled with still more romantic enthusiasm for Don Quixote. On one wall was a bas relief in painted plaster of the incident in the 'enchanted' inn where the knight, dreaming of fighting a giant, lashes out with his sword in his sleep and slices open a bulging wineskin, which his sidekick Sancho Panza, rushing in in the dark on hearing the commotion, thinks is a giant's head, and the red wine his blood.

It's a country that feels like it's been there an awfully long time. One of the descriptions of a Castiblanque wine, Ilex, says in rather a poetic translation into English: 'A dry gust of wind fills the silence … (In) an almost perfect horizon of vineyards, stands a holm oak tree', referring to the presence of ilex oaks, which dot the landscape. These days the red wines are very good. They've discovered stainless steel and controlled fermentation, so gone are the old concrete vats that produced heavy 'cooked wines'. You can see the discarded vessels near the roads on the outskirts of the blue and white towns, and from the distance they look like piles of enormous stone jars.

SALT COD and POTATO PURÉE

Ajoarriero SERVES 4–6 AS A TAPAS OR STARTER

In his excellent book *MoVida*, Frank Camorra says he doesn't really think of salt cod as being fish, that it's been transformed by so much salting and drying into something almost earthy. I think he's got a point. Certainly it's been a part of the diet of inland regions of Spain for so long that it's local. This dish is very like the French *brandade*, a lovely comforting combination of bacalao, potatoes, garlic and olive oil. The name *ajoarriero* means 'muleteer's garlic', and it's because mule drivers could knock this up at the end of a hard day's travel from the ingredients they would be carrying on their animals. This is delicious thickly spread on freshly toasted bread, or stuffed into piquillo peppers as on page 80. If you have floury potatoes you can use a food processor to make this, provided you add the potatoes at the end and use the pulse button a few times so that it does not go gluey. Otherwise pound everything together using a large mortar and pestle.

300g piece of *Bacalao*
    (salt cod; see page 313)
500g peeled floury potatoes,
    such as Maris Piper or
    King Edwards
3 fat garlic cloves
125ml olive oil
1 hard-boiled egg, roughly
    chopped, to garnish
Salt

Soak the *bacalao* in 3–4 litres of water in the fridge for 24–48 hours, depending on its thickness. Change the water when it tastes salty, normally at least twice.

Boil the potatoes in just enough unsalted cold water to cover for 10 minutes, then add the salt cod to the pan and simmer gently for another 10 minutes until the potatoes are tender. Drain, saving a little of the cooking liquor.

Crush the garlic on a board with the blade of a large knife, adding a pinch of salt to help mash it. Flake the salt cod, discarding the skin and any bones, and put it and the garlic into a food processor. Add half the olive oil and blend for a few seconds, then add the potato and blend with the rest of the olive oil and about 6 tablespoons of the cooking liquor if you like the purée quite wet.

Season with salt (how much will depend on how well soaked the cod is), spoon into a shallow terracotta dish or bowl and scatter over the hard-boiled egg.

CRISP FRIED POTATOES
with SPICY TOMATO SAUCE

Patatas bravas SERVES 8–10 AS A TAPAS

Patatas bravas roughly translates as 'fierce potatoes', in the same way that in Cornwall the fishermen talk about a 'brave wind', which is a fierce, strong wind. In *patatas bravas* the fierceness is the amount of chilli in the sauce. It's a much-abused tapas and should be crisp olive-oil-fried potatoes topped with a tomato sauce well-flavoured with hot pimentón and sharpened with a little vinegar. A bar in the heart of Madrid near the Puerta del Sol called Las Bravas is reputed to have invented the sauce, which they also serve with shrimp and octopus; the recipe, as you can imagine, is a fiercely guarded secret.

1.5kg peeled floury potatoes, such as Maris Piper or King Edwards
180ml olive oil, for shallow frying
Salt

FOR THE SALSA BRAVA:
3 tbsp olive oil
1 tsp *pimentón picante* (smoked hot Spanish paprika), plus extra for serving
½ tsp crushed dried chilli flakes
½ tsp Tabasco sauce
1 tbsp red wine vinegar
125ml *Tomato sauce* (see page 306)

For the salsa brava, heat the olive oil over a low heat, add the pimentón, chilli flakes, Tabasco and vinegar and mix together well. Stir in the tomato sauce and taste and adjust the seasoning. Thin with up to 3 tablespoons water if necessary.

Cut the potatoes into small even-sized pieces. Drop into a large pan of well-salted water and cook for 6–7 minutes or until just tender, then drain well. Heat the olive oil in two large, non-stick frying pans, divide the potatoes between them and shallow-fry in a single layer for 10–12 minutes, turning them regularly, until crisp, golden all over and sandy in texture. Spoon the potatoes into one large or individual serving plates, drizzle over the sauce, sprinkle with a pinch of pimentón and serve with some toothpicks and napkins.

QUAIL MARINATED in WINE, VINEGAR, SPICES and HERBS

Codornices en escabeche SERVES 6 AS A STARTER

All countries had ways of preserving meat and fish before refrigeration, such as smoking, drying and salting. *Escabeche* came from the Moors and was a process whereby small game birds like quail or partridge were preserved by first being fried and then steeped in a vinegar-based marinade made from boiling vinegar and the pan juices, together with whatever vegetables were to hand or liked. The reduced marinade was then returned to the pan with the game birds and gently braised, the point being that there was enough vinegar to keep them from going off. Originally there would have been a lot more vinegar, in the same way that kippers were once made with a lot more salt, but these days the slightly tart flavour of a good red wine vinegar is there mostly for pleasure. You can serve these quail at room temperature or warmed through, in which case use some of the tart aromatic juices to dress a bitter-leaf salad. It makes a lovely, unusual first course.

12 farmed quail (or 6 oven-ready partridges)
205ml olive oil
1 medium onion, halved and thinly sliced
100g carrots, halved lengthways and thinly sliced
1 head garlic, halved horizontally
A pinch of crushed dried chillies
4 fresh bay leaves
3 large thyme sprigs
400ml dry white wine
100ml red wine vinegar
4 cloves
12 black peppercorns
3 pared strips orange zest
10cm sprig rosemary or 2 sprigs fresh oregano
A small pinch of saffron strands
1 tsp caster sugar
Salt and freshly ground black pepper
Mixed escarole, radicchio and curly endive salad leaves, and crusty fresh bread, to serve

Season the quail or partridge well with salt and pepper inside and out and tie their legs together with string to give them a neat shape.

Heat 4 tablespoons of the olive oil in a large flameproof casserole in which the birds will fit quite snugly side by side. Add half the birds and fry over a medium-high heat until nicely browned on all sides. Lift out onto a plate and set aside. Repeat with the remainder, adding another tablespoon of oil if you need it.

Add another 3 tablespoons of oil to the casserole with the onion, carrot, garlic halves (cut-side down), chilli, bay leaves, thyme and ½ teaspoon of salt, and cook gently for 10 minutes. Add the wine, vinegar, cloves, peppercorns, orange zest, rosemary or oregano, saffron and sugar. Rest the birds on top of the vegetables and herbs, pour over the remaining oil, add another ½ teaspoon of salt and bring back to the boil. Reduce the heat, cover, and simmer very gently, for 25 minutes for the quail, 40–45 minutes for the partridge.

Lift the birds into a serving dish and snip off and discard the pieces of string. Strain the cooking juices through a sieve set over a bowl. If the skin of the garlic has loosened, remove and discard it. Add the halved bulb to the dish and scatter over the vegetables and herbs from the sieve. Return the cooking liquid to the pan and simmer vigorously until well flavoured and reduced to about 250ml. Adjust the seasoning, pour the juices back over the birds and leave to cool. Then cover and refrigerate for at least 24 hours and up to 3–4 days, turning the birds in the marinade every now and then.

To serve, lift a couple of quail or one of the partridge onto each plate and pile some of the mixed bitter salad leaves alongside. Spoon juices over the leaves and the birds and serve with plenty of bread.

PICKLED AUBERGINES ALMAGRO-STYLE

Berenjenas de Almagro MAKES 2 X 1-LITRE KILNER JARS

The town of Almagro is not only famous for its beautiful Plaza Mayor, its lace and its sixteenth-century theatre, but also these piquant little aubergines, which have been part of the traditional cuisine of La Mancha for over a thousand years, and are today popular in the very best tapas bars of Barcelona and Madrid – and indeed all over Spain, wherever immigrants from La Mancha gather. The small rounded aubergines are about the size of a hen's egg and rather like the green-and-white-streaked Thai aubergine available from many Asian grocers. They are prepared whole with part of their stem still attached, which you hold when eating them. I wouldn't normally give a recipe for something you can buy bottled or canned but I don't think you can get the best ones, produced by Vicente Malagón and called Almagreña, in the UK. I would love these to become more popular because they are so very good. They are also wonderful, by the way, served with smoky barbecued lamb.

1.25kg small aubergines, such as Thai aubergines
3 large *Roasted red peppers* (see page 307)
500ml red wine vinegar
120ml olive oil
3 tbsp caster sugar
½ tsp crushed dried chilli flakes
2 tsp *pimentón dulce* (smoked sweet Spanish paprika)
25g garlic cloves, crushed
2 tsp freshly ground cumin seeds
½ tsp dried oregano
Salt and freshly ground black pepper

Bring a pan of well-salted water to the boil. Make a small slit lengthways into each aubergine, down to within 1cm of the stalk end. Drop the aubergines into the water and cook for 4–5 minutes or until just tender but still crunchy. Drain and leave to cool. Meanwhile, split open the roasted red peppers, discard the stalks and seeds and cut the flesh into strips 5mm wide. Push a couple of strips into the slit of each aubergine and then pack them tightly into 2 sterilized 1-litre Kilner jars.

In a pan, mix together the remaining ingredients with 300ml water, 1 tablespoon of salt and ½ teaspoon freshly ground black pepper. Bring to the boil, pour over the aubergines so they are completely covered, put on the lid and refrigerate. They are ready to eat within 24 hours and will keep for up to 3 weeks.

SCRAMBLED EGGS with KIDNEYS, BACON and LAMB'S BRAINS

Duelos y quebrantos SERVES 4

At the beginning of *Don Quixote de la Mancha*, Cervantes writes that 'his habitual diet consisted of a stew, more beef than mutton, hash most nights, *duelos y quebrantos* on Saturdays, lentils on Fridays, and a young pigeon as a Sunday treat. This took three-quarters of his income.' It's not a bad diet, but if it took so much of his wages I'm inclined to believe that *duelos y quebrantos*, or 'sorrow and sadness', must have been the odds and ends, a pan-fry of what you have to hand. Such a dish can be sublime, or horrid. This particular version of *duelos y quebrantos* is sublime: softly scrambled eggs with onions, bacon and lamb's kidneys all cut up quite small and not overcooked, and then the crowning glory of lightly poached lamb's brains folded in at the end. What is extraordinary is the similarity between the texture and almost the taste of the brains and the egg. If you don't like offal, you're barking!

2 lamb's brains
2 lamb's kidneys
2 tbsp olive oil
1 tbsp butter
50g bacon lardons,
    cut into 5mm pieces
1 medium onion, finely
    chopped
8 large free-range eggs
1 tbsp chopped flat-leaf
    parsley
Salt

Put the lamb's brains into a small pan with 500ml cold water and ½ teaspoon of salt. Bring to the boil, remove from the heat and leave until cool enough for you to handle. Remove from the water and cut into 5mm pieces.

Pull any fat and membrane away from outside the kidneys, cut them in half lengthways and snip out the white cores with kitchen scissors. Chop them into 5mm pieces.

Heat the olive oil and butter in a heavy-based, non-stick frying pan over a medium heat. Add the bacon and onion and fry gently until the onion begins to brown. Add the kidneys, continue to sauté for another 3 minutes then remove from the heat.

Break the eggs into a bowl and beat them with a little salt. Stir the chopped lamb's brains and parsley into the pan, return the frying pan to a low heat and, when hot, pour in the eggs and stir until the eggs are softly scrambled. Serve immediately.

GARLIC SOUP with EGGS

Sopa de ajo con huevos SERVES 4

If I were to describe this soup as hot stock with fried garlic, grilled bread and a poached egg, it would sound rather dull, but the fact that it is made all over Spain and is at the very heart of the cooking of Castilla-La Mancha tells you there is something magical about this combination. The stock is made by gently simmering chicken and a whole ham hock with vegetables for a couple of hours. The garlic, and lots of it – fresh, moist garlic from the beginning of the season is best – is thinly sliced, and gently fried with olive oil and pimentón. The bread has to be something resembling the glorious rustic bread of Spain, ideally grilled over coals, and finally the egg must be the freshest free-range egg you can get. Get all those things right and you have the most glorious combination, justifiably part of Castilian folklore.

1 litre *Chicken stock*
   (see page 306)
1 cured ham bone, such
   as serrano (optional)
1 x 200g gammon steak
1 head of garlic, wet garlic
   if in season
3 tbsp olive oil
1 tsp *pimentón picante*
   (smoked hot Spanish paprika)
4 x 1cm-thick slices
   crusty white bread
4 large, very fresh,
   free-range eggs

Bring the chicken stock to the boil, add the ham bone if using and the gammon steak, cover and simmer for 30 minutes. Remove the ham bone and gammon and season to taste with salt and set aside. The cooked ham can be used for making croquetas (see page 104).

For the soup, separate the cloves of garlic, then peel and thinly slice. Put the oil into a wide, shallow pan over a medium heat, add the sliced garlic and fry gently until lightly golden, but no darker or it will become bitter. Add the pimentón and 1 litre of the broth and bring almost back to a simmer.

Meanwhile, toast the bread on a barbecue, under a grill or singe over a naked flame and finish in the toaster, then put one into the bottom of each large soup plate.

One at a time, crack the eggs into a cup, carefully slide them into the broth and leave them to poach for 3 minutes. Lift one egg into each bowl, resting it on the bread. Ladle over the broth and serve.

CHICKPEA, SALT COD and SPINACH STEW

Potaje de garbanzos, bacalao y espinacas SERVES 4

Interestingly, I have a recipe for a salt cod and chickpea stew from Italy in an earlier book, *Seafood Odyssey*. This one could only be Spanish with its use of pimentón and saffron. It's extremely good and would probably have been a dish for Lent when the eating of meat was prohibited, and salt cod would be the fish of choice in inland areas such as La Mancha. You may notice a lot of alioli cropping up in this book; I just love stirring it into any soup or stew.

350g piece *Home-salted fresh cod* (see page 307) or 175–200g piece *Bacalao* (salt cod; see page 313)

350g dried chickpeas

1 small head of garlic, plus 3–4 cloves, finely chopped

2 medium onions, chopped

3 fresh bay leaves

100ml olive oil

A good pinch of crushed dried chillies

½ tsp *pimentón picante* (smoked hot Spanish paprika)

3 vine-ripened tomatoes, skinned and chopped

½ tsp loosely packed saffron strands

225g spinach, whole baby leaf or ordinary, torn into smaller pieces

4–6 tbsp *Alioli* (see page 307), to serve

Salt

Crusty fresh bread, to serve

If using bacalao, soak it in 3–4 litres of water in the fridge for 24–48 hours, depending on thickness. Change the water when it tastes salty, normally at least twice. Cover the chickpeas with plenty of cold water and soak for 24 hours. If using fresh salted cod, cover with cold water and soak for 1 hour, if you haven't already done so.

Drain the chickpeas and put them into a large flameproof casserole or saucepan. Peel all the loose skin from the head of garlic and add it to the pan with half the chopped onion, the bay leaves, 50ml of the olive oil and 2 litres of cold water. Bring to the boil, then lower the heat and leave to simmer for 1½ hours or until the chickpeas are just tender but not losing their skins and the liquid is now just covering them.

Shortly before the chickpeas are ready, bring 500ml water to the boil in another pan, add the salt cod and simmer for 6–8 minutes or until just cooked through. Lift the fish onto a plate and, when cool enough to handle, break into large flakes, discarding the skin and any bones. Reserve the cooking water.

Heat 3 tablespoons of the oil in a frying pan over a medium heat. Add the remaining onion, the chopped garlic, dried chilli flakes and pimentón and fry for 6–7 minutes until soft and lightly golden. Add the tomatoes and cook for another 10 minutes or until they have broken down into a thick sauce.

Remove and discard the bay leaves from the chickpeas. Lift out the garlic and squeeze the pulp from each clove back into the pan. Discard the skin. Stir in the tomato mixture with the saffron and a little of the salt-cod cooking liquid if the mixture seems a bit too thick and simmer for 15 minutes more, until the chickpeas are properly tender and the liquid has reduced by half.

Add the spinach and cook for 2 minutes. Stir in the salt cod and 1 teaspoon of salt or to taste and simmer for 1–2 minutes more. Serve in warmed shallow soup plates, with a drizzle of oil, a dollop of the alioli and some crusty bread.

EGGS BAKED in a SUMMER VEGETABLE STEW

Pisto manchego con huevos SERVES 2

Don Quixote contains lots of references to the food of La Mancha. It's probable that most people, including Cervantes himself, were hungry much of the time, since they were poor, so food would have been very much on the writer's mind. Indeed Cervantes seems to have lived a life as full of incident as his hero – imprisoned by Algerian pirates, sold into slavery, imprisoned for tax irregularities, wounding someone in a duel, that sort of thing. One can only marvel at the humour he shows in describing life's vicissitudes. Needless to say, dishes like this from the inn where Quixote was knighted by his landlord, La Venta de Don Quixote, are a great comfort in an uncertain world.

4 tbsp olive oil
4 garlic cloves, thinly sliced
1 medium onion, halved
    and thinly sliced
1 green pepper, seeded
    and chopped
1 red pepper, seeded and
    chopped
350g courgettes, thinly sliced
A pinch of crushed dried
    chilli flakes
½ tsp cumin powder
½ tsp *pimentón dulce* (smoked
    sweet Spanish paprika)
400g skinned chopped tomatoes,
    fresh or from a can
4 large free-range eggs
1 *Roasted red pepper*
    (see page 307), stalk, skin
    and seeds discarded and
    flesh cut into strips
Salt and freshly ground
    black pepper
Crusty fresh bread, to serve

Heat the olive oil in a large, deep frying pan over a medium heat. Add the garlic, onion and peppers and cook for 6–7 minutes until the onion is soft and lightly golden. Add the courgettes and fry for 4 minutes more. Stir in the crushed dried chilli flakes, cumin and pimentón and fry for 1 minute more.

Stir in the tomatoes, cover and simmer for 4 minutes, until the tomatoes have broken down into a sauce and thickened slightly and the courgette is tender. Season with ¾ teaspoon of salt and some pepper.

Make 4 shallow dips in the top of the mixture, carefully break in the eggs, and season each one with salt and pepper. Scatter the roasted red pepper strips around the eggs, cover with a lid and simmer for about 8 minutes or until the whites are set but the yolks are still runny. Serve with bread.

LAMB-STUFFED AUBERGINES with MOORISH SPICES and MANCHEGO CHEESE

Berenjenas rellenas SERVES 4

I must say I took a bit of poetic licence with my stuffed aubergines. That's not to say the people of La Mancha don't stuff them, because they do, but I oiled and salted halved aubergines and baked them in the oven until tender, then made a ragu with minced lamb, red pepper, cumin, cinnamon and nutmeg and mixed that with the scooped-out aubergine flesh, filled the cases and sprinkled them with Manchego cheese before baking again. I have to say they are flying out of the door at our deli.

4 aubergines, each weighing
    about 275g
6 tbsp olive oil
1 medium onion, chopped
4 garlic cloves, finely chopped
1 large red pepper, seeded
    and chopped
1½ tsp freshly ground
    cumin seeds
1 tsp ground cinnamon
½ tsp freshly grated nutmeg
1 tsp *pimentón dulce* (smoked
    sweet Spanish paprika)
A large pinch of crushed
    dried chillies
500g minced lamb
6 tbsp *Tomato sauce*
    (see page 306)
100g Manchego cheese,
    coarsely grated
Salt and freshly ground
    black pepper

Preheat the oven to 200°C/gas 6. Cut each aubergine lengthways through the stalk, then score the flesh in a tight criss-cross pattern, taking the knife through the flesh down to the skin, but taking care not to cut through the skin. Place them side by side on a baking tray and drizzle each half with 1½ teaspoons of the oil, season with salt and bake for about 30 minutes or until the flesh is soft and tender but not browned.

Meanwhile, heat the remaining 2 tablespoons of oil in a large non-stick frying pan. Add the onion, garlic, red pepper and spices and fry gently for 10 minutes. Add the minced lamb and fry for 3–4 minutes or until all the meat is lightly browned. Stir in the tomato sauce and leave to simmer for 5 minutes.

Remove the aubergines from the oven and increase the temperature to 220°C/gas 7. Using a dessertspoon, carefully scoop most of the flesh out of the baked aubergine halves, leaving the skins with a layer of flesh about 1cm thick. Stir the flesh into the lamb mixture with ½ teaspoon of salt and some pepper to taste. Spoon the mixture into each aubergine shell and sprinkle with the grated cheese. Bake for 9–10 minutes until golden brown.

SLOW-ROASTED LEG of LAMB with FENNEL SEEDS, PIMENTÓN and POTATOES

SERVES 8

This dish originated in the bakers' ovens of La Mancha, where they would put trays of lamb rubbed with a paste of fennel seeds, pimentón, salt, black pepper, garlic and lard into the oven after baking the bread. The residual heat from the wood fire would slowly cook the meat. I've simply taken the ingredients for *patatas a la pobre*, which is onions, garlic, red and green peppers and thickly sliced potatoes, and cooked them under the lamb so that they end up more like a rich, soft fondue than a crisper, drier dish.

1 x 2.5kg leg of lamb
2 tsp fennel seeds
1 tbsp black peppercorns
1 tbsp sea salt flakes
½ tsp *pimentón picante*
  (smoked hot Spanish paprika)
4 garlic cloves, crushed
1 tbsp lard

FOR THE POTATOES:
2 tbsp olive oil
2 medium onions, halved
  and thinly sliced
3 fresh bay leaves, torn into
  small pieces
2 red peppers, seeded and cut
  lengthways into 1cm wide strips
2 green peppers, seeded and cut
  lengthways into 1cm wide strips
The leaves from 2 sprigs fresh
  thyme
4 garlic cloves, sliced
1.2kg peeled waxy main-crop
  potatoes, such as Desirée
Salt and freshly ground black
  pepper

Preheat the oven to 160°C/gas 3. Using a small, sharp knife, make small deep slits all over the leg of lamb, about 5cm apart.

Coarsely crush the fennel seeds, peppercorns and salt in a mortar, or in a small bowl with the end of a rolling pin. Mix in the pimentón, crushed garlic and lard to make a paste. Spread the mixture over the outside of the leg, pushing some of the mixture into each of the slits. Set to one side.

For the potatoes, heat the olive oil in a large, deep frying pan. Add the onions, bay leaves, peppers, thyme and garlic and fry on a medium heat for 10 minutes. Tip the mixture into a large roasting tin and mix in the potatoes with 1 teaspoon of salt. Spread out in an even layer, pour over 100ml water and rest the lamb on top. Cover the tin tightly with foil and bake in the oven for 3½ to 4 hours until the lamb is almost falling off the bone.

Lift the lamb onto a board, wrap the foil around it and keep it warm. Pour away the excess fat from the tin, then, if there seems to be a lot of liquid in the potatoes, place the tin directly over the heat and leave to simmer vigorously for a minute or two until reduced. Uncover the lamb and pull or carve it into chunks. Serve with the potatoes.

TOLEDO-STYLE RABBIT with SPICES, PINE NUTS and RAISINS

Conejo a la toledano SERVES 4

Toledo, up in the north-western corner of La Mancha, was taken by the Moors in 712, who brought with them exotic spices from the Middle East, such as cinnamon, cloves and saffron, together with the idea of cooking meat with fruits and nuts, in this case raisins and pine nuts. But because this dish is also very much a Spanish dish, it contains some less exotic, more native ingredients too, such as rabbit, which is everyday fare in Spain, carrots and onion, wild herbs, and of course a sprinkling of pimentón. I think these dishes from southern Spain with a clear mix of North African, Middle Eastern and Mediterranean flavours are particularly attractive. I like to serve this with some simply steamed white rice. This would also work very well with chicken.

1 x 1.5kg farmed rabbit
7 tbsp olive oil
350g small shallots, 250g
 peeled but left whole and
 the rest finely chopped
3 garlic cloves, sliced
½ tsp cumin seeds
1 x 10cm cinnamon stick,
 broken in half
4 cloves
½ tsp ground coriander
½ tsp ground ginger
½ tsp *pimentón dulce* (smoked
 sweet Spanish paprika)
175g carrots, sliced
250ml dry white wine
1 tbsp clear honey
4 soft thyme sprigs
Leaves from two 10cm
 rosemary sprigs
500ml *Chicken stock*
 (see page 306)
50g raisins
1½ tbsp sherry vinegar
25g toasted pine nuts
Salt and freshly ground
 black pepper

To joint the rabbit, first remove the head, and then cut off the back legs from either side of the tail. Cut off and discard the tail, then cut off the front legs. Trim away the bony ends of each leg and cut each leg in half at the joint. Remove the kidneys and liver from the body cavity and set to one side. Trim away the belly flap and ribcage from the body, then cut the remaining saddle across into 4 pieces. Reserve the bits and pieces for making stock if you wish.

Season the rabbit pieces well. Heat 4 tablespoons of the olive oil in a large cazuela, shallow flameproof casserole or large sauté pan over a medium heat. Add the rabbit pieces and sauté them for about 8 minutes, turning over halfway through, until lightly browned. Lift out onto a plate and set aside.

Lower the heat, add the whole shallots and shake around until nicely browned all over. Set aside with the rabbit. Add the chopped shallot, garlic, cumin seeds, cinnamon, cloves, coriander, ginger and pimentón to the pan and fry gently for 5–6 minutes. Add the carrots and cook for 2–3 minutes more.

Stir in the wine and simmer for 2–3 minutes, scraping up the bits from the base of the pan with a wooden spoon, then return the rabbit pieces to the pan with the shallots, honey, thyme, rosemary and the stock. Bring to the boil, cover and simmer gently for 45 minutes, turning the rabbit pieces over halfway through.

Uncover the rabbit and add the raisins and sherry vinegar. Increase the heat and simmer a little more vigorously for 15–20 minutes or until the liquid has reduced slightly and is well flavoured and the rabbit is completely tender. Add the rabbit livers and kidneys 5 minutes before the end of cooking. Adjust the seasoning to taste, sprinkle over the pine nuts and serve.

Chapter Eight

EXTREMADURA

When I arrived at the central square of Trujillo in Extremadura, the first thing I noticed was a large storks' nest on top of the cathedral tower. Below was the helmeted statue of the conquistador Pizarro, the conqueror of Peru. He's bearded and looks fierce sitting on a giant horse, his helmet trailing two long ribbons and keeping his face sinisterly in shadow, his sword outstretched. But the storks' nest – would they be allowed to nest on Westminster Abbey, I wondered? It was the sort of detail that drove home the slightly under-cherished quality of a lot of historical sights in Spain: weeds sprouting from the baroque towers of the cathedral at Santiago de Compostela, and the same in Seville too, making them thereby much more real. Much of Trujillo and nearby Cáceres is slightly falling down, a bit like the Lost Gardens of Heligan in Cornwall. You feel that you participate more in enjoying the reality of somewhere that's not perfect. The Pizarro mansion across the square from the statue is quietly crumbling too; even the friezes on the corner of the 'House of the Conquistador' are cracking. The busts of Francisco Pizarro and his wife the princess Inés Yupanqui, sister of the Inca Emperor Atahualpa, look out over a town of towers and turrets. Atahualpa, you may remember, having been capured by Pizarro, offered a large room filled with gold for his freedom. Pizarro took the gold but executed him anyway – by garotte, a kinder way to die than burning at the stake, from which the emperor was spared by having converted to Catholicism. Cruel times.

Apart from the looted gold and silver, the food that such men brought back from the new world – peppers, chillies, aubergines, potatoes, sweetcorn and tomatoes, for example – changed European and Asian cooking for ever. Extremadura is arguably where the most distinctive flavour in Spanish cooking comes from: the smoked sweet paprika, pimentón. It is said that Christopher Colombus brought paprika peppers back and presented them to King Ferdinand and Queen Isabella in the monastery of Guadalupe in 1493. The monks passed this vegetable on to other brothers in their order and developed the art of drying and grinding it into the spicy red powder. The wood they used to smoke-dry the peppers, giving pimentón its characteristic flavour, is the same holm oak whose acorns feed the ibérico pigs and give the hams their smooth savoury taste, tart with slight salty sweetness. These hams are finely marbled with fat, deep red and dense with a perfume both faintly musty and savoury in the same way as a mature cheese.

Extremadura produces the two most special flavours of Spain, and because of the ever-increasing popularity of ibérico ham, the lovely landscape of Extremadura – open rolling country with the dark green of oak and cork trees everywhere – is likely to be preserved. The pigs not only keep these enormous wooded areas tidy by grubbing for roots, which removes the undergrowth, but they also fertilize the soil with their manure. I met a crowd of these marvellous animals, with their ebony-black hooves, slim ankles and elegant elongated haunches, companionably snuffling around under the trees. Extremadura is the sort of landscape where Ferdinand the Bull, in the famous children's story by Munro Leaf, sat down in the shade of one of those cork trees and smelt the flowers rather than charge around like the other young bulls, a pacifist hero in a book that came out just before the Civil War. I went to an ibérico ham producer, Maldonado, and walked through the ageing rooms. The sweet, nutty aroma of mature ham is of the same order of satisfaction as being in a cellar of barrels of red Burgundy.

There are lots of sheep here too, and a cheese from Cáceres called Torta de la Serena produces the same sort of fervency locally as Vacherin Mont d'Or does around the Jura in France and Switzerland. The milk is curdled using cardoons, and in fact the slight bitterness that it gives the cheese put me off to start with, then turned me into a complete fan. It is aged for at least sixty days, by which time, like Vacherin, it's creamy and pungent in the middle, and is eaten by cutting off the top and spooning it out. There's a cheese shop (*formatgeria*) in Barcelona called La Seu, run by Katherine McLaughlin, a Scots affineur (someone whose speciality is maturing and ripening cheese), where you can taste this wonderful delicacy spread on bread or toast.

SERRANO HAM, LEMON and GREEN OLIVE MEATBALLS in TOMATO and SHERRY SAUCE

Albóndigas en salsa de tomate SERVES 4–6

Albóndigas are found all over Spain, tiny ones in tapas bars usually covered in sauce and served in little cazuelitas with cocktail sticks for spearing them, or larger ones on market stalls ready to be cooked at home. They are probably another of those dishes introduced to Spain during the Moorish occupation, reminiscent as they are of the köfte of the Middle East, often spiced with cumin and coriander, but I have to say I like these ones, which are flavoured with some finely chopped green olives, a little serrano ham and some lemon zest.

FOR THE MEATBALLS:
50g crustless white bread
Finely grated zest and juice of 1 lemon
150g thinly sliced serrano ham
350g lean minced pork
350g minced veal or chicken
3 garlic cloves, crushed
50g pitted green olives, finely chopped
2 tbsp chopped flat-leaf parsley
¼ tsp *pimentón picante* (smoked hot Spanish paprika)
4 tbsp olive oil

FOR THE SAUCE:
3 tbsp olive oil
1 medium onion, finely chopped
3 garlic cloves, crushed
½ tsp pimentón, sweet or hot
2 x 400g cans chopped tomatoes
200ml fino sherry or dry white wine
2 fresh bay leaves
200ml *Chicken stock* (see page 306)
Salt

Break the bread into a small bowl and sprinkle with the lemon juice and 1 tablespoon of water. Leave to soak for 5 minutes. Drop the sliced serrano ham into a food processor and process using the pulse button until finely chopped.

Lightly squeeze the excess moisture from the bread and put it into a mixing bowl with the minced pork and minced veal or chicken, serrano ham, garlic, olives, parsley, lemon zest, pimentón and 1 teaspoon of salt and some pepper. Mix together well with your hands then take a little piece of the mixture and fry it in a drop of oil, taste and adjust the seasoning if necessary. Form the mixture into about 60 small, tapas-sized meatballs.

Heat half the olive oil in a large frying pan over a medium heat. Add half the meatballs to the pan and fry for 2–3 minutes, shaking the pan every now and then, until nicely browned all over. Lift them out onto a plate and set to one side. Repeat with the remainder of the meatballs, using the rest of the olive oil.

For the sauce, heat the oil in the frying pan, add the onion, garlic and pimentón and fry gently for 10 minutes. Add the tomatoes, sherry, bay leaves, chicken stock and ½ teaspoon of salt and simmer for 15 minutes or until the sauce has reduced and thickened.

Add the meatballs to the sauce and simmer for 5 minutes until cooked through. Remove and discard the bay leaves, spoon the meatballs and sauce into several small shallow dishes and serve while still warm with some cocktail sticks alongside.

CHICKPEAS with CHORIZO

Garbanzos con chorizo SERVES 4–6 AS A TAPAS OR STARTER

If you were to ask me for the one dish in the world that best celebrates the fabulously earthy quality of chickpeas, it would be *garbanzos con chorizo*. Chorizo goes with all pulses – white beans, brown beans, lentils – but nothing seems better to conjure up an image of those vast plains of La Mancha stretching to Extremadura than these large peas with their slightly firm texture blended with the pork sausage of the region and flavoured with some smoked pimentón, another product of those wide open spaces. While I was cooking during filming, I was often struck by how many Spanish dishes echo the colours of the national flag: the red of pimentón and tomato, and the yellow and golds of the saffron, eggs, cheese, maize and chickpeas. The flavours of Spain are there in their flag.

350g dried chickpeas, soaked
   overnight in plenty of
   cold water
4 fresh bay leaves
4 tbsp olive oil
2 medium onions, finely chopped
100g garlic cloves, crushed
350g cooking *chorizo picante*,
   skinned and cut into 1cm pieces
½ tsp *pimentón dulce* (smoked
   sweet Spanish paprika)
1 tbsp tomato purée
120ml dry white wine
4 large free-range eggs
Extra virgin olive oil, to serve
1 tbsp chopped flat-leaf parsley,
   to garnish
Salt and freshly ground black
   pepper

Drain the chickpeas, put them into a pan and cover by 5cm with fresh cold water. Add 2 of the bay leaves, bring to the boil, lower the heat and leave to simmer for 45 minutes or until the skins just begin to crack and they are tender. Drain, reserving the cooking liquid.

Heat the olive oil in a large saucepan or flameproof casserole over a medium heat. Add the onions, garlic, remaining bay leaves, chorizo and pimentón and fry gently, stirring frequently, for 15 minutes. Add the tomato purée and wine and simmer vigorously until the wine has almost disappeared.

Add the drained chickpeas and 300ml of the reserved cooking liquor and simmer, uncovered, for 8 minutes. Meanwhile, drop the eggs into a pan of boiling water and cook for 8 minutes. Drain and run briefly under cold water until just cool enough to peel.

Season the chickpeas with salt and pepper to taste, and ladle into warm shallow serving bowls or terracotta tapas dishes. Quarter the eggs and garnish each bowl with a few pieces. Drizzle over extra virgin olive oil, scatter with parsley and serve.

TENCH in a SWEET and SOUR MARINADE

Tenca escabeche SERVES 4 AS A STARTER

This recipe was given to me by José Pizarro, a Spanish chef and friend of mine from London. He took me freshwater fishing in Extremadura and we met at a lake just outside Caçeres. It was a public holiday and a lot of José's chums were fishing there. The place looked a bit like Bodmin Moor, but the difference between Britain and Spain is that in Spain it wasn't just about catching the biggest and putting them all back, they were seriously fishing for tench to take home and cook for their families. This escabeche is one of the favourite recipes in the area and José prepared it for me on the camping stove in the back of my camper van. While we were filming him cooking it, a local TV crew asked if they could come and film us filming him, shortly after which another local TV crew asked if they could come and film us too. They waited politely until the first crew had finished. The presenter, a girl in her early twenties, looked shy and inexperienced, but immediately they started filming she transformed into an international superstar: noisy, sexy, in everybody's face, demanding, seeking the limelight and speaking most passionately about Extremaduran cuisine and how very happy she was to have José and me cooking in her part of the country. It made us all laugh. It was a bit like something out of Monty Python. But back to the recipe. It's very good and we now sell it regularly in our deli, but using rainbow trout instead of tench.

2 whole rainbow trout
    (approx. 350g each)
50g plain flour
10 tbsp extra virgin olive oil
1 small onion, halved and
    thinly sliced
2 garlic cloves, sliced
100g carrot, cut into
    matchsticks 5cm long
50g celery, cut into
    matchsticks 5cm long
4 fresh bay leaves
The leaves from 2 x 10cm
    sprigs rosemary
The leaves from 4 sprigs
    fresh thyme
1 tsp black peppercorns
4 tbsp white wine vinegar
4 tbsp dry white wine
Sea salt flakes and freshly
    ground black pepper

Season the trout inside and out with salt and pepper, then dredge the fish in the flour, making sure both sides are lightly covered, and pat off the excess.

Using a frying pan large enough for both fish, heat 2 tablespoons of the oil over a medium heat. Add the trout and cook for 4–5 minutes on each side until golden brown and just cooked through. They should register 58°C at the thickest part, just behind the head. Lift them out of the pan and set aside in a shallow gratin dish while you make the escabeche marinade.

Clean the frying pan, add 2 more tablespoons of the oil, the onion, garlic, carrot and celery, and fry for 10 minutes until soft and lightly golden. Stir in the herbs and peppercorns and pour in the remaining 6 tablespoons of oil, the vinegar and white wine and leave to simmer quite vigorously for 3 minutes. Add 180ml hot water and simmer for another 3 minutes. Season with 1 teaspoon of salt and pour this mixture over the trout. You can eat this immediately, or leave it to cool to room temperature: it's delicious either way and even better the next day.

For ease of serving you can also skin the cooked fish, lift the fillets away from the bones and lay them side by side in the gratin dish before pouring over the escabeche marinade. This also allows the flavour of the marinade to penetrate the fish more easily too.

PEARL BARLEY STEW
with MORCILLA, BACON and WILD FENNEL

SERVES 6

This is my version of a dish called *olla de trigo*. An *olla* is the name of a traditional rounded terracotta cooking pot. I've noticed that a lot of Spanish dishes are named after the pot in which they are cooked, such as *caldereta* or *paella*. The reason I've modified it is that, like the *cocido* on page 34 and the *fabada* on page 70, the original is a grand performance whereas I think this actually lends itself to rather a simple all-in-one-pot treatment for a nourishing and economical lunch. In my view, none of these pulse and meat stews should be eaten at night. They are much more satisfying at lunchtime with a glass or two of Rioja. In some areas this stew is made with whole wheat grains (known as *farro* in Italy, and sometimes called wheat berries in the UK), which gives it a pleasantly chewy texture and makes a change from the bean or dried pea dishes. I've used pearl barley, which is easy to get hold of. The morcilla I use is from Brindisa and is available on mail order (see page 314), but black pudding will work just as well.

1 small green (unsmoked) ham hock
4 fresh bay leaves
225g dried chickpeas, soaked overnight in cold water
1 litre *Chicken stock* (see page 306) or leftover *Cocido stock* (see page 34)
175g pearl barley
3 tbsp olive oil
12 small shallots or button onions
75g cooking chorizo (approx. 1 sausage), sliced
1 large head fennel, fronds reserved, the rest cut into 2.5cm pieces
200g carrots, cut into 2.5cm pieces
2 celery stalks, cut into 2.5cm pieces
200g leeks, cleaned and cut into 2.5cm pieces
150g morcilla or black pudding
1 small bunch fennel herb, wild if possible, chopped
Salt and freshly ground black pepper

Put the ham hock into a large saucepan, cover with cold water and bring to the boil, skimming off the scum as it rises to the surface. Add the bay leaves, cover and leave to simmer for 1½ hours.

Drain the chickpeas, add them to the pan and cook for 45 minutes until tender and the ham is falling off the bone.

Meanwhile, bring the chicken stock to a boil, add the pearl barley and 1 teaspoon of salt, cover and simmer for 30 minutes until it is just cooked but still *al dente* and has absorbed most of the liquid.

Lift the ham out onto a plate and, when cool, remove and discard the bone and fat and break the meat into small, chunky pieces.

Heat 2 tablespoons of the oil in a large flameproof casserole over a medium-high heat, add the onions and chorizo and brown all over. Add the fennel, carrots, celery, leeks, ½ teaspoon of salt and some pepper. Cover and leave to sweat gently for 10 minutes.

Drain the chickpeas, reserving the ham stock. Add the chickpeas to the chorizo and vegetables with the pearl barley, ham hock meat and 600ml of the ham stock or enough to give it a nice stew-like consistency. Cover and leave to simmer for 5 minutes.

Meanwhile, cut the morcilla or black pudding lengthways in half and then across into pieces 5cm long. Heat the remaining tablespoon of oil in a frying pan, add the blood sausage and fry for 1 minute on each side until lightly golden.

Uncover the stew and adjust the seasoning to taste. Stir in the chopped fennel herb and fronds and ladle into large warmed soup plates. Put the pieces of blood pudding on top and serve.

TOMATO and POTATO SOUP with PIMENTÓN

Caldo de tomate y patata con pimentón dulce SERVES 6–8

I watched this very simple soup being made in the valley of La Vera in Extremadura. Before we got there we were told the fields would be bright red with the ripe peppers they use to make the famous pimentón, and indeed in the programme I describe the fields as 'on fire'. After we had watched a cheerful band of Romanians picking the peppers, we went back to the farm where they smoke and dry them. It's simply a matter of hauling the bags of peppers up a rickety wooden ladder to a loft whose floorboards have gaps between them, then an oakwood fire is lit below and the peppers smoke and dry over a few days. They are then taken to a cooperative to be ground into the powder that is a defining flavour of Spain. What everyone loves are the tins in which the pimentón – *dulce*, *agridulce* and *picante* – is sold. The painted labels have a romanticism that is entirely in keeping with the contents. The farmer's wife, Salo Martín, made this soup in one large pot. The ingredients were simple and I remember thinking that surely using plain water rather than stock would make it weak and tasteless. Not at all; testimony then to the depth of flavour of the pimentón and the local sweet ripe tomatoes and peppers and also the velvety thickening power of good Spanish bread.

3 tbsp olive oil, plus extra to serve
1 medium onion, halved and thinly sliced
4 garlic cloves, 1 finely chopped, and the others left whole
2 red peppers, romano if possible, seeded and sliced
1 tbsp *pimentón dulce* (smoked sweet Spanish paprika)
700g peeled floury potatoes, such as Maris Piper or King Edwards, very thinly sliced
600g beef tomatoes, skinned and chopped
2 fresh bay leaves
Leaves from 2 small sprigs mint (approx. 5g), chopped
150g sliced crustless white bread
1 large *Roasted red pepper* (see page 307), seeded and cut into strips
Salt

Heat the olive oil in a large saucepan. Add the onion, the chopped garlic and sliced red pepper and cook gently for 10 minutes until the onions are soft and sweet but not browned. Stir in the pimentón and cook for 1 minute. Add the potatoes, tomatoes, bay leaves, 1.5 litres water and 2 teaspoons of salt and bring to the boil. Simmer for 15 minutes until the potatoes are tender.

Meanwhile, crush the remaining garlic on a board with the blade of a large knife, adding a pinch of salt to help mash it. Add to the pan with the mint and simmer for 1 minute.

Break the bread up into the base of a large soup tureen. Ladle on some soup, leave to soften for 2 minutes, then mash the bread with a fork into a porridge-like mixture. Pour over the remaining soup and stir. Ladle into warmed bowls and garnish with the red pepper strips. Drizzle over a little more oil and serve.

SCRAMBLED EGGS with ASPARAGUS, WILD MUSHROOMS and TRUFFLE OIL

Revuelto de espárragos, setas y aceite de trufa SERVES 2

Scrambled eggs are immensely popular all over Spain, flavoured with things like chorizo or ibérico ham, green garlic shoots or spring onions, tiny shelled prawns, wild asparagus, wild mushrooms or even truffles. The flavouring ingredient is briefly sautéed in a little olive oil before the beaten eggs are added and scrambled over a medium-low heat until soft and creamy. When I make this I'm lucky enough to be able to stir a few truffle shavings in as well as the wild mushrooms, one of the privileges of having a restaurant, but I do think a little truffle oil stirred in makes the dish very special. Wild asparagus (*trigueros*) is not easy to find outside Spain but fine British asparagus is an excellent substitute.

100g wild or fine asparagus
    or 200g ordinary asparagus
225g wild mushrooms, such
    as ceps
3 tbsp olive oil
2 garlic cloves, finely chopped
8 large free-range eggs
15g butter
A few drops of truffle oil,
    or to taste
Salt

If using wild or fine asparagus, lightly trim the ends of each stalk. If using ordinary asparagus, snap off and discard the woody end from each stalk. Cut into 5cm pieces. To prepare the ceps, shave off any dirt and leaf litter from the base of each stem, then brush them clean with a dry pastry brush to remove any stray particles of dirt. Give them a light wipe with a slightly damp cloth if absolutely necessary, then cut them into slices, lengthways through the stem to retain their shape if small enough.

Heat half the olive oil in a large, non-stick frying pan over a medium heat. Add the asparagus and sauté for 5 minutes or until tender, sprinkling over the garlic towards the end of cooking. Tip onto a plate and set to one side.

Add the remaining oil to the pan, increase the heat, add the mushrooms and season them lightly with salt. Toss over a high heat for 4–5 minutes until just tender and any excess liquid has been driven off. Return the asparagus to the pan and toss together briefly. Draw the pan off the heat.

Break the eggs into a bowl, add some salt and beat together lightly with a fork. Return the pan to a medium-low heat and when hot, pour in the eggs and cook, stirring all the time with a wooden spoon, until the eggs are half set. Take the pan off the heat, add the butter and truffle oil, and keep stirring, returning the pan to the heat briefly if necessary, until the eggs are soft and creamy. Immediately spoon onto gently warmed plates and serve.

CRISP-FRIED BREADCRUMBS, EXTREMADURA-STYLE

Migas a la extremeña SERVES 4

This is the best breakfast dish you've probably never had: fried chorizo sausages, eggs and breadcrumbs fried with olive oil and flavoured with garlic and smoky pimentón. A leading characteristic of Spanish cooking is the use of bread everywhere. They have wonderful bread, crusty rustic loaves, off-white in colour and full of wheaty flavour, and they revere it, they never throw it away. They use stale bread in gazpacho, in picadas with almonds for thickening sauces, for coating croquetas, and as a very coarse crumb in *migas*. This humble dish was created by the migrating shepherds who herded sheep between the north and south regions. It was their daily sustenance, being a great way to use up stale bread and the few ingredients they could purchase from the towns they passed through. Gradually this frugal recipe spread throughout Spain. In Aragón, *migas* is usually served with chorizo and grapes, in Extremadura with roasted red peppers and hot pimentón; sometimes crisp bacon bits are stirred through at the end, sometimes it is sprinkled with pomegranate seeds, and often even sweetened with sugar or melted chocolate and eaten as a dessert or sweet snack. You need to be patient when making *migas*: the crumbs need to be constantly stirred while in the pan so they become deliciously crisp and golden brown and don't burn.

450g crustless day-old white bread, thinly sliced

6 tbsp olive oil or 90g lard, plus extra oil for frying the chorizo and eggs

4 garlic cloves, finely chopped

1 tbsp *pimentón dulce* (smoked sweet Spanish paprika)

8 x 100g cooking chorizo (see page 310)

4 large free-range eggs

2 x large *Roasted red peppers* (see page 307)

Salt

Break the bread into a food processor and whiz into very rough crumbs, about the size of grains of rice. Tip them into a large mixing bowl, sprinkle with 4 tablespoons of water, cover with a clean tea towel and set aside for a few minutes to moisten.

Heat the olive oil or lard in a large, approximately 30cm, non-stick frying pan over a medium-high heat. Lower the heat to medium, add the garlic and as soon as it starts to change colour, add the breadcrumbs. Fry them, stirring them around continuously, for 20 minutes or until they are crisp and richly golden. Stir in the pimentón and ½ teaspoon of salt and set to one side.

Heat 2 smaller frying pans over a medium heat. Add 4 tablespoons of oil to each one. Prick the chorizo, add to one pan and fry for 6–7 minutes, turning, until cooked through. Crack the eggs into the second pan and leave them to fry, spooning some of the hot oil over the yolks as they cook, until they are cooked to your liking and have crispy edges. Warm the roasted red peppers through in a third small pan.

Spoon the migas onto warmed plates and put the fried eggs on top. Put the chorizo and red peppers to one side and serve straight away.

ROASTED GOAT with HERBS, ONION, WHITE WINE and GARLIC

Cabrito al horno SERVES 6

I made this recipe with a small leg of lamb. This wasn't ideal because when I ate this dish at the Carlos V restaurant it was made not only with goat, but with milk-fed goat, with the result that a whole back leg weighed about a kilogram and was a generous portion for one. But I was so taken with the way the goat was cooked that I decided to try it with lamb. It had come with a delicious crust, imbued with the flavours of herbs, garlic and salt, and with it were the onions that had been cooked on the bottom of the roasting tin with a great deal of wine and wine vinegar, and were served up with the goat almost like a relish, as you would mint sauce with lamb. In the glossary I have written at some length about buying goat in this country.

1 x 2.25kg leg of lamb, or goat
    if you can get it
3 medium onions, halved
    and thinly sliced
250ml dry white wine
2 tbsp white wine vinegar
4 garlic cloves, roughly chopped
2 pared strips of lemon zest,
    chopped
A small handful of parsley
    leaves, roughly chopped
1 tbsp rosemary leaves,
    chopped
1 tbsp olive oil
Salt
Patatas fritas (see page 146)
    or roast potatoes, to serve

Preheat the oven to 180°C/gas 4. Weigh the leg of lamb or goat and calculate the cooking time at 20 minutes per 500g. This will give you medium-rare meat and will be 1½ hours for a 2.25kg joint. Spread the sliced onions over the base of a roasting tin in which the leg of lamb will fit quite snugly and pour over the wine and vinegar.

Put the garlic, lemon zest, parsley and rosemary leaves into a mini food processor or mortar with ½ teaspoon of salt and grind into a paste. Stir in the olive oil, then rub the mixture all over the outside of the leg of lamb and place it on top of the onions. Slide the roasting tin into the oven and roast for 1½ hours.

Remove the lamb from the oven, lift it onto a carving board, wrap it in foil and leave it to rest for 15 minutes. Meanwhile, pour the excess fat from the roasting tin and season the onions with a little more salt if necessary.

Carve the lamb and serve it with a spoonful of the roasted onions. The Spanish like to serve this with patatas fritas.

PARDINA LENTILS with WHITE WINE, SERRANO HAM and PIMENTÓN

Lentejas con vino blanco, jamón y pimentón SERVES 6

This lentil stew is very pleasant served on its own or with any roasted game birds. I love partridge, as do the Spanish, so to do this, follow my timings on page 117. The tiny dark brown pardina lentils of Castilla y León are very similar to French Puy lentils and have the same earthy flavour. At the Seafood Restaurant we serve ibérico ham sliced off the bone and we use the trimmings for this dish, a deluxe version, if you like. Apart from the sweet, slightly tart flavour of the ham, there is also the flavouring of *pimentón dulce*, which seems almost to increase the earthiness of the dish.

225g green-brown lentils, such as pardina
6 tbsp olive oil
1 head garlic, cloves peeled and thinly sliced
1 medium onion, finely chopped
200g carrot, finely chopped
100g thinly sliced serrano ham, finely chopped
1 tbsp *pimentón dulce* (smoked sweet Spanish paprika)
2 large vine-ripened tomatoes, skinned and chopped
120ml dry white wine
1 tbsp chopped flat-leaf parsley
Salt and freshly ground black pepper

Check over the lentils for any little stones, then rinse in cold water. Tip them into a saucepan, add cold water to cover them by 5cm and bring to the boil over a high heat. Lower the heat and leave them to simmer for about 30 minutes or until just tender but still a little *al dente*. Drain, reserving the cooking liquid, and set to one side.

Put the olive oil, garlic, onion and carrot in a wide, shallow pan over a medium heat and cook gently for 15 minutes or until the vegetables are soft and just beginning to colour. Add the serrano ham and fry for another 5 minutes.

Stir in the pimentón, tomatoes and wine and simmer for 5 minutes or until they have reduced and thickened into a sauce. Stir the lentils into the sauce with 150ml of the reserved cooking liquid, the chopped parsley, 1½ teaspoons of salt and some pepper and simmer together for 5 minutes, then serve.

SLOW-COOKED LAMB with DRIED CHILLI, SUN-DRIED TOMATOES, ROASTED GARLIC and THYME

Caldereta extremeña SERVES 6

How does this sound? A rustic shepherd's stew of lamb slowly cooked in wine with hot peppers in an iron pot over the embers of a fire, thickened with a picada of lightly roasted almonds, smoked pimentón and a splash of sherry vinegar, with some boiled potatoes and cooked artichoke hearts stirred in at the end. It's great on its own or with some crusty fresh bread.

2 x 1kg shoulders of lamb, each one cut into 3 large chunks through the bone (get your butcher to do this)
2 dried guindilla peppers
2 dried ñora peppers
4 tbsp olive oil
1 head garlic, cloves separated, peeled and thinly sliced
1 large onion, halved and thinly sliced
A handful of soft thyme sprigs
The leaves from 1 large sprig rosemary
4 fresh bay leaves
4 pieces sun-dried tomato, thinly sliced
250ml red wine
75g toasted blanched almonds
1 tsp *pimentón dulce* (smoked sweet Spanish paprika)
2–3 tsp sherry vinegar
200g small, peeled main-crop potatoes, halved
200g prepared artichoke bases (about 4 large globe artichokes) (see page 111)
Salt and freshly ground black pepper
Crusty fresh bread, to serve

Sprinkle the pieces of lamb with plenty of salt and pepper and set aside at room temperature for 1 hour. Remove the stalks of the dried guindilla and ñora peppers, slit them open and remove the seeds. Soak in hot water for 1 hour alongside the lamb.

Heat 1 tablespoon of oil in a large flameproof casserole over a medium-high heat. Add the lamb in batches and brown them well all over. Lift out onto a plate and pour the fat from the pan.

Add the rest of the oil to the casserole with the garlic and onion and cook gently for 10 minutes. Add the thyme, rosemary, bay leaves and sun-dried tomatoes and fry for 2 minutes more.

Return the lamb to the casserole with the wine and 1 litre of water, cover and leave to simmer gently for 2 hours or until very tender.

Meanwhile, drain the soaked peppers and scrape the flesh away from the skin, discarding the skins as you go. Set the flesh aside.

Lift the pieces of lamb out of the casserole and put on a plate. Strain the cooking juices through a sieve into a glass bowl or jug so you see the layer of fat, and skim this off. Return the remainder to the pan and boil rapidly until reduced to about 600ml.

Remove and discard the thyme and rosemary stalks and the bay leaves from the residue left in the sieve and transfer the remainder to a liquidizer. Add the red pepper flesh, the almonds, pimentón and 300ml of the reduced cooking liquor and blend to a smooth paste. Stir the mixture back into the casserole with enough vinegar to taste, 1½ teaspoons of salt and some pepper.

Return the lamb to the casserole and simmer for a further 15 minutes. Meanwhile, boil the potatoes in well-salted water for 15 minutes or until just tender, then drain. Cook the artichoke bases in boiling salted water for 10 minutes until tender, then drain and cut into quarters. Stir the potatoes and artichokes into the casserole and serve as it is with just some crusty fresh bread.

Chapter Nine

ANDALUCÍA

I can't get enough of Seville. I've been there about half a dozen times and every time I go I find the city more fascinating and soulful. I went there with Sarah, my fiancée, recently, and we wandered endlessly from tapas bar to tapas bar. At one point, in a particularly old and dusty one near the Alcázar, they were serving *bellota* ham made from the black Iberian pig, which is fed exclusively on a diet of acorns and grass for three or four months before being slaughtered. Whether from the hills of Andalucía or from the *dehesa,* the cork and oak forest of Extremadura, it's the best cured ham in the world and the most expensive. I got quite cross with her because she wouldn't drink a glass of fino sherry with it, in my opinion the greatest combination of flavours in Spain. It was a tad unfair of me, I guess, since she doesn't drink wine, but I get very enthusiastic indeed about great food.

Having got over that we then found ourselves in a small bar just by the bull ring, the Plaza de Toros, owned by an ex-picador. We knew that because there were pictures of him on the walls, sitting on his padded horse wearing a wide-brimmed hat and holding a lance. In the bar he had the look of a rugby front row forward about him, bald and wide. The bar was packed because a bullfight was about to begin. Sarah said, 'Why don't we get a ticket from a tout?' I warned her she would hate it, but she was so taken with the elegance of everyone's clothes and the conviviality of the conversation in the arena, and the messages flowing between one of the matadors and a very ostentatiously dressed matador manager, that I think she might not have really noticed what was going on with the bulls. Interestingly, in Ernest Hemingway's book *Death in the Afternoon*, he writes about how women react to bullfights when watching one, that it is entirely unpredictable: some are disgusted, others find it interesting, even cathartic. But the fact is, love them or hate them, they are still very much a part of Spanish life and I feel not going to one would have been to miss something.

I feel the same about flamenco, too, and this is where the privilege of making TV comes in. Our translator in Andalucía took us to a tiny bar, Casa Matías, in a narrow street between the cathedral and the bullring. It was so packed on a Saturday afternoon that we had to pass the camera over people's heads. As we squeezed our way into a tiny back bar, Matías and his partner Maria, together with guitarist Manuel and a couple of the crowd, started to sing in that distinctive wail you often hear in flamenco music. It wasn't particularly upbeat; indeed, the song was rather melancholic, but in the same way as the blues is melancholic, so that although the words might be about tough times, the music and the dance are anything but – they are electrifying. I had to join in as I was being filmed. Not singing, of course, but drumming my knuckles on the tabletop, and clapping in that difficult, syncopated way that brings you alive, liberates you from your boring self. Matías's partner got up and danced: a tight black dress, dark eyes and long black hair, clicking, flicking and stamping on the floor. Then a blonde Spanish girl stood up joined in the dancing, swaying and sashaying. It lasted only about ten minutes and then we were out of there, but I won't ever forget it, and you can see why that music is such an important part of Spanish life.

Flamenco is part gypsy and part Arab, and the best food in Andalucía is similarly exotic. Take the chicken in pine nut and almond sauce on page 266 for example. It's flavoured with saffron, cardamom, cinnamon, nutmeg, coriander, cloves and black pepper and finished with that mixture so special to Mediterranean Spain, the *picada*, a pounded paste of fried garlic and bread, sometimes hard-boiled egg yolks, toasted pine nuts or almonds and olive oil. I've cooked it on a number of occasions for friends and they are surprised that it's Spanish. The combination of southern Mediterranean and North African cooking is like flamenco, full of fire and colour. There are others like it in this chapter: the *Pinchitos Moruños* on page 258, pork kebabs with cumin, coriander and fennel seed, and, in particular, the beef stew, the *Estofado de buey* on page 270, made with sherry vinegar, orange zest, cinnamon and lots of red pimentón. The use of sherry and sherry vinegar is a distinctive local touch. I'm particularly fond of the clams with oloroso on page 256, and good sherry vinegar is the paramount ingredient in the *Gazpacho* on page 260 too.

BROAD BEANS with SERRANO HAM and MINT

Habas con jamón SERVES 4 AS A TAPAS

Served in a cazuelita, warm from gently cooking shallots, garlic and serrano ham in olive oil, into which the peeled broad beans are then tossed, this could make you determined to give up all other forms of eating and commit to a lifetime of tapas.

800g shelled beans, about 2kg in their fresh pods, or frozen
120ml olive oil
1 small onion, finely chopped
5 garlic cloves, finely chopped
50g sliced serrano ham, finely chopped
The leaves from 2 small sprigs fresh mint, chopped at the last minute
Salt and freshly ground black pepper

Cook the broad beans in boiling, well-salted water for 1–2 minutes until only just tender. Drain and refresh under cold water. When they are cool enough to handle, remove the bright green beans from their outer skins. If the broad beans are very young and small you can omit this stage.

Pour the olive oil into a small cazuela or wide shallow pan and place over a medium heat. Add the onion and garlic and cook gently for 10 minutes until soft and sweet but not at all browned. Reduce the heat to medium-low, add the ham and cook gently for 2 minutes, but do not let it fry or you will lose its subtle sweet flavour.

Add the beans, ¼ teaspoon of salt and a little black pepper. Stir in the mint, spoon into 4 warmed cazuelitas and serve with plenty of fresh bread.

POTATO SALAD
DRESSED with OLIVE OIL,
VINEGAR and TUNA

Papas aliña con melva de almadabra SERVES 6–8 AS A TAPAS

This recipe comes from Ramon's tapas bar-cum-restaurant in Seville called Antigua Abacería de San Lorenzo. If you are travelling to Seville, which I would suggest is a good idea, you might like to pay a visit for a few tapas, since it's right off the visitors' beaten track but still to be found in a very pleasant part of the city. Ramon only has a few dishes on his menu: a chorizo and chickpea stew similar to the one on page 34 with lashings of spinach, plates of jamón which he serves with some superb fino sherry, charcoal-roasted red peppers with hard-boiled egg (see page 250) and this. Not surprising really, since he cooks everything on a tiny two-ring electric cooker, a bit like a Baby Belling, but if you want Andalucían atmosphere, it doesn't get any better. This is one of his most popular tapas, but how do they get such sweet-tasting potatoes in the Mediterranean? Well, they are cut up while still slightly warm and tossed with chopped spring onions, olive oil and sherry vinegar, then topped with what you might think was tinned tuna but is actually a local fish, white bonito.

1kg unpeeled waxy new
    potatoes, such as Charlotte
125g bunch spring onions
The leaves from 1 x 20g bunch
    flat-leaf parsley, chopped
2 tbsp sherry vinegar
6 tbsp extra virgin olive oil
150g good quality tuna steak,
    preserved in olive oil
Coarse sea salt, roughly ground

Boil the potatoes in well-salted water until the skins just break and they are very tender – about 20 minutes. Drain and, when just cool enough to handle, peel off their skins and break into small, coarse chunks directly into a large mixing bowl.

Trim the spring onions, cut away and discard the green top half and very thinly slice the remainder. Add to the bowl with almost all the parsley, then drizzle over the vinegar and oil, sprinkle with some sea salt to taste and mix together lightly, taking care not to break up the potatoes too much. The warm potatoes will absorb the dressing as they cool down.

Divide the potatoes between small tapas-like bowls and scatter some small chunks of tuna on top. Scatter over the remaining parsley and serve with small forks.

ROASTED RED PEPPERS
with SPRING ONIONS
and HARDBOILED EGGS

SERVES 6 AS A TAPAS

This is the second dish from the Antigua Abacería de San Lorenzo in Seville. Interestingly, this tapas bar started as a shop specializing in produce from the Americas: potatoes, peppers, chillies, tomatoes, corn, etc. There used to be many of these little shops called *antiguas abacerías* in the sixteenth and seventeenth century in Seville, and this is possibly the last.

4 large *Roasted red peppers* (see page 307)
3 spring onions, trimmed and very thinly sliced
2 tbsp extra virgin olive oil
1 fat garlic clove, thinly sliced
A large pinch of *pimentón dulce* (smoked sweet Spanish paprika)
2 tsp sherry vinegar
2 hard-boiled eggs, sliced
Salt

Split open the red peppers and remove and discard the stalks, skin and seeds. Cut the flesh lengthways into strips 2.5cm wide and scatter them over the base of a small shallow serving dish. Scatter over the spring onions.

Put the olive oil and garlic into a small shallow pan and put it over a medium-low heat. As soon as the garlic starts to sizzle and change colour, add the pimentón, vinegar and a good pinch of salt. Drizzle the mixture over the red peppers, scatter over the hard-boiled eggs and serve.

CUTTLEFISH BALLS in a CURRY-SPICED TOMATO SAUCE

Albóndigas de chocos SERVES 12 AS A TAPAS OR STARTER

This recipe comes from a fish restaurant right in the heart of the Mercado del Arenal in Seville. The restaurant – called, not unnaturally, El Pesquero – is owned by Antonio Sanchez, who also owns the largest fish counter in the market, and a magnificent counter it is too. So when his chefs run short of fish, all they have to do is walk across the aisle to pick up some more. I remember Antonio's restaurant specifically for some giant Mediterranean gambas called *las carabinas*, a new albariño, Santiago Ruiz (the best fish wine in Spain I'd ever tasted), and the tapas dish they served us when we arrived, *albóndigas de chocos*. The prawns, served whole, had been grilled over sea salt, and for serving, the chefs had made a slit in the head of each of them and inserted a small teaspoon, making it quite clear that the juices there were worth prizing out, and a little more delicately than by chewing on the heads, which is what I normally do. The wine was deliciously fragrant in a citrus way and the cuttlefish balls were inspired, made by chopping up raw cuttlefish, binding it with egg, garlic and salt, then deep-frying to seal them and give them colour. They were then briefly simmered in a mildly curry-flavoured tomato sauce. It was a great lunch, made even better for me by the great enthusiasm the other customers had for their food too. Incidentally, our local Cornish octopus, 'blitzed' (as we say) in a food processor, makes a very tasty alternative to cuttlefish in these seafood balls.

900g prepared cuttlefish
4 small garlic cloves, crushed
1 egg, beaten
1 tbsp dry white wine
10g fresh white breadcrumbs
2 tsp chopped flat-leaf parsley
Olive or vegetable oil, for
   deep-frying
Salt

FOR THE SAUCE:
4 tbsp olive oil
1 medium onion, finely
   chopped
3 fresh bay leaves
125g carrots, finely chopped
1 tsp mild curry powder
250ml *Chicken stock*
   (see page 306)
150ml *Tomato sauce*
   (see page 306)
2 tbsp dry white wine
1 tsp lemon juice

Roughly cut up the cuttlefish, put it into a food processor with the garlic and 1 teaspoon of salt and blend to a coarse paste. Add the beaten egg and blend once more, then scoop the mixture into a bowl and stir in the wine, breadcrumbs and parsley. Cover and chill for at least 30 minutes.

Meanwhile, for the sauce, heat the olive oil in a shallow flameproof casserole or large, deep frying pan over a medium heat. Add the onion, bay leaves, carrots and curry powder and cook gently for 10 minutes. Add the stock, tomato sauce and wine and simmer gently for 10 minutes until well reduced and thickened. Meanwhile, heat some oil for deep-frying to 180°C.

Add the lemon juice and 120ml water to the curry sauce and bring it back to a gentle simmer. Remove the cuttlefish mixture from the fridge. Take heaped teaspoons of the mixture and, using a second teaspoon, shape into balls. Drop about 8 at a time into the hot oil. Fry for 1 minute until lightly golden then remove with a slotted spoon (or the frying basket) and leave to drain on a tray lined with plenty of kitchen paper. You should make about 50 balls.

Drop the cuttlefish balls into the simmering sauce, stir well and leave to heat through for 2 minutes; don't overcook them. Adjust the seasoning to taste, spoon into small, shallow dishes and serve hot, with toothpicks or small forks.

PAN-FRIED KIDNEYS with SHERRY

Riñones al jerez SERVES 8 AS A TAPAS OR 4 AS A MAIN COURSE

It's rare to find kidneys in Spain other than those cooked 'al Jerez', with sherry. Just as a plate of jamón goes perfectly with a glass of fino, the same is true of kidneys sautéed quickly in a pan and finished off with oloroso sherry, olive oil, garlic and parsley. The Spanish like to slightly thicken the sauce, sometimes with breadcrumbs and sometimes with flour. I prefer the latter, which gives the sauce a velvety texture. It's the sort of tapas dish I love, and it goes very well with a buttery rice pilaf as a supper dish too.

750g fresh lamb's or calf's kidneys
5 tbsp olive oil
75g finely chopped shallot
2 garlic cloves, finely chopped
1½ tsp plain flour
165ml oloroso or amontillado sherry
1 tsp chopped parsley
Salt, freshly ground black pepper and *pimentón picante* (smoked hot Spanish paprika)
Crusty fresh bread, to serve

Peel any fat or membrane away from the outside of the kidneys if necessary. Slice the lamb's kidneys in half, or snip the calf's kidneys into separate lobes, then snip out the white fatty cores. Season with ½ teaspoon of salt and some pepper.

Heat 1½ tablespoons of the olive oil in a large, deep frying pan over a high heat. Add half the kidneys and fry briskly for 1 minute, sprinkling them with a little pimentón just before you remove them from the pan to a plate. They need to be a little undercooked in the centre at this stage, but nicely browned. Repeat with another 1½ tablespoons of oil and the rest of the kidneys.

Add the remaining 2 tablespoons of olive oil to the pan with the shallot and garlic and cook for 3–4 minutes until the shallot is soft and lightly golden. Stir in the flour, then gradually stir in the sherry and the juices from the plate of kidneys and simmer, stirring, for about 1 minute. Stir in the kidneys, adjust the seasoning to taste and simmer for 1 minute more, until heated through but still pink and juicy in the centre. Spoon into warmed cazuelitas, sprinkle with the parsley and serve with bread.

ANDALUCIAN SHRIMP and SPRING ONION FRITTERS

Tortillitas de camarones MAKES 16 FRITTERS

These tortillitas bring back happy memories of a holiday I had years ago, staying in a hacienda just outside Jerez. Every night we'd go into the city and be the only customers because we couldn't get used to the fact that eating only started at ten o'clock at night. We'd resort to eating tapas and this was the absolute favourite. It's a shame that we British don't seem to appreciate that it's perfectly OK to eat shrimps in the shell when made into a fritter and crisp-fried like this. You don't notice the shells as long as they are small; Falmouth Bay prawns during the autumn months, for example, would be perfect. But if you still can't take it, use peeled raw prawns instead. It's not the same, though.

175g raw peeled prawns, or 300g
    whole raw unshelled small
    prawns or brown shrimps
175g plain flour
½ tsp baking powder
1 tbsp dry white wine
2 spring onions, thinly sliced
1 tbsp chopped flat-leaf parsley
Olive oil, for shallow frying
Salt

If using raw peeled prawns, cut them across into ½cm-thick slices. If using unshelled prawns, such as those from Falmouth Bay, or brown shrimp, break off and discard the heads but leave the tails unpeeled.

Sift the flour, baking powder and a pinch of salt into a mixing bowl. Make a well in the centre and add 300ml water and the wine. Gradually mix the dry ingredients into the liquid to make a batter, then whisk until you have a thick cream. Fold in the prawns, spring onions and parsley.

Pour ½cm of oil into a large frying pan and place over a high heat. Leave until hot but not smoking, and until a drop of the batter sizzles immediately. Carefully drop large spoonfuls of the batter into the pan and spread each one out a little with the back of the spoon so they develop lovely thin, crispy edges as they cook. Don't be tempted to overcrowd the pan – only do 2–3 at a time.

Cook, turning the fritters over every now and then, for about 2 minutes or until puffed up and golden brown on both sides. Remove with a slotted spoon and drain on a tray lined with plenty of kitchen paper. Eat straight away while they are still hot and crisp.

CLAMS with SERRANO HAM and OLOROSO SHERRY

Almejas al jerez SERVES 4

I'm a great fan of this dish, which marries jamón, sweet sherry and seafood beautifully. I think it's the sweetness of the slow-cooked onions, coupled with the flor in the sherry and again the sweetness of the ham, that makes you want to eat the clams for ever.

4 tbsp olive oil
1 medium onion, finely chopped
2 garlic cloves, finely chopped
100g thinly sliced serrano
    ham, chopped
4 fresh bay leaves
1 kg small clams, such as
    carpetshell
½ tsp plain flour
150ml oloroso sherry
2 tbsp chopped flat-leaf parsley

Heat the olive oil in a large, deep pan over a medium-low heat. Stir in the onion, garlic, ham and bay leaves and leave to cook very gently without browning, stirring now and then, for 10 minutes or until the mixture is soft and sweet. Meanwhile, wash the clams under cold running water, discarding any that don't show signs of closing when squeezed gently.

Stir the flour into the onion mixture. Turn up the heat and add the clams and sherry. Cover and shake over a high heat for 2–3 minutes or until the clams are just opened. Stir in the parsley, and serve.

ALPUJARRAN WILD BOAR STEW with CUMIN, ORANGE and MOSCATEL RAISINS

SERVES 4–6

Chris Stewart wrote a very evocative book about Andalucía in the 1990s called *Driving over Lemons*. So taken was I with this book that I had to go and visit his farm in the Alpujarras to see how his decision to live in the middle of nowhere and eschew most of the trappings of modern life had worked out since then. He named the book thus because the English estate agent who sold him the derelict farm had told him to stop trying to avoid the lemons but to drive over them, and it seemed to him a symbol of the abundance of fresh produce in Andalucía. He and his wife Ana were great, obviously loving their life but not averse to enjoying his success as an author, but I think he was a bit irritated that people still recall him as a founding member of Genesis when he left them while he was still at school. Chris cooked us a tabbouleh, which was delicious, and a friend of his who was helping him, Tara Stevens, a cookery writer, produced this main course for us, which was her take on some aspects of Catalan cooking, such as the inclusion of chocolate, but with a big element of Andalucía in there too: wild boar, cumin, orange and raisins. There is also a clear Moroccan influence. She has since written a book on the cooking of Fez. I do think this is a very successful merging of the flavours of North Africa and Mediterranean Spain.

4 tbsp olive oil
2 large onions, finely chopped
8 garlic cloves (40g approx.), crushed
4 tsp cumin seeds, freshly ground
2 tsp smoked *pimentón picante* (smoked hot Spanish paprika)
900g wild boar meat or boneless pork shoulder, cut into 2.5–3cm pieces
100g plump raisins, moscatel or Malaga if possible
6–8 pared strips of orange zest
150ml freshly squeezed orange juice (approx. 1 large orange)
250ml red wine
35g bitter chocolate (85% cocoa solids is best)
200g skinned and chopped tomatoes, fresh or from a can
3 tbsp roughly chopped parsley leaves
Salt and freshly ground black pepper
Garlicky mashed potatoes, to serve

Heat half the olive oil in a medium-sized flameproof casserole. Add the onions and garlic and cook gently over a medium-low heat for at least 20 minutes, stirring regularly, until soft, sweet and caramelized.

Stir in the cumin seeds and pimentón and cook gently for 2 more minutes then scoop the mixture into a bowl and set to one side.

Add the remaining 2 tablespoons of oil to the casserole, add half the wild boar and some seasoning and cook over a high heat until nicely browned all over. Lift onto a plate and repeat with the remainder. Return the rest of the boar to the casserole with the onion mixture, raisins, orange peel, orange juice and wine. Simmer together for 10 minutes.

Add the chocolate and tomatoes to the pan with ½ teaspoon of salt, cover and leave to simmer gently for 3 hours, stirring now and then to make sure it's not sticking, until the meat is meltingly tender. As with all stews, if you can leave this overnight and reheat it the next day, so much the better. Just before serving check the seasoning, sprinkle with the chopped parsley and serve with mashed potatoes made with a touch of garlic.

SMALL, SPICY MOORISH KEBABS

Pinchitos moruños MAKES 12 SKEWERS

The influence of the Moors on the cuisine of Andalucía is very apparent, and no more so than with these kebabs, which are almost Middle Eastern in their use of spices such as cumin, coriander and fennel seed. However, these are more likely to be made with pork, whereas originally they would have been made with lamb. Grilled over charcoal, they are served as tapas in many a bar and fiesta. You can buy a ready-prepared pinchitos spice mixture in most shops and supermarkets in Spain, although, naturally, grinding your own fresh spices makes all the difference.

1kg lean pork fillet
4 garlic cloves, peeled
2 tsp each cumin, coriander
   and fennel seeds
2 tsp *pimentón picante*
   (smoked hot Spanish paprika)
2 tsp dried thyme or oregano
4 tsp lemon juice
4 tbsp olive oil
2 x 2cm-thick slices crusty white
   bread, cut into 2.5cm cubes
Salt and freshly ground black
   pepper

12 x 22cm thin metal skewers

Cut the pork fillet into 2.5cm cubes and put them in a mixing bowl. Put the garlic cloves on a board, sprinkle with ½ teaspoon of salt and crush under the blade of a large knife into a paste. Add to the pork with another teaspoon of salt and plenty of black pepper.

Put the seed spices into a spice grinder and grind to a fine powder. Add to the bowl with the pimentón, dried thyme, lemon juice and olive oil and mix everything together well. Refrigerate overnight if you wish.

Thread 4 pieces of pork onto each skewer. Barbecue or griddle over a high heat for 7−8 minutes, turning them over as they brown, until cooked through but still moist and juicy in the centre. Spear a chunk of bread onto the end of each skewer and serve hot.

TRADITIONAL ANDALUCIAN GAZPACHO

Gazpacho andaluz SERVES 6

'Gazpacho' is actually the name given to a whole family of soups, all based on the same basic ingredients: bread, garlic and olive oil, and was originally the food of peasants who, working in the fields, would be given rations of bread and oil for their meals. When the bread was soaked in water and pounded with garlic, oil, vinegar and salt for flavour, it provided a nutritious meal that would satisfy their hunger and quench their thirst, as well as replenishing the salts and minerals lost whilst working in the hot sun. The rest is just embellishment, but what delightful embellishment. It's a celebration of summer vegetables: tomatoes, cucumber, spring onions, a quality sherry vinegar, and in my case roasted red peppers to enhance the sweetness. Gazpacho in Spain is often paler and creamier with bread than we are used to, but I like my gazpacho really concentrated, so there's not a great deal of bread in it, or water, but if you like a thicker and less intense flavour, add double the bread and a little more iced water to your taste.

50g slightly stale, white
   crusty bread
2 large red peppers
1kg really ripe vine-ripened
   tomatoes, skinned
1 cucumber
2–3 garlic cloves, crushed
150ml good quality olive oil,
   plus extra to serve (optional)
4 tbsp good quality sherry vinegar
1 tsp caster sugar (only if your
   tomatoes lack sweetness)
Salt

FOR THE GARNISHES:
25g white bread
1 tbsp good olive oil, for the
   croutons, plus extra to serve
1 large vine-ripened tomato,
   skinned, seeded and cut
   into small dice
¼ cucumber, peeled, seeded
   and cut into small dice
2 spring onions, trimmed
   and thinly sliced
1 hard-boiled egg, peeled
   and cut into small dice
25g piece serrano ham, cut
   into small dice (optional)

Preheat the oven to 220°C/gas 7. Cover the bread with 100ml cold water and leave to soak for at least 30 minutes. Place the red peppers on a baking tray and roast them in the oven for 20–25 minutes, turning them 2–3 times, until the skins are quite black. Leave to cool, then remove and discard the stalks, seeds and skin, and roughly chop the flesh. Add to the juices in the bowl and set to one side. Lower the oven temperature to 200°C/gas 6.

Quarter the tomatoes and scoop out the seeds into a sieve set over another bowl. Rub the juices from the seeds through the sieve. Peel the cucumber, cut it in half lengthways, scoop out the seeds with a teaspoon and discard. Roughly chop the remainder.

Put half the roasted red peppers, tomatoes and tomato juices, cucumber, soaked bread, garlic, olive oil, vinegar, sugar if using and ¾ teaspoon of salt into a liquidizer (not a food processor as they don't seem to get things smooth enough) and blend until very smooth. Tip into a large mixing bowl and repeat with the rest of the ingredients. Thin to the required consistency if you wish with cold water. Cover and chill for at least 2 hours.

Meanwhile, for the croutons, tear the bread into little rough pieces and toss with 1 tablespoon of oil. Spread on a baking sheet and bake for 4–5 minutes or until crisp and golden. Remove and leave to cool.

To serve, put the garnishes into separate small bowls for everyone to help themselves from. Ladle the soup into chilled bowls and drizzle with a little more olive oil, if you wish.

WHITE GAZPACHO with GARLIC SPRINKLED with GRAPES

Ajo blanco de Málaga SERVES 6

As with the traditional gazpacho on page 260, this is all about stale country bread, garlic and olive oil with the judicious addition of a good quality sherry vinegar and, in this case, almonds and seedless white grapes. We also serve it at our café garnished with some cubes of chilled charentais melon instead of the grapes. This is at its best made with wet new-season garlic, which we see from time to time in our supermarkets.

200g slightly stale, crustless
    white bread
800–900ml ice-cold water
15g garlic cloves, thinly sliced
100g blanched almonds
150ml good quality olive oil,
    plus extra to serve
4 tbsp sherry vinegar
About 24 seedless white
    grapes, halved
Salt

Break the bread into a bowl and sprinkle with 400ml of the ice-cold water. Set aside to soak for at least 30 minutes.

Put the bread into a liquidizer with the garlic and almonds and blend to a smooth paste. Then, with the motor still running, gradually add the olive oil, followed by the vinegar, 1 teaspoon of salt and enough of the ice-cold water to give the soup a good texture, neither too thick nor too watery.

Tip the soup into a large mixing bowl and adjust the vinegar and seasoning to taste. Chill for at least 2 hours.

To serve, ladle the soup into small, chilled bowls and sprinkle grapes into the centre of each. Drizzle over a little more olive oil and serve straight away.

CRISP-FRIED FISH MALAGA-STYLE
Pescado frito

Andalucía is known as the *zona de los fritos*, the seafront bars and restaurants of Huelva, Sanlucar, Cadiz and especially Malaga being renowned for their superb fried fish. I still remember years ago eating tiny red mullet and baby hake called *pescadilla* together with some gambas in Sanlúcar de Barrameda, and drinking the local manzanilla sherry, which I swear tasted salty from the fact that it is matured in oak barrels right by the sea. It was all fabulous, though I recall a pang of guilt at the time that these tiny fish must be illegally caught. However, I subsequently found out that they weren't illegal, they were just the least saleable. But even had they been illegal, this would be so much less disturbing than the reality that many fishermen today throw undersized and unwanted fish back into the water, dead. Here I've substituted thin steaks of small hake and fillets of red mullet for those tiny fish. (See page 314 for where to find the coarse flour called *harina de trigo especial para freir*.)

Olive oil, for deep-frying
Harina de trigo especial para freir, or fine-ground semolina
Wedges of lemon, to serve
Sea salt

Allow about 180g mixed fish per person:
40g piece red mullet fillet, pin-boned
A 1cm-thick, 60g steak of hake, whiting or sea bass, cut through the bone of a small fish
40g large, raw peeled prawns, with the last tail section of the shell still in place
40g prepared squid rings

Heat some oil for deep-frying to 190°C.

Prepare the fish. Working with one person's portion of fish at a time, season each piece well with salt and dredge heavily in the flour. Give it a vigorous shake to remove the excess flour, then drop it into the hot oil and fry until crisp and golden. Cook the red mullet, hake or other fish and prawns for 30 seconds, then add the squid to the oil and cook for a further 30 seconds, by which time all the fish should be cooked through. Lift the fish out of the oil as soon as it is ready, drain briefly on a baking tray lined with plenty of kitchen paper, and then arrange on a warmed serving plate. Garnish with the lemon wedges and serve as fast as you can while it is still piping hot, then go on to cook the next portion.

CHICKEN in a MILDLY SPICED SAFFRON, PINE NUT and ALMOND SAUCE

Pollo en pepitoria SERVES 4

The Australian chef Luke Mangan opened a restaurant in Bondi called Moorish, about five years ago. Sadly, it didn't last that long because the Australians at that time weren't ready for Spanish/North African food, but I thought it was fabulous, as I also think Moro in London is. Dishes that encompass Spanish Mediterranean and North African cooking are enormously attractive, partly because the cooking traditions of countries such as Morocco and Tunisia come from far further afield, all the way from Persia, in fact. This Moorish dish of chicken braised in sherry with the mild spices of cloves, nutmeg and saffron, thickened with hard-boiled egg yolks, almonds and pine nuts, is popular all over Spain at Christmas, and has to me a distinct flavour of Persia in it. If you ever needed confirmation of how profound the Moorish influence on southern Spain has been, this dish would be a good place to find it.

2 large free-range eggs
1 x 1.5kg free-range chicken
1 tsp green cardamom pods (approx. 10)
½ tsp loosely packed saffron strands
½ tsp coriander seeds
2 cloves
1 cm piece cinnamon stick
¼ tsp freshly grated nutmeg
10 black peppercorns
6 tbsp olive oil
2 garlic cloves, peeled but left whole
20g slice crustless white bread
1 large onion, finely chopped
200ml dry sherry or dry white wine
200ml *Chicken stock* (see page 306)
2 fresh bay leaves
65g blanched almonds
40g pine nuts
1 tbsp freshly squeezed lemon juice
1 tsp chopped flat-leaf parsley, to garnish
Salt and freshly ground black pepper

Boil the eggs for 10 minutes. Cool, then peel.

To joint the chicken, cut the legs away from the body, cut them in half at the joint, then skin each of the pieces. Remove the breasts from either side of the carcass, taking with them the wings. Cut off the bottom two joints of each wing and set aside with the rest of the carcass for making stock. Skin the breasts and detach the little fillets from the underside of each one. Cut the breasts into 2 evenly sized pieces and set aside with the thighs, drumsticks and fillets.

Lightly crush the cardamom pods so the husks split open and remove the seeds from inside. Discard the husks and add the seeds to a spice grinder with the saffron, coriander seeds, cloves, cinnamon, nutmeg and peppercorns and grind to a fine powder.

Heat 4 tablespoons of the olive oil in shallow flameproof casserole or large, deep frying pan over a medium heat. Add the whole garlic cloves and slice of bread and fry, turning over once, for about 2 minutes until golden on both sides. Transfer to the bowl of a mini food processor.

Season the chicken pieces lightly, add them to the pan, and fry until lightly golden on both sides. Remove and set aside on a plate. Add another tablespoon of oil and the onion to the pan and fry for 10 minutes until soft and sweet but not browned. Stir in the ground spices, cook for 1 minute, then stir in the sherry or wine and stock. Return the chicken to the pan, add the bay leaves and season with ½ teaspoon of salt. Bring to a simmer, cover and leave to cook gently for 40 minutes, turning the chicken pieces over every now and then, until very tender.

Heat a frying pan and dry-roast the pine nuts for 1 minute and 40g of the almonds for 2 minutes. Leave to cool, then add to the mini food processor with the yolks from the hardboiled eggs and 10–12 tablespoons of the chicken cooking liquid. Grind everything to a smooth paste. Coarsely chop the remaining almonds and set to one side.

Uncover the pan and lift the pieces of chicken out onto a warmed serving dish. Cover and keep warm. Add the paste to the sauce, return to a low heat and simmer, stirring, for a minute or two until nicely thickened. Stir in the lemon juice, adjust the seasoning to taste and pour back over the chicken.

Heat the remaining tablespoon of oil in a small frying pan over a medium heat, add the coarsely chopped almonds and stir-fry for a few seconds until lightly golden. Scatter over the chicken with the chopped parsley and serve straight away.

ANDALUCIAN ESTOPHADE with SHERRY VINEGAR, ORANGE and OLIVES

Estofado de buey a la andaluza SERVES 4–6

You could say this was an Andalucían version of a Provençal daube, the big difference being that this contains pimentón and a great deal of cinnamon, reflecting its Moorish connections. It's often made with the meat from bullfights, but actually bull meat is quite hard to come by, even in Spain. I haven't partnered much of the food in this book with wine but this calls out for a seriously strong bottle of tempranillo, maybe one from Extremadura or La Mancha.

1kg stewing beef, such as
    chuck or blade steak
2 tbsp plain flour
4 tbsp olive oil
150g bacon lardons
4 tbsp sherry vinegar
2 medium onions, halved
    and thinly sliced
6 garlic cloves, crushed
2 tsp *pimentón picante*
    (smoked hot Spanish paprika)
2 tbsp tomato purée
300ml red wine
300ml *Beef stock* (see page 306)
3 fresh bay leaves
The leaves from 4 sprigs
    fresh thyme
2 pared strips of orange zest
2 x 5cm cinnamon sticks
6 cloves
100g small green olives
Salt and freshly ground
    black pepper

Cut the meat into 4–5cm chunks. Season the meat well all over with salt and pepper and then dust in the flour, shaking off but reserving the excess.

Heat 2 tablespoons of the oil in a large, flameproof casserole over a medium-high heat, add the bacon lardons and fry briefly until lightly golden. Remove with a slotted spoon to a mixing bowl. Next, brown the beef in small batches and set aside with the bacon.

Add the sherry vinegar to the casserole and leave it to bubble up, rubbing the caramelized juices from the bottom of the pan with a wooden spoon as you do so, until reduced by half. Pour over the bacon and beef in the bowl.

Add the remaining 2 tablespoons of oil to the pan with the onions and garlic and fry gently for 10 minutes until the onions are soft and sweet and nicely caramelized. Add the pimentón and tomato purée and fry for 1 minute more.

Return the beef, bacon and juices to the casserole and add the red wine, stock, bay leaves, thyme, orange peel, cinnamon sticks, cloves, green olives, ½ teaspoon salt and ½ teaspoon of black pepper. Give everything a good stir, cover with a well-fitting lid, and leave to simmer very gently on the top of the stove for 2½ hours, by which time the meat should be meltingly tender. Remove and discard the bay leaves, adjust the seasoning to taste and serve.

Chapter Ten

SPANISH DESSERTS

While on holiday in my house in Mollymook on the south coast of New South Wales, I made a Spanish rice pudding with lemon and cinnamon for twenty-three people. I also made a Spanish mixed salad. I found some tins of asparagus at the supermarket, bought a couple of cos lettuces, some beef tomatoes and spring onions, boiled some eggs for it, and made a dressing with Spanish olive oil and sherry vinegar. I'd ordered aged beef, rib-eye on the bone, for *chuletón*, and sautéed potatoes and tossed them with hot sliced chorizos. I bought some best ends of young lamb and cut them into lamb chops for *chuletillas*. I cooked these on the barbecue along with the rib-eye chops. I made an alioli, hot with garlic, and a romesco sauce with smoked paprika, lots of romano peppers, which I roasted till blistering on the barbecue, olive oil, garlic, pine nuts and a couple of egg yolks. I bought shiraz from the Barossa Valley to emulate the strong Spanish reds from Extremadura. I got prawns and made the same sauce I used for the Cantabrian prawn cocktail on page 50. Everything was eaten, but the complete star was the rice pudding on page 276. I thought the baked rice pudding of my childhood was good, but this was better.

I wonder if it is generally recognized how good Spanish desserts and sweets are. If you were to judge this only by the desserts you get in most Spanish restaurants, you would be missing something. There will be the rice pudding, and *flan*, crema catalana and ice cream, but generally they are bought in and suffer accordingly. Made at home, these sweets are fabulous. Most large towns and cities have very attractive *pastelerías* (cake shops) filled with countless almond or custard-based pastries, meringues, *milhojas* (millefeuilles) and large glazed fruit tarts and gateaux.

Puddings in Spain are sophisticated, and I'm sure much of this is to do with the eight hundred years that Spain was ruled by the Moors, because in Muslim countries, the love of sweet, nutty and spicy mouthfuls is very apparent. Most Spanish puddings are delicious, and pastries such as the almond cake from Santiago or the cherry one from San Sebastián, are as good as anything you'd find in Italy or France. In fact, just at this moment I crave a slice of that sour cherry tart and a cup of tea …

RICE PUDDING with a CARAMEL TOPPING

Arroz con leche requemado SERVES 4

While there is a great variety of sweet things in Spanish cooking, few are meant as puddings to have after a meal; they are more to have with a cup of *café con leche*, mid-morning. On the whole, after a meal they prefer fresh fruit and nuts or ice cream, but rice pudding and *flan* (see page 300) are the desserts eaten with any regularity, in the home and in restaurants. Asturias claims to be home for this pudding, the region being famous for its milk. Instead of baking the rice and milk as we do in Britain, they are simmered together on top of the stove, flavoured with lemon and cinnamon, then left to cool to room temperature and served finished with a crunchy layer of caramel on top. You can get a half-decent topping by sliding the rice pudding under your grill, but it's better to use a blowtorch or a *quemador*, a thick cast-iron disc attached to a long handle. You heat this in a gas flame until extremely hot, then lower it onto the surface of the sugar, which caramelizes is a matter of seconds. Don't, like me, buy a cheap aluminium one though. It's got to be cast-iron, or you'll end up with a pool of molten aluminium on top of your stove.

1 litre full-cream milk
1 x 10cm cinnamon stick
Pared zest of 1 lemon
125g short-grain pudding rice
100g caster sugar, plus extra
    for the tops
30g unsalted butter
Pinch of salt

Bring the milk, cinnamon stick, lemon zest and rice to the boil in a large saucepan, stirring frequently to loosen the rice sticking to the base of the pan. Lower the heat and leave to simmer for 30–35 minutes, stirring regularly, until the rice is tender and the mixture is creamy and thick.

Remove and discard the cinnamon stick and pieces of lemon zest, stir in the sugar and simmer for a further 10 minutes, continuing to stir regularly.

Remove the pan from the heat, stir in the butter and a small pinch of salt, then spoon the mixture into 4 small, shallow ovenproof dishes. Level the tops and leave to cool but do not refrigerate.

Just before serving, finish the tops. Sprinkle a generous tablespoon of sugar in a thick layer on each pudding and, holding the blowtorch about 5cm away, caramelize it. Allow to cool for just a moment, then serve, while the topping is still brittle.

BAKED CHEESECAKE

Tarta de queso SERVES AT LEAST 12

On the front wall of the Bar la Viña, in the Calle 31 de Agosto in the old quarter of San Sebastián, there are some appetizing paintings of what you can expect to find inside: a sliced beef chop grilled over charcoal, a whole hake split open and cooked on the plancha with caramelized garlic, a seafood cocktail salad and a big wedge of the dark, almost blackened, cheesecake for which this tapas bar is famous. You go in and there are at least four whole cheesecakes on the bar. It was one of those occasions when I say to myself 'I know they won't give us the recipe', but they did. They are extremely easy to make, though they say getting just the right amount of the caramelized exterior is what makes them so special. I urge you to have a go. They serve it with thin slices of *membrillo*, quince 'cheese', in the sit-down restaurant part and it goes extremely well.

1kg full-fat cream cheese,
    at room temperature
7 large free-range eggs
400g caster sugar
500ml double cream
30g plain flour
Membrillo, to serve (optional)

Bring the cream cheese back to room temperature if you haven't already done so. This is important to the finished texture of the cheesecake.

Preheat the oven to 220°C/gas 7. Line a round 23–24cm loose-bottomed or clip-sided cake tin with a double-thickness of non-stick baking paper.

Break the eggs into a jug and beat together well. Put the cream cheese into a bowl and beat with a hand-held electric mixer, then gradually beat in the eggs. Mix in the sugar, then the cream, then the flour, until the mixture is very smooth.

Pour the mixture into the prepared tin and bake for 45–50 minutes, until well browned on top and almost set but still wobbly in the centre. It will firm up as it cools. Turn off the oven, leave the door slightly ajar and leave it to cool inside. This is what helps give it a silky-smooth texture.

Undo the sides of the tin, carefully peel the paper away then invert the cake onto a plate, peel the paper off the base and turn right side up again onto a serving plate. Serve, cut into slices, with thin slices of membrillo if you wish.

SANTIAGO ALMOND TART with MEMBRILLO

SERVES 10–12

The *tarta de Santiago* is probably the best-known cake in Spain: a deliciously moist, flourless, almond-rich sponge, sometimes cooked in a crisp, buttery pastry case, which can be found in every bakery, hotel, restaurant and souvenir shop in Galicia. It is always decorated with the cross of the knights of St James, stencilled into the icing-sugar-coated surface and I always come home from Galicia with one in a box. I've added a little embellishment to the classic recipe by putting a layer of quince paste, *membrillo*, under the almond sponge, along the lines of a walnut tart in one of my previous books, *Food Heroes*, and it works really well. Some time later I noticed in Sam and Eddie Hart's excellent book, *Modern Spanish Cooking*, a very similar recipe. It happens so often that you think you're being clever and then discover others have done it too.

1 x larger quantity of *Sweet pastry* (see page 307), plus a little beaten egg for brushing
200g *membrillo* (quince paste) or 8 tbsp quince or apricot jam
1½ tbsp lemon juice
450g blanched almonds, Spanish Marcona if possible
50g plain flour
4 large free-range eggs
150g caster sugar
Finely grated zest of 1 large lemon
½ tsp ground cinnamon
Icing sugar, for dusting

Roll out the pastry thinly on a lightly floured surface and use it to line a lightly greased 26cm, 4cm-deep loose-bottomed flan tin. Prick the base here and there with a fork and chill for 20 minutes. Preheat the oven to 200°C/gas 6. Line the pastry case with a sheet of crumpled greaseproof paper and a thin layer of baking beans and bake blind for 12–15 minutes or until the edges are biscuit-coloured. Carefully remove the paper and beans and return to the oven for 5 minutes. Remove, brush the inside of the case with a little beaten egg and return to the oven once more for 2–3 minutes until richly golden. Remove and set to one side. Lower the oven temperature to 180°C/gas 4.

Put the *membrillo* into a small pan with the lemon juice and 1½ tablespoons of water and warm over a low heat, stirring, until it has melted. If using jam, simply warm through if necessary, without the lemon juice or water, until spreadable. Spread over the base of the baked pastry case.

For the filling, put the almonds into a food processor and grind briefly until chopped. Add the flour and grind once more until fine.

Break the eggs into a large mixing bowl, add the sugar and whisk together with a hand-held electric whisk for 5 minutes or until thick and moussey and the mixture leaves a trail behind when dribbled back over the surface from the beaters. Whisk in the lemon zest and cinnamon, then fold in the ground almond mixture.

Pour the mixture into the pastry case and bake for 35–40 minutes, covering with a sheet of foil if it starts to brown too quickly, until a skewer pushed into the centre comes out clean. Remove from the oven and leave to cool. Remove from the tin, dust heavily with icing sugar and serve, cut into wedges.

JUNKET with HONEY
Cuajada SERVES 6

The cheese Idiazabal is almost as distinctive a symbol of Basque nationalism as the language itself. I went to the town of Ordizia to visit the market there, which is like a Palladian church with its Romanesque pillars and high roof. I remember doing a slightly over-the-top piece to camera saying something like any artisan produce you bought at that market would inevitably seem like the best you'd ever purchased because of the splendour of the place. Thus this ewe's milk cheese, when slivers of the fresh, matured and aged were presented to me, seemed up there with the cheeses of Corsica in terms of character. I bought a kilo of the fresh and the mature on the spot, a jar of chestnut honey, two jars of chillies pickled in vinegar, a slab of the extremely dense cornbread, and I couldn't resist some homemade membrillo set in a recycled tin can. I was also tempted by the Tolosa black beans and, as ever, by the local chorizo, *txorizoa*. I don't know whether it was the proliferation of 't', 'k' and 'x' in every word, or the unusual produce, but even the vegetables looked especially appetizing. After that, I just had to visit an Idiazabal maker, outside the town of Olaberria. What really struck me there was the making of *cuajada* (*mamia* in Basque), by Amelia Jaureqin in her tiny farmhouse kitchen. She used a natural rennet made from the stomach of lambs that had died during or soon after birth, and the milk from her *latxa* ewes. There's something a bit off-putting about the thought of junket made from milk that had been curdled using an enzyme from the stomach, so when the *cuajada* came out of the fridge in its terracotta pots I was expecting to give a forced smile and a polite comment, and yet it was the very heart of fresh milk, cold and silky smooth, the sort of texture you always hope *panna cotta* will have but never quite does. It was accompanied by a sprinkling of granulated sugar, but it's also lovely with honey or Demerara sugar.

1 litre full-cream milk
    (unpasteurized if you can get it)
1 tsp bottled rennet
Clear honey, granulated sugar
    or Demerara sugar, to serve

Pour the milk into a heavy-based pan and warm through very briefly over a low heat until it reaches 37°C. Quickly remove the pan from the heat and pour the milk into 6 terracotta *cuajada* pots or 200ml glass tumblers.

Using a pipette or a very keen eye, add an equal amount of the teaspoon of rennet to each pot and quickly stir it in with the handle of a spoon. Chill overnight until cold and set. Serve drizzled with honey or sprinkled with sugar.

MATILDE'S
TURRÓN CUAJADA

SERVES 4

Matilde Sulian Perrero lives in Tronchón, a small picturesque village just a few miles from Morella, in Valencia. Here, she cooks daily and serves her food up to locals and visitors alike in various dining rooms dotted around her home. This was on offer the day I was there and seemed to me near perfect; it left me marvelling at how good the Spanish are at desserts. You can get *turrón*, which is a Spanish version of nougat, from importers such as Brindisa (see page 314).

500ml full-cream milk
(unpasteurized if you can get it)
150g soft *turrón blando*, very
thinly sliced
25g caster sugar
½ tsp bottled rennet

Put the milk and *turrón* into a pan and warm very gently, stirring from time to time, until it has melted. Stir in the sugar, then continue as for the recipe on page 282.

FENNEL SEED FRITTERS
with THICK HOT CHOCOLATE

Buñuelos con chocolate SERVES 4

Buñuelos, or *bunyols* in Catalan, are addictive little balls of batter, well flavoured with fennel seed, which are deep-fried, rolled in sugar and served with small cups of thick hot chocolate for dunking. You can also fill them with pastry cream if you wish. Make the pastry cream according to the instructions on page 288, but without the cream cheese, and pipe some into each freshly cooked fritter before rolling them in the sugar.

Sunflower oil, for deep-frying
65g butter
1 tsp fennel seeds
120g plain flour
2 tsp caster sugar, plus 100g
     for coating
4 medium free-range eggs,
     beaten
Salt

FOR THE HOT CHOCOLATE:
225ml full-cream milk
¼ tsp ground cinnamon
100g good quality plain chocolate,
     with 70% cocoa solids
1 tbsp cornflour
4 tbsp sweetened condensed milk

For the fritters, heat some oil for deep-frying to 190°C. Meanwhile, put the butter and 250ml cold water into a medium-sized saucepan. Leave over a low heat until the butter has melted. Finely grind the fennel seeds in a mortar or briefly in a spice grinder. Mix into the flour with the sugar and ¼ teaspoon of salt.

When the butter has melted, increase the heat and bring quickly to the boil. Add the flour, take the pan off the heat and beat vigorously with a wooden spoon until the mixture is smooth and leaves the sides of the pan. Leave to cool for a few minutes, then gradually beat in enough of the egg to make a smooth, glossy paste with a dropping consistency. You might not need to add it all.

For the hot chocolate, put the milk, 225ml water and the ground cinnamon into a saucepan and bring to the boil. Take off the heat, break in the chocolate and stir until smooth. Mix the cornflour with 2 teaspoons of cold water. Stir into the hot chocolate together with the condensed milk and set to one side.

Drop 4–5 heaped teaspoons of the fritter batter at a time, spaced well apart, into the hot oil and leave them to cook for 7 minutes, turning them over now and then. They will continuously puff up and get bigger as they cook. When they have stopped expanding, the sizzling noises have stopped and they are nicely golden all over, they are ready. Lift them out with a slotted spoon onto a tray lined with plenty of kitchen paper and leave to drain briefly, then roll in caster sugar. Return the hot chocolate to a medium heat and cook gently, stirring, until smooth and thick. Pour into small cups and serve straight away with the fritters.

SPANISH TOASTED ALMOND and LEMON MERINGUES

Soplillos de almendras y limón MAKES ABOUT 16–18

Drinking coffee is almost as important a ritual to the Spanish as it is to the Italians, so naturally they adore anything sweet to go with a café con leche or a cortado (an espresso with a drop of steamed milk, served in a small glass). They are particularly fond of meringues and this is one of the most popular flavourings. They are very nice served with some whipped cream, or even Cornish clotted cream.

200g blanched almonds
150g very fresh, free-range egg whites (about 4 medium)
150g caster sugar
150g icing sugar, from a newly opened packet, sifted
Finely grated zest of 1 lemon

Preheat the oven to 200°C/gas 6. Spread the almonds on a baking tray and roast for 6–8 minutes until lightly golden. Remove and leave to cool, then roughly chop by hand into pieces about the size of pine kernels.

Lower the oven temperature to 110°C/gas ¼. Line 2 large, heavy-duty baking sheets with non-stick baking paper.

Put the egg whites into a large, spotlessly clean china, glass or metal mixing bowl and whisk with a hand-held electric mixer until they form stiff peaks.

With the hand mixer still going, add the caster sugar 1 dessertspoonful at a time, whisking for about 10 seconds between each addition. When you have added it all, the mixture should be stiff and glossy.

Next, sift over one-third of the icing sugar and gently fold in with a large metal spoon. Repeat twice more, taking care not to over-mix. The finished mixture should look very smooth and airy. Gently fold in the toasted chopped almonds and lemon zest.

Using 2 large metal serving spoons, scoop up a generous amount of the mixture with one, and use the other to scrape it off onto the paper-lined tray. Leave a good 8cm between each one to allow them plenty of room to expand. Shape each spoonful into a tennis-ball-sized meringue then swirl the tops a little with the back of the spoon.

Slide them into the oven and bake for 1¼–1½ hours, until they are crisp and dry and sound hollow when tapped on the base. Remove from the oven and leave to go cold. They can be stored in an airtight container for up to 2 weeks.

A MILLEFEUILLE of ORANGE SCENTED PASTRY CREAM

Milhojas SERVES 8

Milhojas is the Spanish version of a millefeuille. I have memories of making a millefeuille in a practical pastry exam at Camborne College about thirty-five years ago, where everything had to be neatly squared off and covered with melted white fondant on which thin contrasting lines of melted brown fondant were to be piped, then feathered by dragging a skewer across in opposite directions. I just scraped through the exam. I remember the City and Guilds examiner being incredulous that I took a timer in. I think to start with he thought it was illegal. Doing that and icing Christmas cakes are not my forte, so I took to the Spanish version with great gusto. Basically all you need to do is to bake three rectangles of puff pastry (and it even comes ready-rolled these days), one topped with flaked almonds, layer them with pastry cream flavoured with orange, and then dust with icing sugar. That's what a lot of Spanish patisserie is like, much more homemade-looking, which is what appeals to me.

1 x 375g packet ready-rolled
　　puff pastry
1 free-range egg white
1 heaped tbsp flaked almonds
2 tbsp caster sugar
1 tsp icing sugar

FOR THE PASTRY CREAM:
2 large free-range egg yolks
Finely grated zest of ½ lemon
110g caster sugar
20g plain flour
20g cornflour
300ml full-cream milk
Finely grated zest of 1 large orange
150ml double cream

For the pastry cream, mix the egg yolks, lemon zest, sugar, plain flour, cornflour and 3 tablespoons of the milk together in a mixing bowl until smooth. Bring the rest of the milk to the boil in a non-stick pan. Gradually beat the hot milk into the egg yolk mixture, then return the mixture to the pan and cook over a medium heat, whisking all the time, until smooth and very thick. Simmer gently for 2 minutes, stirring, then remove from the heat, spoon into a bowl and press a sheet of cling film onto the surface to prevent it from forming a skin. Leave to go cold, then chill until needed.

Preheat the oven to 200°C/gas 6. Unroll the sheet of pastry and cut it across into three rectangles, approximately 11cm x 28cm, but this will all depend on the brand of pastry that you use. Put side by side onto a large, greased baking sheet, and chill for 20 minutes.

Beat the egg white until slightly frothy and brush over the pastry rectangles, taking care not to let any run over the edges or it will stop the pastry from puffing up. Scatter the flaked almonds over one rectangle, sprinkle the caster sugar evenly over all three and bake for 20 minutes until risen and golden. Remove from the oven, transfer to a wire rack and leave to cool.

Shortly before serving, beat the pastry cream to loosen it a little, then beat in the orange zest. Whip the cream into soft peaks and gently fold in.

Take the 2 plain pastry rectangles and press down on them lightly to flatten slightly. Spread each one with half the pastry cream, then place one on top of the other. Place the almond-coated rectangle on top, dust lightly with the icing sugar and cut across into pieces with a sharp serrated knife to serve.

ORANGE CARAMEL CREAMS

Flan de naranja SERVES 6–8

'Flan', or crème caramel as we know it, is Spain's national pudding. This one, however, from the Valencia region, is made with orange juice instead of milk, and is yet still deliciously creamy with an intense flavour of orange.

4 large oranges
300g caster sugar
14 large free-range egg yolks
2 large free-range eggs

FOR THE CARAMEL:
100g caster sugar
45ml water

Preheat the oven to 160°C/gas 3. Put six 175ml pudding basins or eight dariole moulds into a small roasting tin and bring a kettle full of water to the boil.

For the caramel, put the sugar and water into a small, heavy-based pan and leave over a very low heat until the sugar has completely dissolved. Then increase the heat to high and leave to boil rapidly, without stirring, until the syrup has turned into a brick-red caramel. Remove from the heat and quickly pour a little into the base of each dish, twisting to coat the bottom and slightly up the sides. Be careful because the dishes might be hot.

Finely grate the zest from 2 of the oranges, then squeeze the juice from them all and measure 400ml into a pan. Add the orange zest and caster sugar and bring to the boil over a low heat, stirring now and then to dissolve the sugar.

Meanwhile, put the egg yolks and whole eggs into a mixing bowl and whisk together. When the orange juice comes to the boil, turn down the heat slightly and simmer rapidly for 2 minutes. Pour the mixture onto the eggs, stirring, then strain through a fine sieve into a large jug.

Pour the mixture equally into each dish and pour boiling water around them to come two-thirds of the way up the sides of the dishes. Bake for 20 minutes for the pudding basins, 15 minutes for the dariole moulds, then remove from the oven and lift out of the water. Cover and chill for at least 4 hours or overnight. To serve, carefully invert each dish onto a small serving plate and pour some of the caramel syrup around each one. If too much caramel has stuck to the base of the pots, put them back into a small roasting tin, pour boiling water into the tin and leave until it has melted.

APPLE TARTS with a CHEESE PASTRY CREAM

Tarta de manzana MAKES 8 TARTLETS

As far as I can remember, I had one of these little apple tarts in Tudella while waiting for Floren to take me off to his *huerta* to cook *menestra* next to his artichokes (see page 111). The thing that really interested me about it was the pastry cream, which seemed to have a slightly cheesy flavour to it. I came back and described it to Debbie, who is the queen of all desserts. She suggested beating some cream cheese into a simple crème patissiere and poaching slices of apple in apple juice flavoured with cloves and nutmeg for the top.

1 smaller quantity *Sweet pastry*
  (see page 307)
75g white chocolate

FOR THE APPLES:
400ml pressed apple juice
3 tbsp caster sugar
2 cloves
¼ tsp freshly grated nutmeg
4 small dessert apples,
  such as Cox's

FOR THE CHEESY
  PASTRY CREAM:
2 large free-range egg yolks
Finely grated zest of ½ lemon
60g caster sugar
20g plain flour
20g cornflour
300ml full-cream milk
100g full-fat cream cheese

FOR THE BUTTERSCOTCH
  GLAZE:
75g light soft brown sugar
2 tbsp single cream
15g butter
Pinch of salt

Preheat the oven to 200°C/gas 6. Briefly re-knead the pastry, then cut into 8 pieces. Roll each piece out on a lightly floured work surface to a 3mm thickness and use to line eight lightly buttered, 8cm loose-bottomed tartlet tins. Chill in the fridge for 20 minutes. Prick the bases with a fork and line with squares of crumpled greaseproof paper and a thin layer of baking beans. Bake the tartlet cases for 10 minutes or until the edges are biscuit-coloured. Carefully remove the paper and beans and return the tartlets to the oven for 2–3 minutes or until golden brown. Remove and leave to cool. Meanwhile, break the white chocolate into a small heatproof bowl. Bring 3cm of water to the boil in a small pan, remove from the heat and rest the bowl of chocolate on top. When it has melted, brush a very thin layer of chocolate over the inside of each tartlet case. Leave to cool and set.

Put the apple juice, sugar, cloves and nutmeg into a wide shallow pan and simmer until reduced by half. Quarter, core and peel the apples, thinly slice them into the syrup and simmer for 1 minute. Leave to cool in the syrup.

For the cheesy pastry cream, mix the egg yolks, lemon zest, sugar, plain flour, cornflour and 2 tablespoons of the milk together in a mixing bowl until smooth. Bring the rest of the milk to the boil in a non-stick pan. Gradually beat into the egg yolk mixture, return the mixture to the pan and stir over a medium heat, until smooth and thick. Simmer gently for 2 minutes, stirring, then spoon into a bowl and press a sheet of cling film onto the surface to prevent it from forming a skin. Cool, then chill until needed.

To assemble the tarts, put the cream cheese into a mixing bowl and beat with an electric hand-held whisk for a minute or two until smooth and light. Gradually beat in the chilled pastry cream. Spoon the mixture into the tartlet cases and lightly level the tops. Lift the apple slices out of the syrup and arrange them, slightly overlapping, over the top of the pastry cream.

For the butterscotch glaze, put all the ingredients into a small pan and heat gently until the sugar has dissolved. Brush the mixture over the top of the apples and leave to cool, then serve.

APPLE, CINNAMON and CIDER CAKE

Tarta de manzana, canela y sidre SERVES 8–10

What I like about Asturias above all is the people's enormous affection for their locally produced cider, and there could be no better celebration of that than this sponge cake, layered with apples tossed with cinnamon, sugar, vanilla, cream and cider, then baked and drizzled with a glacé-style icing made from sugar and reduced cider. Make sure you use a good quality fruity, vintage cider; it will make all the difference to the flavour.

3 large dessert apples, such
   as Braeburn or Cox's
3 tbsp cider
½ tsp ground cinnamon
40g caster sugar, plus 1 teaspoon
1 tsp good quality vanilla extract
3 tbsp double cream

FOR THE SPONGE:
175g butter, at room temperature
75g light soft brown sugar
75g caster sugar
3 medium free-range eggs,
   lightly beaten
150g plain flour
½ tsp ground cinnamon
1 tsp baking powder
50g ground almonds
1–2 tbsp cider

FOR THE GLAZE:
300ml cider
6 tbsp icing sugar

Preheat the oven to 190°C/gas 5. Grease and line the base of a round 23cm loose-bottomed or clip-sided cake tin with greaseproof paper.

Quarter, core and peel the apples and slice them thinly into a bowl. Stir in the cider, cinnamon, sugar, vanilla extract and cream.

For the sponge, cream the butter and both sugars together in a mixing bowl using an electric hand whisk for 5 minutes until light and fluffy. Gradually beat in the eggs, adding a tablespoon of flour with the last couple of additions to prevent curdling. Strain off any liquid from the apples and beat it into the mixture, then sift over the flour, cinnamon and baking powder and gently fold in. Stir in the ground almonds and enough cider to give a dropping consistency.

Spoon half the sponge mixture into the prepared tin and scatter over half the apples in a thin even layer. Spoon over the remainder of the sponge mixture, then scatter over the remaining apple slices. Sprinkle lightly with the teaspoon of sugar.

Place on the middle shelf of the oven and bake for about 50 minutes until a deep golden brown and cooked through. A skewer pushed into the centre of the cake should come away clean. Leave to cool in the tin for 10 minutes, then remove and leave to cool.

For the glaze, put the cider into a small pan and boil rapidly until reduced to 2 tablespoons. Tip into a small bowl and leave to cool. Beat in the icing sugar, drizzle over the cake and leave for a few minutes to set. Serve cut into wedges.

BASQUE SOUR CHERRY TART

Pastel vasco MAKES 1 X 23CM TART TO SERVE 8–12

Go into any bakery in the Basque Country and they will no doubt have these little pastry tarts on sale, filled with sour cherries flavoured with *pacharán*, the local anise-flavoured sloe liqueur, which have a criss-cross design of fine lines marked into the egg-washed top with a fork. What makes them so special is the shortcake-like pastry, which is buttery and crumbly, and only slightly sweet so that it contrasts well with the filling. There's a very nice pastry shop in the Parte Vieja of San Sebastián called Pastelería Otaegui which sells them. With a café con leche they make an excellent breakfast. I have made one large tart for ease, but do make eight smaller tartlets if you wish.

FOR THE PASTRY:
210g plain flour, plus extra
    for dusting
40g ground almonds
1 tsp baking powder
¼ tsp salt
150g caster sugar
115g butter, at room temperature,
    plus extra for greasing
1 large free-range egg
1 large free-range egg yolk
1 tsp vanilla extract

FOR THE FILLING:
250g good quality sour or
    morello cherry conserve
2 tsp anise-flavoured liqueur,
    such as Pernod
Finely grated zest of 1 small lemon

FOR THE GLAZE:
1 large free-range egg yolk
1 tsp milk

For the pastry, put the flour, ground almonds, baking powder, salt and sugar into a food processor. Cut the butter into small pieces, add to the flour mixture and process briefly until it looks like breadcrumbs. Beat the whole egg and egg yolk together with the vanilla extract, add the mixture to the bowl and pulse until it just starts to stick together in lumps. Tip onto a lightly floured work surface and knead briefly into a ball. Cut the dough into 2 pieces, one very slightly larger than the other, flatten into thick discs and wrap in clingfilm. Chill for 30 minutes.

Put a baking sheet onto the middle shelf of the oven and preheat it to 180°C/gas 4. Grease a 23cm, 2cm-deep loose-bottomed tart tin. For the filling, mix the cherry conserve with the Pernod and lemon zest. Remove the smaller piece of pastry from the fridge and thinly roll out on a lightly floured surface. Cut out a 23cm disc using the base of the tin as a template. Set to one side.

Roll out the other piece of pastry and cut out a 28cm disc. Use it to line the tart tin. Spread the cherry jam filling evenly over the base, then gently lay the second disc on top of the jam. Brush the edge of the lid with a little water, then fold over the edges of the pastry case and press them together lightly with your fingertips to make a good seal.

Beat the egg yolk with the milk and brush it generously over the surface of the tart. Run the tines of a fork first one way across the surface then the other to create a crosshatch design.

Slide the tart onto the baking sheet and bake for 30 minutes or until the pastry is richly golden. Remove from the oven and leave to cool for 10 minutes. Remove from the tin and leave to cool on a wire rack. Serve cut into thin wedges.

ORANGE BLOSSOM WATER ICE CREAM

Helado de agua de azahar SERVES 8

I have to admit this recipe is not as good as Joaquín Liriano's. Joaquín gave up architecture to open his artisan ice-cream business – Heladeria la Fiorentina in Calle Zaragoza in Seville – and I doubt if you'd find anywhere more inspired in the world. Some of his flavours read like Heston Blumenthal, things such as lemon sorbet with mint and manzanilla, chamomile sorbet, watermelon and rosemary sorbet, French toast ice cream, sweet pine-nut ice cream. To me, the orange blossom water ice cream was the star. He described it as summoning up the colours and scents of Seville in one dish. He was such an artist that it seemed in rather bad taste to ask him for the recipe. Still, in trying to get near to what he'd created, I managed to produce a pretty fine ice cream. I suspect my main failing lies in not having got hold of the absolutely very best orange blossom water, but you can get very good ones from large supermarkets or online.

150g caster sugar
3 large nicely tart oranges
150ml double cream
2 tsp orange blossom water
50g good-quality chopped
    candied orange peel

Put the sugar and 120ml water into a pan and bring slowly to the boil, stirring occasionally to dissolve the sugar. Remove from the heat and leave to cool. Meanwhile, finely grate the zest from 2 of the oranges and then juice all 3. If they are not very tart, use a little lemon juice too. Stir the orange zest and 300ml of the strained juice into the syrup, cover and chill overnight.

The next day, strain the orange syrup mixture to remove the zest, then stir in the double cream and the orange blossom water.

Churn the mixture in an ice-cream maker, adding the candied peel 2–3 minutes before the end of churning, then transfer to a rigid plastic container and freeze. If you do not have an ice-cream maker, pour the mixture into a shallow plastic container and freeze until almost solid. Scrape it into a food processor and blend until smooth, then return it to the container and freeze once more. Repeat this 2–3 times until the mixture is very smooth. Stir in the chopped candied peel and freeze, ideally overnight, until very firm.

MALAGA RAISIN ICE CREAM
with PEDRO XIMÉNEZ SHERRY

SERVES 8

We've long had a simple vanilla ice cream on the menu at the Seafood Restaurant, which we serve with the unctuous Pedro Ximénez sherry, so rich and sweet that it is viscous and flows over the ice cream like olive oil. I thought it would be a great idea to expand on the theme and make the same ice cream with some of the famous raisins from Malaga steeped in sherry too, and I have to say it is pretty good.

2 fresh vanilla pods
400ml full-cream milk
6 large free-range egg yolks
200g caster sugar
500ml double cream
100g Malaga raisins
4 tbsp Pedro Ximénez sherry,
     plus extra to serve

Slit open the vanilla pods lengthways and scrape out the seeds with the tip of a knife. Put the milk and the vanilla pods into a non-stick pan and bring to the boil, then remove from the heat and set aside for 30 minutes to infuse the milk with the flavour of the vanilla.

Put the egg yolks, vanilla seeds and caster sugar into a mixing bowl and, using an electric hand-held whisk, whisk for 3 minutes or until pale and moussey. Bring the milk back to the boil, strain onto the egg yolk mixture and mix until well combined. Return to the pan and cook over a low heat, stirring, for 3–4 minutes or until the mixture lightly coats the back of a wooden spoon, but do not let the mixture boil or it will scramble. Remove from heat and set aside to cool slightly, then stir in the cream. Cover and chill overnight.

Put the raisins and sherry into a small bowl, cover and leave to soak at room temperature for at least 2 hours.

Either churn the mixture in your ice-cream machine, or pour it into a shallow container and freeze until almost solid. Scrape the mixture either into a bowl or a food processor and beat until smooth, then return to the box and freeze once more. Repeat this 2–3 times more until the mixture is very smooth. Stir in the soaked raisins and any remaining liquid just before you finish churning or freezing for the last time.

To serve, scoop some of the ice cream into glasses or bowls and pour 1 tablespoon of Pedro Ximénez sherry over the top.

CARAMEL BAKED CUSTARD

Flan SERVES 8

When I first saw 'flan' on the menu in a Spanish restaurant I avoided it because I thought it was going to be some kind of stodgy tart, and indeed I didn't try one until a pepper-grower's wife in Extremadura gave me a slice after a bowl of her red pepper, tomato and pimentón soup (see page 228). Only then did I realize it was a crème caramel. 'Crème caramel' is a pretty thing to say and conjures up an image of what you are going to get. I have a friend with a Burmese cat called Caramel. 'Flan' doesn't do it for me, but it's all part of that take-it-or-leave-it attitude that I mentioned in the introduction to the book. As it happens, flan is as good a pudding as you will find anywhere, and I especially like the way they tend to cook it in a tray and serve it up in a slice.

1 litre full-cream milk
8 large free-range eggs
4 large free-range egg yolks
200g caster sugar
2 tsp vanilla extract

FOR THE CARAMEL:
175g caster sugar
75ml water

Preheat the oven to 160°C/gas 3 and bring a kettle full of water to the boil. Place a 1.5-litre shallow rectangular baking dish (one that measures about 29cm x 20cm x 5cm deep as this will give your custard about the right depth) in a roasting tin. Slide it into the oven to warm. This will prevent it from cracking when you pour in the boiling hot caramel.

For the caramel, put the sugar and water into a heavy-based pan and leave over a very low heat, swirling the pan every now and then, until the sugar has completely dissolved. Then increase the heat to high and leave to boil rapidly, without stirring, until the syrup has turned into a brick-red caramel. Quickly remove from the heat and pour into the warmed baking dish, then tilt the dish forwards and backwards until the base is coated in an even layer.

Bring the milk to the boil in another pan. Meanwhile, break the eggs into a large mixing bowl, add the egg yolks, sugar and vanilla extract and whisk together lightly to break up the eggs and mix in the sugar, but try not to incorporate too much air.

Once the milk has boiled, take off the heat and leave to cool for 1 minute. Whisk into the eggs, then strain the mixture through a sieve into the baking dish. Slide the roasting tin onto the middle shelf of the oven and pour hot water from the kettle into the roasting tin until it comes halfway up the sides of the dish. Bake for 45–50 minutes until almost set but still slightly wobbly in the centre. It will continue to firm up as it cools.

Carefully remove from the oven and lift the baking dish out of the hot water. Leave to cool, then cover and refrigerate overnight.

To serve, carefully run a round-bladed knife around the edge of the custard, then cut it lengthways in half and across into 8 rectangular slices. Carefully lift the pieces out with a palette knife, invert onto serving plates and spoon over plenty of the caramel syrup.

CINNAMON, ORANGE and LEMON CUSTARDS with a BURNT SUGAR CRUST

Crema catalana SERVES 6

It almost goes without saying that if you are going to make crema catalana you must have the proper little terracotta dishes to make it in. The dishes ensure you get the right proportion of crisp caramel topping to set custard underneath. We British share with the Spanish an enthusiasm for all manner of custard dishes, such as *flan* (opposite) and *leche frite* (see page 302). It's hard to think of a more elegant dessert than this.

375ml full-cream milk
375ml single or double cream
Finely grated zest of 1 lemon
Finely grated zest of 1 small orange
1 x 5cm cinnamon stick
6 large free-range egg yolks
115g caster sugar, plus 6 heaped
   tbsp extra for the tops
25g cornflour

Put the milk, cream, lemon zest, orange zest and cinnamon stick into a non-stick saucepan. Bring to the boil, then set aside to cool for 1 hour, during which time the flavour of the lemon, orange and cinnamon will infuse the milk.

Put the egg yolks and sugar into a mixing bowl and beat together with a hand-held mixer until thick, pale and creamy. Whisk in the cornflour. Bring the milk back to the boil and strain a little over the egg yolk mixture. Mix together well to loosen it slightly, then strain over and stir in the remainder.

Pour the mixture back into the pan and cook over a low heat, stirring constantly, for 4–5 minutes or until the mixture thickly coats the back of the wooden spoon. Do not let the mixture boil.

Pour the custard into 6 wide, shallow dishes measuring about 10cm across, leave to cool then chill for at least 2 hours or overnight. Leave them uncovered so that a thin skin can form, which will make caramelizing the tops easier the next day.

Just before serving, sprinkle a generous tablespoon of sugar in a thick layer over the surface of each custard. Holding a blowtorch about 5cm away from the surface, caramelize the sugar. Leave to cool briefly then serve, while the topping is still brittle.

CRUNCHY CUSTARD CREAM FRITTERS

Leche frite SERVES 6

The literal translation for this dessert, which originated in the Basque country, is 'fried milk', but it is in fact a very thick vanilla- and lemon-flavoured custard, which is then cut up into small pieces, coated in egg and sometimes breadcrumbs and deep-fried, then dusted in cinnamon sugar. It's quite often just fried without any coating but that can be a bit greasy. I think flour, egg and breadcrumbs make it superb. To me, it's the perfect accompaniment to a café con leche at any time of day.

500ml milk
Finely grated zest of ½ lemon
1 large vanilla pod, split open
   and the seeds scraped out
4 large, free-range egg yolks
100g caster sugar
30g plain flour
40g cornflour
Vegetable oil, for deep-frying

FOR THE CRUNCHY
   COATING:
40g plain flour
2 large free-range eggs, beaten
200g white breadcrumbs,
   made from day-old bread
25g caster sugar
¼ tsp ground cinnamon

Grease a 19cm shallow square baking tin with a little oil. Put the milk, lemon zest, vanilla pod and its seeds into a non-stick pan and bring to the boil. Remove from the heat and set aside for 1 hour so the flavours can infuse the milk.

Put the egg yolks, sugar, flour, cornflour and a small splash of the milk into a bowl and mix to a smooth paste with a wooden spoon. Bring the rest of the milk back to the boil and gradually strain it over the egg yolk mixture, stirring all the time. Return the mixture to a clean pan and place over a medium heat. Cook, stirring, for 5 minutes or until you have a very thick custard. Pour the mixture in the tin and leave to cool, then chill, for a minimum of 2 hours or overnight until really firm.

To finish, turn the set custard out onto a board and cut into 5cm squares, then each square diagonally in half into triangles. Put the flour, beaten eggs and breadcrumbs into 3 shallow dishes.

Heat some oil for deep-frying to 180°C. Dip 4 triangles at a time into the flour, then the beaten egg and then the breadcrumbs, making sure they take on a good coating. Drop them into the hot oil and fry for 2½ minutes or until crisp and golden brown. Remove with a slotted spoon and leave to drain on a tray lined with plenty of kitchen paper.

Mix the caster sugar and cinnamon powder together, sprinkle over both sides of the custard triangles and serve straight away.

THE SPANISH CHEESEBOARD

Manchego is possibly the best known cheese, but much of the country is home to the sheep and goat, and much of northern Spain provides lush grazing for cattle as well. Cheese is generally served on its own, as tapas, maybe with a little sliced chorizo sausage and a few olives, or as a dessert, where the Spanish have a predilection for something sweet to go with it. Fresh fruit such as grapes, apples or figs, membrillo (see page 312) and honey are all popular.

MANCHEGO

A hard ewe's milk cheese from Castilla-La Mancha, which is sold at various stages of maturity: *fresco* (put on sale after about 8 weeks), *semi-curado* (a cheese of up to 6 months old), *curado* (a cheese matured for more than 6 months), and *viejo* or *añejo* (the oldest, matured for anything up to 24 months). It has a slightly waxy rind marked with a tight herring-bone pattern, originally from the esparto grass baskets in which the cheeses were formed, but now re-created with plastic moulds. Inside it has a firm and dry, yet rich and creamy texture, studded with very small, irregular sized holes, with a beautifully nutty, slightly piquant flavour.

TETILLA & SAN SIMON

The two best-known cheeses from the north-western region of Galicia, shaped like a breast. Tetilla is a cow's milk cheese with a thin, slightly ridged yellow exterior and firm, smooth interior with a buttery flavour, not dissimilar to a very young gouda. San Simon is gently smoked, giving it a reddish-brown exterior and slightly woody flavour.

IDIAZÀBAL

This is one of my favourite cheeses. A hard cheese made from ewe's milk with a buttery-rich texture due to a fat content of almost 45 per cent, and a very slightly sweet yet sharp flavour. You can find it smoked, which gives it a darker rind. To carry the *Denominación de Origen* (DO) stamp, the smoking must have been carried out over beech or hawthorn.

TORTA DEL CASAR & LA SERENA

Two ewe's milk cheeses from the region of Extremadura, where a rennet-like agent made from cardoons is used to coagulate the milk. This gives them a pleasing bitterness and a runny, creamy consistency. A round hole is usually cut into the top of a Torta del Casar cheese before the contents are spooned out for eating. Like a really ripe Vacherin Mont d'Or, but possibly even better.

CABRALES & VALDEÓN

The range of mountains running along the coast of north-western Spain, called the Picos de Europa, are a warren of small limestone caves, home to millions of spores which work their way into the cavities of the cheeses stored there, to produce the characteristic irregular blue veins. Cabrales, Spain's most famous blue cheese, is made with varying percentages of cow's, goat's or ewe's milk depending on the season, the best being produced in the spring, and has a sticky orange-yellow rind, a buttery texture and sweet yet piquant flavour. Valdeón, more commonly known as Picos de Europa, is eaten locally with wild honey.

RONCAL

A ewe's milk cheese from Navarra, a hard, close-textured cheese a little like a medium-hard Parmesan, with a pungent aroma and sweet yet punchy almost nutty flavour, which goes very well with some of the local roasted piquillo peppers.

GARROTXA

A relatively new addition to Spain's list of great cheeses, created in the 1980s in the region of Catalonia. It is a semi-hard goat's cheese whose skin is rubbed with charcoal and left to produce a soft, velvety coat, which contrasts beautifully with its smooth and creamy stark white interior.

MATÓ

Another cheese from Catalonia, this time an unsalted fresh curd cheese, traditionally served with honey as the classic dessert *mel y mató*; honey goes well with its slightly tangy flavour.

QUESO IBORES

A goat's cheese from the Extremadura region. First immersed in olive oil, it is rubbed with pimentón to give it a deep red rind. It can also be bought without the pimentón rind and at different maturities (the photo shows a young Ibores with a natural rind and an Ibores con pimentón). The peppery tang of the rind goes well with the slightly sharp, creamy, white interior.

COOKING EQUIPMENT

CAZUELAS & CAZUELITAS

These are wide, shallow, terracotta-red earthenware cooking dishes, glazed on the inside and rough and unfinished on the outside. Spanish cooks like them because they heat evenly, without hot spots, and retain heat long after being removed from the stove. They can be used directly over a flame on a gas hob (though not on an electric hob), where I also like to use a heat diffuser, or in the oven. Cazuelitas are smaller, about 12cm across, ideal for hot tapas that you take straight to the table. Take care not to put a hot cazuela on a cold surface, or ice-cold liquid into a hot cazuela, because it may crack.

PAELLA PANS

I have two, one made from steel and one with an enamelled surface, and both work well on a domestic gas hob. Stainless-steel ones have a naturally non-stick finish and don't rust, but cost twice as much, so I'm happy to give my steel pan a good scrub each time before I use it, and lightly rub it with oil before I put it away. The only problem with a paella pan on a domestic hob is their size, being too large to fit over one burner. I have found that you can cook in one quite easily if you position it over 2 or 4 burners, depending on the configuration of your stove, and give the pan a small turn every few minutes, to ensure the liquid is always at a simmer so the rice cooks evenly.

MORTAR & PESTLE

A standard piece of equipment in the Spanish kitchen, and indispensable, so they say, for obtaining the right consistency for a *picada*, the all-important paste used to thicken soups and stews. But most mortars outside Spain are too small for the job. If you can, go for a granite one from Thailand. I use one that's 17cm deep and 23cm wide; the larger and deeper the better.

CUAJADA POTS

When you are served or buy ready-made cuajada in Spain, it always comes in attractive little terracotta pots. I haven't yet been able to find a supplier in the UK. Cuajada pots hold about 150ml, so any ramekin of the same volume would do.

BASIC RECIPES

FISH STOCK
Makes approx. 1.2 litres
For a deeper-flavoured stock, make this with 500g cheap white fish fillet, cut into 2cm slices, instead of the bones.

1 onion, chopped
1 fennel bulb, chopped
100g celery, sliced
100g carrot, chopped
25g white button mushrooms, sliced
1 sprig of thyme
2.25 litres water
1kg flatfish bones, such as lemon
    sole, brill and plaice

Put all the ingredients except for the fish bones into a large pan, bring just to the boil and simmer for 40 minutes. Add the fish bones (or fillet), bring back to a simmer, skimming off any scum as it rises to the surface, and simmer for a further 20 minutes. Strain through a sieve into a clean pan, and simmer a little longer if necessary until reduced to about 1.2 litres. Use or store as required.

BEEF STOCK
Makes approx. 2.4 litres

2 celery stalks
2 carrots
2 onions
900g shin of beef, cut into small chunks
5 litres water
1 tbsp salt
2 bay leaves
2 thyme sprigs
2 tbsp sunflower oil (darker stock only)
2 tbsp tomato purée (optional, darker
    stock only)

For a lighter-coloured stock, put the vegetables, beef and water into a large pan and bring to the boil, skimming off the scum as it appears. Reduce the heat and simmer for 2 ½ hours, adding the salt and herbs 15 minutes before the end. For a deeper-coloured, richer stock, heat the sunflower oil in the pan, add the vegetables, beef and tomato purée, if using, and fry for 10–15 minutes until nicely browned, before adding the water and continuing as before. Use or store as required.

CHICKEN STOCK
Makes approx. 1.75 litres
If you have them, use the bones from a roasted chicken for a slightly deeper-flavoured stock.

Bones from a 1.5kg uncooked chicken
    or 450g chicken wings or drumsticks
1 large carrot, chopped
2 celery sticks, sliced
2 leeks, cleaned and sliced
2 fresh or dried bay leaves
2 sprigs of thyme
2.25 litres water

Put all the ingredients into a large pan and bring just to the boil, skimming off any scum from the surface as it appears. Leave to simmer very gently for 2 hours – it is important not to let it boil as this will force the fat from even the leanest chicken and make the stock cloudy. Strain the stock through a sieve and leave to simmer a little longer to concentrate in flavour if necessary. Use or store as required.

TOMATO SAUCE
Makes approx. 600ml
You can make this sauce with either fresh tomatoes or canned. If using fresh, make sure they have a good deep colour and are juicy with lots of flavour. Good tomatoes are not always easy to come by – if you can't get good fresh ones, you will get a better-tasting sauce using canned instead.

125ml olive oil
225g onions, finely chopped
2 garlic cloves, crushed
400g skinned chopped tomatoes,
    fresh or from a can
150ml water
3 fresh bay leaves
¾ tsp salt
¾ tsp sugar

Heat the olive oil in a wide shallow pan over a medium heat. Add the onions and garlic and sauté for 15 minutes, stirring every now and then, until soft and sweet and very lightly golden. Add the tomatoes, water, bay leaves, salt and sugar, bring to the boil, lower the heat and leave to simmer very gently, uncovered, stirring now and then, for 45 minutes to 1 hour until it has almost reduced to a purée. Leave to cool slightly then remove the bay leaves, tip into a food processor and blend until smooth. Leave to cool, cover and refrigerate or freeze until needed.

SLOW-COOKED ONION CONFIT
A great standby for dishes that start off with slow-cooked onions in olive oil. It cuts down on the cooking time no end. Keeps for 2–3 weeks.

1.2kg onions, chopped according to the
    recipe in which you want to use them
4 fresh bay leaves, 3 kept whole and
    1 finely shredded
10 black peppercorns
200ml olive oil
2 tsp sea salt flakes

Put the onions into a wide-based pan with the whole and shredded bay leaves, the peppercorns, olive oil and sea salt flakes, and leave to cook over a low heat at a very gentle bubble for 2 hours until they are meltingly soft and sweet. Stir every now and then to make sure they are not sticking to the base of the pan and browning. Leave to cool, then spoon into a container with a lid and refrigerate.

SLOW-COOKED GARLIC
Like the onion confit, this is another good standby to have in the fridge, especially for dishes where you want the taste of sweet but not overly browned garlic. It is much easier to control the caramelization of garlic when it is cooked in a large quantity, in lots of olive oil. Keeps for 2–3 weeks.

125g garlic cloves, roughly chopped
90ml olive oil
¼ tsp salt

Put the garlic and olive oil into a small pan and cook over a very gentle heat for 20 minutes, stirring every now and then, and mashing it up with a potato masher after about 15 minutes, until the garlic is soft and sweet. Season with the salt, leave to cool, then spoon into a container with a lid and refrigerate.

MAYONNAISE (MAHONESA)
Makes 300ml
The Spanish claim to have invented mayonnaise, in the town of Mahón in Menorca. They love it and use it for enriching soups, as a dipping sauce for asparagus or fried squid, for dressing salads, and to accompany cooked prawns and lobster. Traditionally, it's made with olive oil, but this recipe can be made with any oil you choose. You can make it in a liquidizer or by hand. When made mechanically, you use a whole egg and the result is lighter, while mayonnaise made by hand is softer and richer.

1 egg or 2 egg yolks
2 tsp white wine vinegar
½ tsp salt
1 tsp Dijon mustard
300ml oil such as sunflower, olive oil
    or a mixture of the two

To make the mayonnaise by hand:
Make sure all the ingredients are at room temperature before you start. Put the egg yolks, vinegar, mustard and salt into a mixing bowl and then rest the bowl on a cloth to stop it slipping. Using a wire whisk or an electric hand mixer on medium speed, lightly whisk to break the yolks, then gradually beat the oil into the egg mixture a little at a time, until you have incorporated it all.

To make the mayonnaise in a machine:
Put the whole egg, vinegar, salt and mustard into a liquidizer or food processor. Turn on the machine and then slowly add the oil through the hole in the lid until you have a thick emulsion.

ALIOLI
Makes approx. 175ml
This is a punchy sauce, traditionally made from just olive oil and garlic, but an egg yolk is often added to make the mixture more stable. It is usually served with fish or stirred into fish stews but also goes well with rice dishes, grilled lamb and vegetables.

4 unpeeled garlic cloves
½ tsp salt
1 medium egg yolk
175ml extra virgin olive oil

Put the garlic cloves onto a chopping board and crush them under the blade of a large knife. Remove the papery skins, sprinkle the garlic with the salt and work into a smooth paste using the knife blade. Scrape the garlic paste into a bowl and add the egg yolk. Whisk everything together and then very gradually whisk in the olive oil (as described above) to make a thick mayonnaise-like mixture.

ROASTED RED PEPPERS
There are 3 ways to roast peppers:
Either: spear the stalk end of each pepper on a fork and turn it over in the flame of a gas burner or blowtorch until the skin has blistered and blackened.
Or: roast the peppers at 220°C/gas 7 for 20–25 minutes, turning over halfway through, until the skin is black.
Or: cook the peppers on a barbecue over a high heat for 15–20 minutes, turning them every now and then until the skins have charred black. Leave them to cool then remove and discard the stalk, skin and seeds. The flesh is now ready to use.

ROMESCO SAUCE
Makes approx. 300ml
This is another classic Spanish sauce, originating in Tarragona in Catalonia, and most often served alongside seafood but also used to thicken seafood stews. There are many versions – this is one I have been making for years. Do replace the hazelnuts with blanched almonds if you wish.

1 dried ñora pepper
225g small vine-ripened tomatoes, halved
15g blanched hazelnuts
120ml olive oil
4 fat garlic cloves, peeled
15g slice of day-old white bread, crusts removed
A pinch of crushed dried chilli flakes
1 tbsp sherry vinegar
½ tsp salt
Freshly ground black pepper

Remove the stalk from the dried pepper, slit it open and remove all the seeds. Soak the pepper in hot water for 1 hour.
   Meanwhile, preheat the oven to 200°C/gas 6. Put the tomatoes into a small roasting tin and roast for 20 minutes. Add the nuts to the tin and roast for a further 5–6 minutes or until the nuts are lightly golden brown. Leave to cool, then remove the skins from the tomatoes.
   Heat 2 tablespoons of the olive oil in a frying pan, add the garlic cloves and slice of bread and fry them gently, until golden brown on both sides. Leave to cool, then break the bread into the bowl of a food processor, and add the garlic and hazelnuts. Drain the soaked pepper, scrape the flesh away from the skin and add to the food processor with the roasted tomatoes, chilli flakes, sherry vinegar, salt and some black pepper. Blend until smooth, then, with the motor still running, gradually pour in the rest of the olive oil to produce a mayonnaise-like sauce.

HOME-SALTED FRESH COD
Sprinkle salt over the base of a plastic container in a layer 1cm thick. Put a thick piece of unskinned cod fillet (taken from the head end of a large fish) on top and completely cover it in another thick layer of salt. Cover and refrigerate overnight. By the next day the salt will have turned to brine. Remove the cod and rinse it under cold water. Cover with fresh water and leave it to soak for 1 hour. It is now ready to use.

RICH SHORTCRUST PASTRY
100g plain flour
¼ tsp salt
40g chilled butter, cut into pieces
25g chilled lard, cut into pieces
1–1½ tbsp cold water

Sift the flour and salt into a food processor or a mixing bowl. Add the pieces of chilled butter and lard and work together until the mixture looks like fine breadcrumbs. Stir in the water with a round-bladed knife until it comes together into a ball, turn out onto a lightly floured work surface and knead briefly until smooth. Use as required.

SWEET PASTRY
Sufficient for a 23cm, 4cm-deep flan tin or 8 x 8cm shallow tartlet cases:
175g plain flour
pinch of salt
50g icing sugar
100g chilled butter, cut into small pieces
1 large egg yolk
1–1½ tsp cold water

Sufficient for a 26cm, 4cm-deep flan tin:
250g plain flour
¼ tsp salt
75g icing sugar
150g chilled butter, cut into small pieces
2 medium egg yolks
1 tbsp cold water

Sift the flour, salt and icing sugar into a food processor or a bowl, add the pieces of chilled butter and work together briefly, either in the food processor or with your fingertips, until the mixture looks like fine breadcrumbs. Tip the mixture into a bowl and stir in the egg yolk(s) and enough water until the mixture starts to come together into a ball. Turn out onto a lightly floured surface and knead briefly until smooth. Use as required.

THE SPANISH LARDER

ALMONDS (*almendras*)

Almonds are an important food in Spain, not only as a snack to serve with drinks, but as an ingredient in the all-important picadas for thickening sauces and stews, and in cakes, pastries, desserts and sweetmeats, particularly marzipan. Most almonds sold in the UK are from America and, in my opinion, don't have the flavour or texture of the Spanish ones. The marcona variety, which is shorter, rounder, sweeter and softer in texture than some other varieties, originated in Spain and is a good one to choose, especially for the almond tart on page 279. The recipes in this book call for blanched almonds, not those with their ridged brown skins still on, and make sure they are fresh. Nuts go stale quickly and their flavour will spoil a dish.

BACON (*panceta* or *baicon*)

Panceta, like pancetta in Italy, is the Spanish equivalent of streaky bacon, the cured, and sometimes smoked, belly of the pig. It is a common ingredient in Spanish cooking, especially in *cocido*, bean dishes and other stews. If you need one large piece, as for the *fabada* on page 70, go to a butcher who slices his own bacon and ask him to cut you off a bit. Ready-prepared pancetta or bacon lardons from the supermarket are perfect for dishes that use chopped bacon.

BEANS, DRIED (*alubias secas*)

No longer just the food of the poor, dried beans are an important and much-loved ingredient in Spain, and every region has its local varieties and favourites, particularly in the north where the bean has almost a cult status. The new season's dried beans, which become available in autumn, are much sought after and can command quite high prices. Beans also store very well through the winter months (although the older they get, the longer they need to cook, and they lose some of their prized creamy texture). In Asturias, look out for *fabes asturianes*, a white bean of remarkable tenderness, or the *fabes de la granja* ('beans from the farm'), another popular but rather expensive bean, about the size of the first joint of a little finger and with a buttery, almost melt-in-the-mouth texture, favoured for use in their classic bean stew, *fabada*. The *alubia planchada* is an all-purpose, small dried white bean which is good in such dishes as the Galician soup *Caldo Gallego*, on page 28. The *garrofó* bean, should you be able to find it, is a large white bean used in the classic Valencian paella, but the *judión blanco* and *judión de la granja*, large creamy-white butter beans, which once soaked measure almost 5cm across, are also commonly used. They have a creamy flavour and firm texture, and hold their shape beautifully once cooked. However, our own white haricot and butter beans and Italian cannellini beans all make adequate substitutes. All dried beans need to be soaked in copious amounts of cold water for at least 12 hours before using them.

BEANS, FRESH (*judias verdes*)

Fresh green beans are popular in Spanish cooking. The long flat green bean, known locally as the *ferraura* and rather like our own runner bean, is an important ingredient in the traditional Valencian paella. Freshly podded beans, those that then go on to be dried, are also popular but cannot take the place of dried beans in any of the recipes.

BREAD (*pan*)

Bread is the most important foodstuff of Spain. No meal would be complete without it and no leftover pieces are ever wasted. Day-old and dried bread have many uses in the Spanish kitchen. Spanish bread varies from area to area and region to region, but is usually white, although you sometimes come across wholemeal loaves in certain areas of the north. It is freshly baked every day, and sold first thing in the morning from the local *panadería*. The best bread for the recipes in this book is any rustic, artisan bread made from unbleached flour, which produces a hard crust and a moist, dense, firm crumb, packed full of wheaty flavour.

BUTIFARRA NEGRA

Catalan sausage, made from pork and pig's blood together with spices and garlic. It is not easy to come by outside Spain, but our own black pudding is an adequate substitute.

CHICKPEAS (*garbanzos*)

All dried pulses are important to the Spanish, and especially the chickpea, which was around long before the potato arrived from the new world and once even rivalled bread as one of the most common foodstuffs. The plants thrived on poor soil and could adapt well to the Spanish climate. Not only are they an essential part of the famous dinner called the cocido, as well as many other *platos de cuchara* (stew-like dishes to be eaten with a spoon), but they are regularly sold cooked and salted as a tapas or fiesta-time snack. The most famous are the *garbanzos de Liébana* of Catalonia and those from Extremadura and Andalucía, but any type of dried chickpea will be fine for the recipes in this book. One of the most economical ways to buy them is in bulk from an Indian grocery store. As with other types of dried bean, they need to be soaked in plenty of water for at least 12 hours before cooking. Don't be tempted to use canned chickpeas; freshly cooked chickpeas are superior in taste and texture.

CHORIZO

The chorizo, the most famous of Spanish sausages, is thought to have originated in Extremadura, but was initially a rather pale affair. It was not until the conquistadors introduced the red pepper from the new world that it became what it is today, a dark red-hued coarse pork sausage, flavoured with garlic and lots of pimentón. It comes in various types, shapes and sizes: fresh or cured then air-dried, thick or thin, plain or smoked, spicy hot (*picante*) or mild (*dulce*), hard and lean for serving as tapas or softer and more fatty for frying and using in other dishes. Chorizos vary from region to region but, as a general rule, the harder, drier, cured chorizo can be sliced and eaten raw as a tapas, whereas the softer, raw varieties are used for cooking and are smaller and often sold in a string (*en ristra*). When I talk of a cooking chorizo in the recipes in this book, I mean those that measure about 10–12cm in length and each weigh approximately 100g. Those linked by scarlet-coloured string are *picante*, far hotter than those with plain string. Chistorra is a thin red chorizo-like sausage from the Navarra, and longaniza is another hard, chorizo-like sausage found all over Spain, whose seasoning varies from region to region.

CIDER (*sidra*)

Cider is a popular drink in northern Spain, especially in Asturias, Cantabria and the Basque Country. Unlike most British cider, it is not naturally sparkling, and is aerated by being poured from a height into the glass. To me it most resembles the ciders from the West

Country, especially our own local Cornish scrumpy. It is an acidic, very dry cider, which also makes it ideal for cooking. If you can't find the real thing in a Spanish delicatessen, use the driest aged British cider you can find.

FIDEUA NOODLES
Catalonia, once a kingdom together with Sardinia, Sicily and Naples, is the only part of the Iberian peninsula where pasta became established. *Fideua* or *fideo* noodles are short, thin pieces of dried pasta, similar in thickness and texture to spaghettini, which are fried in olive oil in a shallow paella-like pan until golden and then cooked with a well-flavoured stock until tender. There are many varieties of *fideua* noodles on the market. Don't go for the one that has a hole in the middle and looks like thin macaroni as it won't give you the correct finished texture for the dish in this book. One I particularly like, and which gives a perfect *al dente* texture, is the *clásica fideo No 2* noodle. However, if you can't get hold of that, simply break some dried spaghettini pasta into 2.5cm lengths.

FLOUR (*harina*)
In Spain they have a special type of wheat flour (*harina de trigo*) they reserve for deep-frying, distinguished by the words *especial para freir* on the packet. It is slightly more coarse in texture than normal flour, giving the fried food a lighter, crisper, drier finish. It is only available in Spanish delicatessens, but fine-ground semolina gives a similar result. *Masa harina* is a flour ground from maize. Maize or corn was brought to Spain from Mexico by the conquistadors in the sixteenth century and was quickly embraced by the more northerly, mountainous regions, where the soil was considered too poor for growing wheat, barley or rye. Here they soon learnt to make a new-world style of flatbread or tortilla, known locally as the *tortos*, an unleavened bread made with maize flour, flattened between soaked dried chestnut or maple leaves and cooked in a dry pan without the need for any butter or oil. *Masa harina* is available online (see page 314) and from some delicatessens and specialist food shops.

GOAT (*cabra*)
Much of the goat meat previously eaten in Britain was the waste meat taken from the cull of dairy herds and was not of a good quality, potentially being dry, tough and stringy and with an overly strong flavour, really best only for processing or long cooking in stews. But there is some very good goat meat to be had, if you know what to look for and where. Most of the best meat comes from the Boer goat, a breed that originated in South Africa, or a Boer-cross goat, which is tender and full of flavour. Good quality meat will come from an animal that is between 6 and 18 months old, although the majority will be about 9–12 months old, and will yield legs of 2–2.25kg in weight, perfect for the recipe in this book. The depth of flavour will subtly improve with age without becoming too 'goaty', and, despite being slightly more fatty (which helps to tenderize it during cooking) than the poorer quality meat, it produces less fat in the tin than an average leg of lamb, and surprisingly has ounce for ounce less fat than a chicken. Because there are only a limited number of farmers producing high quality goat meat in the UK at present, and demand outstrips supply, it could be relatively expensive, but no more so than good quality lamb purchased directly from the producer. I urge you to give it a try. It was a revelation to me and is absolutely delicious. See page 314 for a list of suppliers. In Spain, milk-fed kid goat, *cabretto*, is also popular, but can be difficult to get in the UK.

GRELOS
This is a type of leafy brassica popular in the northern regions of Spain, particularly Galicia where it is positively revered when in season during the winter months. Known as *rapini* in Italian, it is a little like turnip greens. It is usually well cooked and served as the classic accompaniment to *cocido*. The leaves have a slightly bitter-hot flavour. The best alternative in the UK, though it is not at all similar in texture, would probably be curly kale or *cavolo nero*, which is sold in some supermarkets.

HAM, CURED (*jamón curado*)
There are two main types of Spanish cured ham: *jamón serrano*, which is the general name given to Spanish air-dried ham, made from various breeds of white-coated pig depending on the region, and *jamón ibérico*, air-dried ham from the black-coated ibérico pig. All hams are covered in coarse salt and left for about 2 weeks. They are then rinsed off, hung up and left to dry and air-cure in special cool rooms or naturally ventilated *secaderos*, drying warehouses, for at least 8 months and up to 20 months or longer, during which time they lose up to 30 per cent of their weight. The resulting ham is dark red in colour, marbled with fat and deliciously salty yet sweet.

Jamón serrano is generally made from farmed pigs rather than wild. It has an excellent flavour, though the fat is usually to be found on the surface rather than marbled throughout the meat. This is the only ham used for cooking. For most of the recipes in this book, ready-sliced serrano ham is fine to use, and other air-dried hams, such as Italian Parma ham, make an adequate substitute. For dishes where slightly larger pieces of ham are required, get a delicatessen to cut you a slice about 5mm thick, ready for dicing.

Other, better quality ibérico hams are not used for cooking, but are eaten as they are so their fine flavour and texture can be enjoyed and savoured. *Jamón ibérico* is any air-dried ham from the ibérico pig, which is tender, with fat marbled though the meat as well as on the surface. *Jamón de recebo* is considered a second-class ham from ibérico pigs that have been reared on grain, then fed acorns for the last few months of their lives. *Jamón de Jabugo* is a high quality ham, from the village of the same name in the Sierra de Aracena region of Andalucía, and has its own *Denominación de Origen* (DO) status. *Jamón de Bellota*, the very best air-dried ham, comes from free-range ibérico pigs raised only on the *dehesa*, vast grazing meadows and woodlands of oak and cork, where they eat acorns and grass for the last four months before slaughter. The national demand for jamón ibérico is so large and the production so limited that this is reflected in its high price, but it's worth every penny.

The bones left over once all the meat has been carved away are much prized, and usually sold separately for flavouring soups and bean dishes.

LENTILS (*lentejas*)
Lentils are a standard Spanish store cupboard item and each region has its own variety and traditional dishes. The three best-known Spanish varieties are the tiny dark brown *pardina* lentils, similar to the French *lentilles de Puy*; the *lentejas de Armuña* of the Castilla y Leon region, and the big, flat, pale green-brown *rubia castellana* lentils

from Castilla-La Mancha. They all have a
good flavour and texture and stay whole
and slightly *al dente* after cooking. Lentils
do age and become stale. The fresher
they are, the less time they take to cook.

MEMBRILLO
Membrillo, or what should more
correctly be called *dulce de membrillo*,
and what we know as a 'fruit cheese', is
quince that has been boiled down with
sugar into a stiff paste, which then sets
quite firm. It is often served thinly sliced
with Manchego cheese, or used in cakes
and pastries. It is usually sold in blocks.
Interestingly, quince cheese is known
as *mermelada* in Portugal, from where
we get the name 'marmalade'.

MORCILLA
This is another blood sausage from
Spain (*see also butifarra negra*). Morcilla
from Burgos is fat, firm and made with
cooked rice; in Asturias they are softer,
smaller and smoked over oakwood, and
those from La Mancha and Extremadura
are made with a lot of onion, giving them
a rich, almost sweet flavour. They can also
be flavoured with pine nuts or cinnamon.
In Galicia there is even a sweet morcilla,
which is fried and served as a dessert.
They can all be fried or boiled, whole
or cut into slices, but always need to be
cooked before eating. For the recipes
in this book I recommend the Asturias-
style morcilla, and be sure to use the
smoked ones when making fabada.
Our own black pudding, however,
makes an adequate substitute.

OCTOPUS (*pulpo*)
I have a confession to make. Though in
the back of my book *Seafood*, I listed the
most common octopi throughout the
world, along with every other seafood
species I could find, I had assumed that
the Atlantic octopus we get in Cornwall
was the same as the Spanish one i.e. the
Common Octopus (*Octopus Vulgaris*).
Rather than notice the blindingly
obvious, I spent days trying to work out
what I was doing wrong in tenderizing
and cooking them to serve them up as
succulent and tender as I'd had in
Northern Spain. It wasn't until my friend
and excellent seafood cook, Mitch Tonks,
pointed out that the Spanish octopus
has two rows of suckers on each tentacle
and the UK one has only one that I finally
realised ours are a different species. It's
called the Lesser, Curled or Horned
Octopus (*Eledone cirrhosa*). This species

also occurs in the Mediterranean, so
next time you see a Greek bashing an
octopus on a rock, I bet it's only got
single rows of suckers. The Common
Octopus is the one to go for. They are
found in UK waters, although rarely
further north than the Channel Islands,
but are, however, quite easy to get from
Spanish ingredient suppliers. They
come frozen, weighing anything from
1kg to 3kg. The Common Octopus needs
to be simmered for 45 minutes to 1 hour
in well-salted water – that's all. There's
no need for any bashing, freezing or
dunking. If you do get hold of a Lesser
Octopus, simmer it for 1 hour. It will be
a lot tougher, but will still taste superb.

OLIVES (*aceitunas*)
There are many varieties of olive, both
green and black, but some of the best to
look out for are the tiny purple arbequina
olive from Catalonia, the slightly larger
green manzanilla olive, which is often
stuffed with a sliver of anchovy, garlic,
red pepper or a whole blanched almond,
the purple-black empeltre, and the
huge green queen olives called gordal.
Don't be tempted to cook with pitted
olives from a can – you will get a much
better flavour from a good quality
whole olive that you pit yourself.

OLIVE OIL (*aceite de oliva*)
Spain is the largest producer of olive
oil in the world. Its best olive oils are
as good as some of the better-known
Italian oils. The percentage of acidity
given on the label is a helpful indication
of the quality, the lower the acid, the
better the oil. As with Italian oils, *aceite
de virgen extra* is reserved for salads
and drizzling and *aceite de oliva* is
the one to use for cooking.

ORANGE FLOWER WATER
(*agua de azahar*)
Distilled from orange blossoms, orange
flower water is a popular flavouring in
the Middle East and was introduced to
Spain by the Arabs. It is used to give a
unique, slightly perfumed flavour to
desserts, pastries and cakes.

PEPPERS (*pimientos*), DRIED
Dried peppers are an indispensable
ingredient in Spanish cuisine and come
in all shapes and sizes. The *choricero*
pepper is the most widely used. It is a
large red variety, similar in size and
shape to our 'bell' pepper, but a much
darker red colour. When dried, it has

a sweet pepper-rich flavour and imparts
a deep red colour to any sauce or dish
in which it is included.

The *ñora* pepper is smaller, more
squat and round. It is similar in colour
and texture to the *choricero* pepper
and an essential ingredient in romesco
sauce, which goes very well indeed
with grilled meat or fish.

The *guindilla* is more like a chilli
in shape as it is long and thin, and it is
hot. In its dark red dried form, it is used
sparingly in Spanish dishes, both the
soaked flesh and as a powder. When
green and ripening, however, it is the
chilli of choice for making the slender
pickled chillies that are commonly
found in jars throughout Spain.

PEPPERS (*pimientos*), FRESH
Red and green peppers, in dozens of
different varieties, are widely used in
Spain. For us, the uniformly shaped
'bell' peppers are an ideal substitute.
The longer, thinner, more pointed red
'romano' peppers are best used raw
in salad-like dishes. Padrón peppers
(*pimientos de Padrón*) are unique to
Spain. These small, stubby little fresh
green peppers are similar in size to
some varieties of green chilli. They are
always served cooked, fried in olive oil
and sprinkled with salt as a tapas, and
though most are sweet, one in every
dozen packs a chilli-hot punch!

PEPPERS, PRESERVED
The small red *piquillo* pepper from
Rioja is rarely seen fresh outside the
region, but can be bought ready-roasted,
skinned and seeded and preserved in
jars or cans in most Spanish delicatessens
and some supermarkets.

PIMENTÓN
Not only is pimentón the most
commonly used spice in the Spanish
kitchen, it is also essential for giving the
classic deep-red colour to many pork
products, such as the chorizo sausage.
Pimentón can be smoked or unsmoked,
but this is not always made clear on
the tin. Generally, that from the
Extremadura region is made from
peppers which have been dried over
oakwood, giving the finished powder
a smoky flavour, whereas that from
in Murcia to the east is made from
sun-dried peppers which have not been
smoked, and is more similar in taste to
Hungarian sweet paprika. *Pimentón de
la Vera* from Extremadura is considered

to be the very best in Spain and was the world's first pepper spice to be given its own DO status. Pimentón comes in three varieties: *dulce* (sweet or mild), *agridulce* (sweet and sour, mildly spicy) and *picante* (hot and spicy).

RABBIT (*conejo*)
The Spanish love to go hunting and love to eat rabbit. I have found that, outside Spain, farmed rabbit is the one to go for. It's a plumper animal that takes less time to cook and is tender. Wild rabbit can be very tough, if you don't know what you are looking for and don't have a good butcher or game dealer.

RAISINS (*pasas*)
Raisins, of course, are dried grapes, harvested and left in the sun for 2–3 weeks. It is the variety of grape that determines the quality and flavour of the raisin, and most are made using Thompson seedless grapes. Muscat or moscatel raisins tend to be larger and sweeter, while Spanish Malaga raisins, which are dried by the bunch and are large, plump and richly flavoured but not always seeded, are best of all.

RICE (*arroz*)
Spain, especially the area along the eastern Mediterranean coast, from Catalonia in the north to Murcia in the south and particularly around Valencia, is one of the most famous and best rice-growing areas in Europe. Here they produce varieties of a short- to medium-grain rice which have the ability to absorb a lot of liquid, and thus flavour, without developing any stickiness; leaving each grain separate yet still moist and firm at the end of cooking. These are the qualities most sought after in a paella and other *arroz* dishes. I particularly like the variety called 'bomba', and rice from the Calasparra province of Murcia.

ROSE VEAL (*ternera*)
The RSPCA and CIWF (Compassion in World Farming) are trying to redeem veal in the eyes of the conscientious consumer. Known as rose veal, because of its rich, pink colour, the meat comes from humanely reared calves which have had unlimited access to their mothers' milk and fresh, natural pasture. It is full of flavour, tender and very low in fat. Free-range rose veal is available online and from good butchers (though you may need to give them a little notice).

SAFFRON (*azafrán*)
From the Arabic word for yellow, *azafrán* (saffron) is one of the most expensive and highly prized spices in the world. Much of the world's saffron is grown in Spain, particularly on the Castilian plateau of La Mancha. Saffron comes from the red-orange stigma of the purple crocus, the *Crocus sativus*. In October the flowers open up and must be harvested immediately. During a harvesting period that barely lasts ten days, the flowers are picked by hand and taken back to the farm, where the three stigma from each flower are removed by hand. The threads are gently dried over gas burners before being packaged for sale. It takes about 200 flowers to yield 1 gram of saffron. Saffron is sold either as threads or in powdered form; I prefer the threads, which have a superior, fresher flavour. Use saffron sparingly, not just because of its price but because it can taste medicinal in large amounts. For cooking, I like to use the threads whole. Most recipes ask for saffron to be soaked in a few tablespoons of warm water before using, particularly in dishes where the colour needs to be evenly distributed. Mancha saffron is considered by many to be the best in the world. Because saffron is so expensive, the Spanish often use a powdered yellow food colouring known locally as *colorante* to colour their rice dishes instead.

SALT COD (*bacalao*)
Salt cod is not well known in UK, yet in Spain and Portugal it remains enormously popular. It was first introduced in Spain by Basque fishermen who were the first to bring home vast quantities of cod preserved in salt from the Grand Banks off Nova Scotia. It became an important source of protein to the less wealthy and the land-locked regions. It comes in many different cuts and grades but thick pieces of fish without too many bones are the best. *Morro* and *lomo* are thick, square-shaped pieces of bone-free fish, which provide neat, portion-sized pieces and large, moist and juicy flakes of fish. All salt cod needs to be soaked in 3 or 4 litres of water in the fridge for 24 to 48 hours depending on the thickness. Change the water when it tastes salty, normally at least twice. Spanish cod is available from Spanish or Portuguese ingredient suppliers (see page 314).

SHERRY (*jerez*)
Sherry is a fortified wine produced in southern Spain around the towns of Jerez, Sanlúcar de Barrameda and El Puerto de Santa María. Most of it is made from the palomino grape. As the wine is aged in the barrel, a naturally occurring yeast from the region, known as flor, helps to develop each sherry's flavour and style. Going from dry to sweet are fino, manzanilla, amontillado (which can be dry or slightly sweetened), oloroso (dry or sweet), palo cortado, cream (pale, or rich and dark) and pedro ximénez. Where a dry sherry is called for, use either a dry manzanilla or fino. Where oloroso is called for, a sweet amontillado will do; but there is no substitute for the rich, raisin-sweet flavour of a good pedro ximénez.

TURRÓN
This is a Spanish almond and honey nougat, especially popular at Christmas. It comes in two varieties: the hard, brittle Alicante style and the softer, marshmallow-like Jihona style, also sometimes called *turrón blando granulado*. It is the softer variety that you need for the recipe on page 284. Italy also makes some wonderful soft nougat known as torrone, if you can't get hold of Spanish turrón.

VINEGAR (*vinagre*)
Spanish cooks use mainly red or white wine vinegars in cooking, adding them to salads, cold soups, pickles and escabeche-style dishes. However, Spain's most distinctive and noteworthy vinegar is the *vinagre de Jerez*, a sherry vinegar that is slightly more viscous than ordinary wine vinegars, darker in colour and more aromatic, with a stronger, deeper flavour and a hint of caramel sweetness about it. I love it, not only for dressing salads and making hot vinaigrettes for serving with fish, but also for adding a little piquant kick to savoury sauces, casseroles and stews. According to its DO regulations, it must be aged in oak or chestnut casks for a minimum of six months, and the quality will vary depending on the method of aging, and the type and quality of sherry used as its base. Buy the best vinegar you can find and afford. The bodega-bottled ones are always a good bet.

COOK'S NOTES

A note about serving sizes
The particular element to Spanish food that makes it special is tapas. What makes tapas bars work is having lots of them. I don't think the concept works too well if there's just one. It's the sense of anticipation, the constant journey with a group of friends from one place to another, rather than the arrival at one place, which makes them enjoyable: here for ibérico ham and a glass of fino sherry, there for some padrón peppers fried in olive oil, another for some spicy albóndigas meatballs with a curry and tomato sauce and a glass of beer – small glasses in the south so that it's drunk before it warms up.

Getting on for half the recipes in the book are either for tapas or could be used as tapas. The slight dilemma I've had is: how big is a tapas? And, therefore, how many does a recipe serve? In bars the menu, if there is one, will often have three columns: tapas, media ración and ración. Tapas is an individual bite for one person, a single croqueta or 3–4 credit-card sized slices of ibérico ham. A media ración is a plate for a few people to share and a ración is twice as big, i.e. for quite a crowd. It's not exact, but a first course for four would make about eight tapas, and a main course for four about sixteen.

❧ All teaspoon and tablespoon measurements are level unless otherwise stated and are based on measuring spoons:
1 teaspoon = 5ml
1 tablespoon = 15ml
(1 Australian tablespoon = 20ml)
❧ All preparation and cooking times are approximate.
❧ All recipes have been tested in a conventional oven. If you have a fan oven, reduce the temperature by between 10°C and 20°C.
❧ All ovens vary; I keep an oven thermometer hanging from one of the racks to check the exact temperature.
❧ Free-range eggs are recommended in all recipes and all eggs are large unless otherwise stated. Recipes made with raw or lightly cooked eggs should be avoided by anyone who is pregnant or in a vulnerable health group.

❧ The cooking times for dried beans, chickpeas and lentils may vary.
❧ It might be useful to know what I mean in weight when I'm talking about the amount of garlic and onion to use. As a rule of thumb:
Garlic 1 average clove = 5g
Onions 1 small = 100g, unpeeled weight;
1 medium = 175g, unpeeled weight;
1 large = 225g, unpeeled weight
❧ A medium-sized squid has pouches about 15–17cm in length – this size will give you flesh of the right thickness or the right-sized rings for the recipes in this book. With the exception of octopus and prawns, all fish and shellfish should be fresh rather than frozen.
❧ Well-salted water means water salted at the rate of 1 teaspoon per 600ml.
❧ Lighting barbecues. Always give your barbecue plenty of time to get to the right temperature before cooking. If you have a charcoal barbecue, light it 30 minutes before you want to cook, by which time there should be no flames and the coals should be covered in a layer of light grey ash. If you have a gas barbecue, light it 10 minutes beforehand.

SUPPLIERS

UK
www.rickstein.com
Stocks specialist ingredients such as *harina de trigo*.
www.brindisa.com
One of the very first companies to import high quality Spanish ingredients into the UK. They have an online retail store. Brindisa tel: 020 8772 1600
Casa Brindisa tel: 020 7590 0008
www.cafegarcia.co.uk
R. Garcia & Sons is one of London's oldest and largest Spanish delicatessens. Tel: 020 7221 6119
www.ibericalondon.co.uk
A delicatessen, restaurant and online store offering foods and wines.
Tel: 020 7636 8650
www.josepizarro.com
A new and expanding online store for all good quality Spanish ingredients.
www.purespain.co.uk
All things Spanish, including a wide range of earthenware and paella pans.
Tel: 01305 458166
www.delicioso.co.uk
A good online deli with a wide range of Spanish products. Tel: 01865 340055

www.flavourofspain.co.uk
A site specializing in Galician ingredients and artisan foods. Tel: 01634 407458
www.saborear.co.uk
Ingredients and cooking equipment sold online. Good for paella burners.
Tel: 01189 753838
www.goat-meat.co.uk
Sharon and Chris Peacock take the rearing of goats very seriously. Their website also lists other goat meat suppliers in the UK. Tel: 07962 812528
www.wellhungmeat.com
The Well Hung Meat Company, veal suppliers. Tel: 0845 230 3131
www.scottish-roseveal.com
Drumachloy Farm, Scottish Rosé Veal
Tel: 01700 503312
www.bocaddonfarmveal.com
Bocaddon Farm Veal, The Real Veal Company. Tel: 01503 220995

AUSTRALIA & NEW ZEALAND
Torres Cellars & Delicatessen
Found on Liverpool Street, in Sydney's Spanish quarter. Tel: 02 9264 6862
www.elchoto.com.au
Sell Spanish ingredients and cookware from their delicatessen in Adelaide.
Tel: 08 8346 1267

www.spanishflavours.com.au
Serving Perth since 2002. Call the suppliers number below or pop into the store in Wembley. Tel: 08 9284 1313
www.losimportadores.com.au
Los Importadores, based in Sydney, imports products to sell in delicatessens around Australia. Tel: 04 1587 9613
Casa Iberica Deli
Based in Melbourne, Casa Iberica supply deli items, cookware and spices.
Tel: 03 9419 4420
www.farrofresh.co.nz
Stocks artisan Spanish produce, based in Auckland. Tel: 09 478 0020
www.noshfoodmarket.com
Supplies a range of international ingredients, which includes Spanish produce. Based in Auckland.
Tel: 09 632 1034
www.sabato.co.nz
You can order some ingredients and cookware online or call the shop for a full range of deli items, including meats and cheeses. Tel: 09 630 8751
www.spanishgoods.co.nz
A Christchurch based supplier of Spanish sausages, made in New Zealand but to a traditional Spanish recipe.
Tel: 03 379 5122

BIBLIOGRAPHY

Andrews, Colman, *Catalan Cuisine. Europe's Last Great Culinary Secret* (Grub Street 1997)

Aris, Pepita, *Recipes from a Spanish Village* (Conran Octopus 1990)

Aris, Pepita, *The Spanishwoman's Kitchen* (Cassell 1992)

Barlow, John, *Everything but the Squeal. A year of pigging out in Northern Spain* (Summersdale Publishers 2009)

Barrenechea, Teresa, *The Cuisines of Spain. Exploring Regional Home Cooking* (Ten Speed Press 2005)

Bennison, Vicky, *The Taste of a Place, Andalucía* (Chakula Press)

Butcher, Nicholas, *The Spanish Kitchen* (Macmillan London 1990)

Camorra, Frank and Richard Cornish, *MoVida. Spanish Culinary Adventures* (Murdoch Books 2007)

Camorra, Frank and Richard Cornish, *MoVida Rustica. Spanish Traditions and Recipes* (Murdoch Books 2009)

Casas, Penelope, *The Foods and Wines of Spain* (Penguin Books 1979)

Casas, Penelope, *Discovering Spain, The Complete Guide* (Pavilion Books 1992)

Casas, Penelope, *La Cocina de Mamá. The Great Home Cooking of Spain* (Broadway Books)

Chandler, Jenny, *The Food of Northern Spain* (Pavilion Books 2005)

Chandler, Jenny, *The Real Taste of Spain* (Pavilion Books 2007)

Clark, Sam & Sam, *Moro. The Cookbook* (Ebury Press 2001)

Clark, Sam & Sam, *Casa Moro. The Second Cookbook* (Ebury Press 2004)

Culinaria Spain – Spanish Specialities (H.F Ullman 2004/2007)

Daft, Rohan, *Menú del Día* (Simon & Schuster 2008)

Hart, Sam & Eddie, *Modern Spanish Cooking* (Quadrille 2006)

Hooper, John, *The New Spaniards* (Penguin. 2nd Revised Edition 2006)

Kurlansky, Mark, *Cod. A Biography of the Fish that Changed the World* (Vintage 1999)

Luard, Elisabeth, *The Flavours of Andalucía* (Collins & Brown 1991)

Luard, Elisabeth, *The Food of Spain & Portugal* (Kyle Cathie 2004)

Mendel, Janet, *My Kitchen in Spain* (Frances Lincoln 2002)

Mendel, Janet, *Cooking from the Heart of Spain. Food of La Mancha* (William Morrow 2006)

Mendel, Janet, *Traditional Spanish Cooking* (Frances Lincoln 2006)

Mendel, Janet, *Cooking in Spain (Second Edition)* (Santana Books 2006)

Morris, Jan, *Spain* (Faber & Faber 2008)

Pizarro, José, *Seasonal Spanish Food* (Kyle Cathie 2009)

Richardson, Paul, *A Late Dinner. Discovering the Food of Spain* (Bloomsbury 2008)

Sevilla, María José, *Life and Food in the Basque Country* (Weidenfeld & Nicolson 1989)

Sevilla, María José, *Spain on a Plate*, (BBC Books 1992)

Weir, Joanne, *From Tapas to Meze* (Ten Speed Press 2004)

ACKNOWLEDGEMENTS

I would like to thank Debbie Major for the key role she played in the production of this book. Whether researching and testing, writing up recipes or cooking and styling the dishes for James Murphy's photography, she has been indispensable to me. James's photos are spot on in that it's almost impossible to tell whether the dishes were shot on location or in a studio. Praise should also go to Penny Markham for her incredibly accurate choice of props and to Alex Smith, the designer, whose enthusiasm for making this book really feel like Spain influenced everyone and who accompanied James on the photography trip.

My commissioning editor, Shirley Patton, has been the sort of constant, sensible and thoughtful presence, right from the early discussions, that all writers need. It was Shirley who said that I should make this a personal journey through Spain and make the recipes my own. I would like to thank the managing director of Ebury Publishing, Fiona MacIntyre, who went to Galicia while I was working hard on the book and came back full of enthusiasm – sometimes you need others to see what you see in a place. On that note, I'd like to thank Mari Roberts, the copy editor, who knows Spain much better than me and said I'd got it right. And Laura Higginson for tirelessly making sure all my copy was delivered on time.

I'd like to thank Claire Heron-Maxwell for assisting on food photography, as well as various others: my PA Viv Taylor, who somehow manages to juggle my time so I can film and write books, and not forgetting Jessica Barwell, Ollie Clarke, who helped on all the recipe testing, and Matthew Stephens and Garry Dutton for supplying such good fish and meat.

The book accompanies a TV series and for that I would like to thank the director/producer David Pritchard, my mate, and assistant producer Arezoo Farhazad, cameraman Chris Topliss and sound recordist Peter Underwood, as well as Steve Briers and other occasional cameramen. Thanks to Maria Jose Sevilla and the helpful fixers and translators that guided us around each region.

Many of the anecdotes in this book came from that memorable journey. I loved filming in Spain but above all I love working with David, Arezoo and the boys. It's like being on holidays, especially when Sarah's there.

Index
316

Index

319